Adventure Vacations

FOR

Animal Lovers

ALSO BY STEPHANIE OCKO

Spiritual Adventures
Fantasy Vacations

Adventure Vacations
FOR
Animal Lovers

EXPLORING NATURE
ON UNFORGETTABLE GETAWAYS

Stephanie Ocko

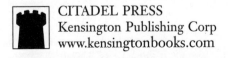

CITADEL PRESS
Kensington Publishing Corp
www.kensingtonbooks.com

CITADEL PRESS BOOKS are published by

Kensington Publishing Corp.
850 Third Avenue
New York, NY 10022

All Kensington titles, imprints, and distributed lines are available at special
quantity discounts for bulk purchases for sales promotions, premiums, fund-
raising, educational, or institutional use. Special book excerpts or customized
printings can also be created to fit specific needs. For details, write or phone
the office of the Kensington special sales manager: Kensington Publishing
Corp., 850 Third Avenue, New York, NY 10022, attn: Special Sales
Department; phone 1-800-221-2647.

CITADEL PRESS and the Citadel logo are Reg. U.S. Pat. & TM Off.

First printing: November 2004

10 9 8 7 6 5 4 3 2 1

Printed in the United States of America

Library of Congress Control Number: 2004106172

ISBN 0-8065-2598-3

Contents

Preface

The purpose of this book is to gather together some opportunities for people to interact with animals, in order to better understand some of the creatures with which we share the planet.

The book does not pretend to be a complete list. It does not focus on birds, except for one or two, such as the African Hornbill rescued by a lodge in Zambia, which shows no desire to leave its monkey friends and return to the wild. Nor does the book mention snakes, except in explaining a matter of life or death.

Some of the wild animals in this book are *habituated*, meaning they are used to seeing tourists. Generally, like chimps or gorillas, habituated animals are indifferent to people. Others are *bicultural*, meaning they have been rehabilitated and released to the wild, but still come back to the rehab center to visit, as orangutans at Camp Leakey in Borneo.

But some animals are truly wild. If they have had little interaction with human beings, they will be as curious about you as you are about them, such as sea lions and finches in the Galapagos, or grizzlies in Kamchatka. Most animals are so busy trying to survive, they will include you as part of the landscape. Nevertheless, follow the advice of regional guides who know how to deal with close encounters. Distance and a certain fine indifference go a long way in human-animal diplomacy. African guides will tell you to freeze if an elephant or a lion charges you. It's counterintuitive, but it works. Baby animals present themselves sometimes irresistibly, but don't touch! Their mothers might attack you, or reject the babies, having been touched by human beings.

The trips described in this book are naturally subject to change, but the companies offer such an imaginative banquet that alternatives should be easily arranged. If you're going to remote parts of the world, most companies will custom-design a trip with you.

No guarantee goes with Website addresses or even telephone numbers. Nevertheless, the book is offered with the hope that some understanding and inspiration might grow from its pages. The material is presented in good faith without bias or preference. On many of these trips, travelers are warned that the weather can alter plans. Neither the publisher nor the author takes responsibility for a company's incompetence or for any accident or injury to any participant incurred while undertaking a project mentioned in this book.

Travel safely.

Please visit www.stephanieocko.com.

Acknowledgments

Thanks to Citadel's Bruce Bender and Gary Goldstein; to the hundreds of people who answered the call for animal tours, especially from Florida, flusa.com; to Andrew Logan of Kamchatka Peninsula.com; Gary Lemmer in Madagascar and Boris Pasek of Remote Rivers Expeditions, remoterivers.com; Barb Gaskell and Gary Lane of Wapiti River Guides in Idaho, doryfun.com; the helpful staff at Siyabona Africa.com; Bob Berghaier at premiertours.com; Blue Magruder of Earthwatch at Earth watch.org. Thanks especially to Roger Archibald; and to Oscar, Jeremy, and Avery, three guys who can save us all, along with the animals, to whom the book is dedicated.

What do you say to a chimpanzee that levels its gaze at you? Of all apes, chimps are most like humans. This one lives with a Bonobo at the Jacksonville Zoo. *Roger Archibald*

Introduction

If we were all Dr. Doolittle, would we understand what animals have to say? We've come a long way from Descartes who believed animals were without souls or minds, just instinctual muscular masses. Recent researchers are exploring exactly what animals think and how, if they are self-conscious and aware that they think, and if they know what they don't know. What, for example, is the experience of Kanzi, the University of Georgia bonobo who understands human speech, when he watches Tarzan movies—his favorite? Even Jane Goodall who has spent her adult life in the company of chimps said her one wish is to see the world through their eyes.

In a Kenya elephant study, researcher Katy Payne recounted an event with a bull elephant in *musth* (looking for mates), which was angry at the researchers' intrusion. He approached their jeep, put his trunk in the open driver's seat window, then pounded the hood of the Jeep with his trunk three times, before moving away. Payne was instantly reminded of an earlier incident when she was studying whales off the coast of Patagonia. She and another researcher were in a small boat and very close to a whale that showed some displeasure at their presence. The whale surfaced, eyed them, disappeared under the boat, then lifted the boat about six inches into the air, not once, but three times.

Being careful not to read her own meaning into the incidents, but to try to view them from the elephant's and the whale's points of view, Payne said in her book *Sudden Thunder*, she saw "that there was forbearance. That it was deliberate. And that it was communicated in a manner that was both subtle and clear."

So, if they speak to us, do we always know it? Psychologist Mark Hauser says that our history with animal communication has been one-sided: we count them, hunt them, manage them, even teach them symbols, but "we overlooked what they have to say to us."

Human beings organize experience in little bits of information that we form into words, sentences, and pictures, in any combination. Animals might not, says Hauser, but that doesn't mean their experience isn't rich. He once observed an elk engaged in a series of complex behaviors around mating season. The elk walked away, but not before stopping, looking over his shoulder, and giving a final grunt. That grunt, for all we know, says Hauser, might be the equivalent of a microchip, full of ones and zeros and loaded with information. Or maybe the grunt was rich and complete.

Investigating communication is just one of the exciting fields around animals these days. Computer scientists study ant behavior to learn how to design robots and look at swarming insects to create computer systems. Researchers in the Americas, using global positioning system (GPS), track collared wolves and jaguars to see exactly where they go and how often and why, so conservationists can design "corridors," wildlife paths that will let the animals travel from the Yukon to Yellowstone, and from Mexico to Argentina. The corridors would be off-limits to hunters and would not interrupt the animals' ranges to hunt and to breed, or people's farms and livestock corrals.

Figuring out how a lot of people on Earth can live happily next to what's left of wildlife is not easy. Conservation groups have begun working with foreign companies, such as mining or logging firms. Poor countries need the income and jobs that these companies provide. The problem arises when the companies take chunks out of animals' backyards, forcing hungry animals to steal food from farms.

But hungry people who are poor shoot wild animals to feed their families. Recently, coalitions between conservationists and miners and loggers have begun to be established: if everyone gives up something—some acres and decent salaries to local people (the companies), a couple of cattle to a hungry predator (the local farmers), and their usual range (the animals)—a workable peace might prevail.

Animals are remarkably adaptive. But the world market is a fierce predator. In places where poaching is rampant because people are poor, wildlife organizations are protecting animals by encouraging tourism, which brings in money to the people and adds perceived value to wild animals: a live tiger that tourists pay to see is worth more than a dead tiger sold for parts. Hundreds of centuries ago, Greek philosopher Aristotle counted the number of species on Earth. He found there were about 800. But he suggested paying attention to every one of them, because "in each one of them is something natural and something beautiful."

Guests return from looking for tigers on elephant back at Tiger Tops Jungle Lodge in the Royal Chitwan National Park, Nepal. *Sanu Raja Bajrachrya, www.tigermountain.com*

Adventure Vacations
FOR
Animal Lovers

1

AFRICA

THE GREAT MIGRATION

You can hear them coming from miles away a half hour before you even see the dust they stir: more than a million wildebeest, each weighing several hundred pounds, with hundreds of thousands of zebras. They move in a twenty-five-mile-long herd from the dry Serengeti Plains in Tanzania to the wet grasslands of the Maasai Mara in Kenya, where they will stay for a few months until the rains return to the Serengeti.

The Great Migration of Africa happens every year, heading west and north around May and June, south around November, not always to the same exact place, not always with every wildebeest. For two to three months, driven by inexorable instinct for water, they travel their ancient routes about 500 miles, stopping only to eat and drink at occasional waterholes, protecting their young from the sudden attack of crocodiles, lions, jaguars, or cheetahs, which have the annual wildebeest migrations flagged on their calendars like a national holiday. Wild dogs and hyenas hope for the best; great vultures cast a cool eye from above.

PREDATOR VERSUS PREY

Altogether, this is what African wildlife is about: herd animals preyed upon by predators. The drama is played out every day in many ways.

1

The prey are herd species, grazers like antelopes and their relatives, and buffalo, wildebeest, and zebra; some are browsers, such as gerenuks, giraffes, and elephants. The predators are lions, leopards, cheetahs, and wild dogs. All need an occasional stream or waterhole. All can be victimized by drought, floods, wildfires, and diseases, such as canine distemper virus and rabies from the domesticated dogs of the neighboring villages, as well as by villagers who kill them for meat or by poachers who kill them for marketable body parts. Living and dying are active here.

Even without a migration, the savannah makes for some incredible photo ops, especially at dawn and sunset when many species graze or browse together. Keep an eye open for fast animals like cheetahs, ostriches, and warthogs, and elusive (because critically endangered) species like black rhinos. The birds will send you to the books to find their names.

WAYS TO DO THE SAFARI

First, Pick Your Place

Southern Africa is where wild game congregates in the greatest numbers on the planet. Kenya, Tanzania, Zambia, Namibia, Zimbabwe, Botswana, and South Africa each boast a healthy number of national parks and game reserves (hunting is off-limits; poachers are often killed on sight), as well as private game reserves. Some parks have greater numbers of one species than another—Zimbabwe's Matusadona National Park is famous for lions, for example; the Ruaha National Park in Tanzania has more than a fair share of hippos. The animals' territory, however, does not necessarily fall within the political entity. Two seasons dominate: wet (roughly between November and May) and dry (June to October). Close to the equator (which runs slightly north of Nairobi in Kenya), the sun rises at 6 A.M. and sets at 6 P.M. sharp.

Endangered rhinos do breed in captivity, like this pair at the New Orleans Zoo that recently became the parents of Satchmo, named after Louis Armstrong.
Roger Archibald

Best Times

All safaris work around the best times to see animals, which as a rule are the hours shortly after dawn and before and after sunset, when you are most likely to see the "Big Five Plus" (lions, giraffes, hippos, rhinos, and elephants; plus buffalos, cheetahs, and leopards). But lions take their time eating their kill, and you might come upon a lion family in the middle of the day eating or resting nearby, or a leopard draped in a tree, catching a nap until the sun goes down.

Throughout the day across the savannah, the grazers are at work: herds of zebra and wildebeest, Cape buffalo, and various species of antelope. Rhinos, single or in pairs, occasionally appear from behind a bush, and a small herd of elephants, sometimes called the quietest animal in Africa, suddenly crosses the road a few feet ahead, stopping to flap their ears in your direction.

Bringing You to the Playing Fields

The differences in safaris lie in the means of transport from which you see the animals and in the level of creature comforts you enjoy when the sun goes down. Aside from the traditional "game drive," which is a van (sometimes painted with zebra stripes) with a few passengers and lots of cameras wending its way through the bush, you can choose from the following.

Walking Tours

Currently the most popular way to see game, walking tours also please tourism officials whose aerial photos show more and more tire ruts throughout the savannah. They are safe, because you are accompanied by an armed guide who knows the territory and probably can hear things stir in the bush long before you will. And they are exciting, because wild animals have a way of simply turning up on the path, whether it's warthogs chasing each other or bull elephants having a fight. You learn bush skills: how to identify tracks—what species they belong to, when the creature was there, if it was running; and how to read dung—how recent it is, and whose it might be (hyenas produce white spoor from bone calcium; giraffes produce small black pellets dropped from a height along a path).

Your guide will teach you the totally counterintuitive technique of what to do if an elephant or a lion charges you: **Freeze!** Watch out for spider webs strung out along the path: some of them contain sleeping giants in the center.

- A *wilderness-trails* safari is a trek with a ranger guide and helpers who carry gear. You stop at night to set up camp.
- A *backed-up* walking safari follows a specific wilderness path to points where you rendezvous with a support team that has already set up camp.
- A *fixed-base* walking safari starts from a lodge or camp usually within the park. Accompanied by a guide, you walk out and back at the best viewing times.

On Elephantback

Once your heart is back in its proper place and the elephant is up and you are still strapped into your seat, relax and enjoy the ride. From about fifteen feet up, the view is overwhelming: you pass tree-tops and see lions below almost in miniature. The pace is magnificently slow; one rider likened it to riding a "living bulldozer." If you like elephants, riders say you will have a deeper appreciation after the ride. The camps that have elephants have raised them from their orphaned youths (their mothers were poached for their ivory). Birders find the trip unparalleled for viewing.

On Horseback

Reserved for confident riders, horseback safaris depend on speed to ride with the herds and avoid tricky situations—such as young lions that like to chase, jump, and play. It is an excellent way to explore the bush off the beaten track, and useful if the terrain is mixed dry savannah and shallow wetlands. Horseback safaris can be organized for a week or so, with mobile camps.

Paddling the Rivers

Yes, there are crocodiles and pods of submerged hippos: just staying in the boat pumps adrenaline like you wouldn't believe. And adrenaline is the generator that allows you to stay cool if a hippo surfaces and threatens your float or canoe. Fortunately, guides know the rivers and manage to stay in shallow enough waters to avoid hippo attacks, and they travel at times when the sleepy large reptiles on shore are still sluggish. Views are magnificent: everything comes to the lake or the pool or river for a drink, and sometimes birds by the tens of thousands.

You don't have to be in fantastic shape to paddle a canoe, or even have any prior experience. The person in the rear takes the burden, and with luck that will be the guide.

With a Scientist

Some say the main advantage of working with a scientist in the field is that you are so busy concentrating on your tasks, you fit right in to the area without a second thought. Insects seem indifferent to you; you just pluck off the leeches and toss them, and you just know when to run and when to stay. Whatever project you contribute your time and energy to is probably for the good of the animals, and no matter how tiny your task, whether it's transcribing numbers in a logbook or counting the number of eggs in a nest, you are making a unique contribution.

By Plane

Anything that gets you up there—helicopter, balloon, or light plane—is ideal for seeing the Big Five Plus in the "big picture." Planes are also great for viewing big falls, such as Victoria Falls, and they are able to move you quickly over the great distances, especially in Africa. Balloons are ideal for quietly fitting into the environment (many lodges have connections to balloonists for a one-to two-hour dawn or sunset trip).

By Train

Trains are good for people who create their safari experience from within and without: you see lots of game from the windows, and can go back to reading a book about the area during the long stretches in between. Many train trips (mostly in South Africa) can be customized to your interests, and arrange stops at game parks along the way.

ACCOMMODATIONS

- The most basic is a fly camp, which can be a mosquito net strung between two oars, resorted to on long bush treks.
- Up from that is a simple tent you pitch yourself, which you tote with you.

On these options, your guide, necessary in any park and reserve, will advise on water and food, as well as how you will dig a temporary latrine.

- The tented camp is a more civilized situation, in which the latrine is dug and the tents are ready before you arrive. Permanent tented camps have a terrific "African" feel, lots of khaki canvas, showers with pails. A mobile tented camp follows your progress on a river, sets up camp, and takes you on bush drives, if you wish.

- Luxury tented camps can be quite elaborate, in the style of British army officers at the turn of the twentieth century—a raised platform, tables, chairs, and beds with mosquito netting, as well as linens and provision for a hot water shower. Often the furniture is made of mahogany, and woven carpets cover the floor.

- Bandas, or roundavels—native-style houses—are small thatched-roof permanent structures with a door and a porch, usually a bathroom with limited water, and electricity on a meter (lights out at 10).

- Luxury camps, with cabins made of wood, often have fireplaces for cool nights.

- Lodges have most hotel amenities.

Most national parks charge an entrance fee (less than $50); some charge an overnight fee as well, no matter where you stay in the park (less than $10).

THE RIFT VALLEY: KENYA AND TANZANIA

Volcanoes tore this place apart 40 million years ago, but not enough to make East Africa a separate continent. What remains is one very big split, surrounded by dramatic escarpments, with mountains, craters, salty lakes, and long swaths of green savannah. Life here goes way back, including human life.

Kenya

For information on Kenya's national parks:

Kenya Wildlife Service   P.O. Box 40241, Nairobi, Kenya. Tel: 011 (254-020) 600800; Fax: (254-020) 603792; Website: www.kws.org.
   Most lodges in Kenya can connect you to drivers who will take you from park to park, called lodge safaris.

Amboseli National Park   Warden, P.O. Box 18, Namanga, Kenya. Tel: 011 (254-0456) 22261; Fax: (254-0456) 22250; E-mail: amboseli.nga@africaonline.co.ke.
   Amboseli National Park, about 100 miles southwest of Nairobi, is one of the oldest parks in Africa, the place where Hemingway was inspired to write *The Snows of Kilimanjaro*, whose elusive snow-capped peaks dominate the park, visible briefly at dawn and sundown. Home to about fifty-six species from baboons to black rhino, it is most famous for its resident herds of elephants, the subject of study for almost three decades by animal behaviorist Cynthia Moss and several others, who discovered that they have three-generation, matriarch-dominated families [see chapter 3, "Elephants"]. Three lodges are inside the park; the Masai run campsites outside the park and provide most of the excellent guides.

Maasai Mara Game Reserve   Website:www.gamereserve.com.
   Maasai Mara Game Reserve, the well-watered end point of the Great Migration, the Kenyan extension of the Serengeti Plain, is a 700-square-mile reserve full of various game, including lots of permanent resident wildebeest and zebras. It's a vibrant place at all times of the year, and it is high and cool, about 4,800 feet. Campsites, tented camps ($100–$150), one used in the film *Out of Africa* ($475), lodge ($100). Many have pools and access to ballooning.

Koija Starbeds   Moses Kanene. E-mail: mkanene@awf.org
   Samburu Game Reserve is north of the equator in view of Mount Kenya, with some species not found in the south of Kenya

A giraffe in the Los Angeles Zoo trades views with a photographer. *Roger Archibald*

such as the reticulated giraffe (chestnut with white lines), Beisa oryx (or gemsbok), and the Somali ostrich. This relatively dry scrub desert, sixty-four-square-mile reserve is watered by the Ewaso Ngiro River, which attracts Grevy's zebra (smaller, gentler, with browner stripes, and endangered), gerenuk (called the "giraffe gazelle" because of its long neck and ability to eat leaves from treetops), and lots of elephants and lions. In fact elephants have their own migration route through the Samburu area. Accommodations are near the riverbanks: two luxury tent camps (one with a pool), a lodge, and campsites are within the reserve; a new ecolodge, built and run by local villagers, is located just outside the reserve. Walking tours are permitted just outside the reserve.

Elephant Watch Safaris   P.O. Box 54667, Nairobi, Kenya.
Tel: 011 (254-2) 334868; Fax: (254-2) 243976; E-mail: info@
elephantwatchsafaris.com; Website: www.elephantwatchsafaris.com.

Oria and Iain Douglas-Hamilton are well-known conservators of
elephants. Iain was among the first to spot poachers from the air
shooting elephants for their ivory in the 1970s and began a crusade
to stop the slaughter. Together, they have written books and made
films on elephants, and organized a group called Save the Elephants,
which conducts scientific research on monitored elephants in the
wild. Oria is a cousin of Laurent de Brunhoff, the creator of *Babar*.

An Elephant Watch safari in the Samburu Game Reserve is based
on the idea of a whale watch: you travel to where they are, accompanied by a guide, and watch. You can also stay in the eco-friendly
Elephant Watch Safari Camp on the banks of the Ewaso Nyiro
River, where the furniture is made of fallen trees. About $475 per
person includes all meals, guides, two game drives, and visits to a
Samburu village and elephant research center.

Wild Frontiers   Helen Douglas-Dufresne, P.O. Box 15165,
Nairobi, Kenya. Tel: 011 (254-2) 884258/9; Fax: (254-2) 891394;
E-mail: wildfrontiers@pyramide.net; Website: www.pyramide.net.

On this unusual trip you go through the largely unexplored
region of the Matthews and Ndoto mountains, in the Samburu
region, accompanied by Samburu guides and camels. Ride the
camels, or let them carry your gear, as you walk through areas
where few tourists go, and where wildlife is as curious about you.
Customized trips; call.

Tsavo East National Park   Assistant Director, P.O. Box 14,
Voi, Kenya. Tel: 011 (254-043) 2228; Fax: (254-0147) 30034;
E-mail: tenp@africaonline.co.ke.

Tsavo East National Park (and Tsavo West NP) is located southwest of Nairobi on the road to the coast. Kenya's oldest national
park, it has more than 7,000 square miles and lots of rock outcrops
and flat ridges, which create bowls that catch water. In the dry

season, hundreds of species, including aardwolves (a smaller light-colored hyena), wild cats, Kirk's dik-dik (dwarf antelopes), Coke's hartebeest (an antelope with long lyre-shaped horns), and black rhinos, come from the acacia scrub, grasslands, and woodlands to congregate here, especially elephants.

Tsavo East is the famous place of the man-killing lions. Although they might not have been vengeful railroad-worker killers, the Tsavo lions are interesting because they are different; in fact, some scientists believe they constitute a subspecies. Males, for one thing, never develop huge manes. Tsavo suffered greatly in the great drought of 1970 when much of it was reduced to desert. Accommodations include a lodge, numerous tented camps, and campsites. Walking tours are permitted along the Galana River that cuts through the park.

The Pride of Safaris   P.O. Box 24696, Nairobi, Kenya. Tel: 011-254-2-884258; Fax: 011-254-2-884445; E-mail: thepride@prideofsafaris.com; Website: www.prideofsafaris.com.

Denys Finch-Hatton, played by Robert Redford in the film *Out of Africa*, was the dashing lover of writer Isak Dinesen (a.k.a. Countess Karen von Blixen), played by Meryl Streep. When he wasn't flying in and out of her camp, he was a sought-after safari guide, and at his tragic death left behind a tented camp. That camp today has been bestowed with the ultimate of bush luxury, winning Kenya's Best Tented Camp award. You can stay here in the southwest corner of Tsavo West National Park among wildlife in the style of the best hunters of a hundred years ago.

Tanzania

Tanzania's parks and reserves   Website: www.tanzania-web.com. More than 25 percent of Tanzania is set aside for wildlife, in thirteen national parks and seventeen game reserves. In addition, the Ngorongoro Conservation Area which contains the Ngorongoro Crater—a collapsed volcano—the permanent home of more than 20,000 animals.

The heavy rainy season in Tanzania is roughly April and May, with lighter rains in November and December. Tourists crowd its parks in January, February, and August.

American Museum of Natural History   Discovery Tours, Central Park West at 79th Street, New York, New York 10024-5192. Tel: 800-462-8687 (toll-free); 212-769-5700; Fax: 212-769-5755; Website: www.discoverytours.org.

The Masai call it "*Siringitu*, the place where the land moves on forever." Tanzania's **Serengeti National Park**, about 9,000 square miles of savannah, contains about 3 million large animals representing thirty-five species, and is the start- and end-point of the Great Migration for wildebeest and zebras. Walking tours are permitted.

The *AMNH Family Safari in the Serengeti* will introduce your children six to sixteen to penpals in Tanzania before they go and will arrange a meeting with them when they visit Sakila Village and School. The trip continues into the Serengeti Park for the Great Migration, travels to Ngorongoro Crater, Olduvai Gorge and the Museum, and Tangangire National Park, staying in tented camps and lodges. Fourteen days, about $7,000 per adult, $6,300 per child, includes international airfare from New York.

Ngorongoro Crater Rim   For detailed information on hiking, including maps and helpful tips, contact: NCAA Tourism Office, P.O. Box 1, Ngorongoro, Tanzania. Tel:/Fax: 011 255 57 4619; E-mail: ncaa_hq@habari.co.tz.

Ngorongoro Conservation Area in the Great Rift Valley includes nine astounding old volcanic peaks, one of which is still active. In the center of the park is the Ngorongoro Crater, a collapsed caldera 1,800 feet deep, about fourteen miles wide. Within the crater are swamps, a lake, an acacia forest, and open grasslands—varied real estate that can create fog, but make for happy animals, among them lions, wildebeest, zebra, and hippo. If you are going to see an endangered black rhino, it will probably be here. The crater is exciting to see if you climb to the cloud forest where the view from the rim of the crater (an easy hike) is breathtaking.

Walking tours with a guide are permitted on the rim of the crater. Overnight camping walks require permission; bring your own gear. You must always be accompanied by an NCA guide.

African Walking Safaris   P.O. Box 12727, Arusha, Tanzania. Tel: 011-255-744 324649; E-mail: info@africanwalkingsafaris.com; Website: www.walkingsafaris.com.

Native Tanzanian Emmanuel Ninja will accommodate all walking tours in the national parks that permit them, with comfortable lodging included. Armed ranger guides who are of the Masai warrior class accompany the tours. Ninja's specialty is a three-day trek around Ngorongoro Crater, where donkeys carry your gear and the ranger turns into chef at dinner. The trip includes a trek up the Mountain of God—Oldonyo Lengai—the only active volcano in Ngorongoro, which begins at 12:30 A.M. under the brilliant stars after a wake-up snack of tea and candies. You arrive at the peak at dawn. Ninja's trips can be customized, average about $130 to $180 a day camping; $250 a day with lodge stays.

Natural Habitat Adventures   2945 Center Green Court, Suite H, Boulder, Colorado 80301-9539. Tel: 800-543-8917 (toll-free); Website: www.nathab.com.

Kilimanjaro National Park consists of the actual peaks, the tallest of which is about 19,000 feet high, and the savannah and forest that you hike through to get there. Elephants, buffalos, and elands (an antelope with spiral horns) take advantage of the savannah; monkeys, including blue monkeys, and black and white colobus monkeys, inhabit the forests. Leopards like this area as well. Lodging in hotels in Arusha, Moshi, and Marangu. See www.habari.co.tz. A helpful site on which route to choose if you climb to the top is www.game-reserve.com.

World Expeditions   580 Market Street, Suite 525, San Francisco, California 94104. Tel: 888-646-TREK[8725] (toll-free); Tel:/Fax: 415-989-2212; E-mail: Michelle@WEadventures.com; Website: www.WEadventures.com.

Tanzania on Foot is the name of the seventeen-day trip that will take you on guided day walks in the Serengeti, Ngorongoro, and up the Rongai Route to the peak of Kilimanjaro. Moderate to strenuous; about $3,000.

Mountain Travel Sobek   6420 Fairmount Avenue, El Cerrito, California 95430-9962. Tel: 800-687-6235 (toll-free); 510-527-8100; Fax: 510-525-7710; E-mail: info@mtsobek.com; Website: www.mtsobek.com.

Mountain Travel Sobek runs several trips to Kenya and Tanzania, many of which include walking safaris and climbs up Mount Kilimanjaro.

Arusha National Park, part of the northern Masai Steppe that includes Lake Manyara and Tangangira national parks, is high and cool: about 4,600 feet and loaded with interesting species in its fifty-three square miles, with the 19,000-foot Mount Kilimanjaro and 15,000-foot Mount Meru for backdrops. In the forest trees are black and white colobus monkeys and blue monkeys; in the grasslands live baboons, bush duiker (small antelope), hyenas, and zebras. In its seven lakes thrive waterbucks and hippos and spectacular birds. Lodging is in four campsites: two small rest houses and two lodges (about $25 to $75 a night). See www.tanzania-web.org.

Two-thirds of **Lake Manyara National Park**, an International Biosphere Reserve, is the Lake Manyara itself, whose size depends on rains, set against the dramatic escarpment of the Great Rift Valley. Forty species of raptors visit the lake to make it a world-class raptor-viewing site. They join 450 other species of birds including saddle-billed storks, hornbills, crowned eagles, pelicans, and pink flamingos that also prefer the salt Lake Manyara. Elephants roam the forest, eating the fruits of the sausage, fig, and mahogany trees; lions climb the acacia trees for a snooze on a branch (lions don't usually climb trees). (Best season is any but April and May, when the roads are very muddy.) Lake Manyara has a couple of spectacular lodges, including the spacious Lake Manyara Tree Lodge, actually in the park, a collection of ten luxury tree-

houses (on stilts). See www.ccafrica.com; Tel: 27-11-809-4300;
between $600 to $1,000 per night for two, includes lodging, food,
guides. Also has a hotel, tented camps, and a campsite. See
www.game-reserve.com.

Tarangire National Park is one of the areas involved in the
Great Migration, but because so many new villages have blocked
the old migration routes, tens of thousands of wildebeest and zebra
remain in this park all year, drinking from the Tarangire River. Lots
of other species occupy this 1,000-square-mile park with nine vegetation zones: an amazing 5,000 elephants, 5,000 elands, 5,000 buffalos, 2,500 giraffes, and 1,000 fringe-eared oryx (with long, straight,
ringed horns). Lots of gazelles, reedbuck, bushbuck, gerenuk,
impala, hartebeest, and kudu (spiral-horned antelope), plus lions and
cheetah and bat-eared fox roam the baobab and acacia forest.
Lodges and tented camps offer guides and walks and drives through
the park.

Thomson Safaris   14 Mount Auburn Street, Watertown,
Massachusetts 02472. Tel: 800-235-0289 (toll-free); 617-923-0425;
Fax: 617-923-0940. E-mail: info@thomsonsafaris.com; Website:
www.thomsonsafaris.com.

This company specializes in Tanzania, runs several family trips
that include Tanganire, Serengeti, Ngorongoro, and Olduvai Gorge.
Thirteen days, about $5,000, includes international airfare. Child
discounts are available.

Ruaha National Park in central Tanzania attracts lots of elephants, giraffes, warthogs, elands, buffalo, ostriches, and cheetahs.
But it is well known for its hippo (and crocodile) population in
the Great Ruaha River. Plant-lovers, bird-lovers, and archaeologists
love this place as well: paleolithic tools have been excavated near
the Ruaha River Lodge.

The ecosystem for **Selous Game Reserve**, the largest game
reserve on the continent, covers about 30,000 square miles. The
19,000-square-mile reserve is a World Heritage Site, with guaran-
teed unspoiled wilderness. The Ruaha and Rufiji rivers channel

through steep escarpments; lakes and hot springs are scattered throughout. You can take a cable car across Stiegler's Gorge, 300 feet down, to get a better view. Expect a variety and lots of each species: elephant and buffalo; an amazing collection of water birds along the banks of the Ruiji River and the salt Lake Tagalala; and hippos, colobus monkeys, Coke's hartebeest, and the Roosevelt sable antelope (large black antelope with long horns that curve over its head). Accommodations in the north of the reserve include tented camps and lodges. An organized safari is recommended: see www.tanzania-web.org for a list of tour operators. Go with a set date group or with your own group in a 4-WD-with-guide. Seven days, lodge accommodation, about $2,300 (includes everything). Walking tours are permitted.

Remote Rivers Expeditions   P.O. Box 544, Boulder, Colorado 80306. Tel: 800-558-1083 (toll-free); E-mail: gary@remoterivers. com; Website: www.remoterivers.com.

This experienced company runs a rafting trip down the Rufiji River, over some rather thrilling rapids, and through the dramatic bottom of Steigler's Gorge. The put-in point is reached by a short ride on the Tazara railway in the north of the reserve, followed by a bush drive in a 4-WD. Bush walks are scheduled each morning and evening. Camping and tented camps: seventeen days in July, about $3,800.

Mountain Travel Sobek   6420 Fairmount Avenue, El Cerrito, California 94530. Tel: 888-687-6235 (toll-free); 510-527-8100. E-mail: info@mtsobek.com; Website: www.mtsobek.com.

Float down the Rufiji River for a day, then spend three days on a walking safari with a guide in the Selous Game Reserve, stopping at night to set up fly camps in the bush (these can be simply mosquito netting over a frame). This trip then picks up a charter flight to go on to Ruaha National Park and the little-visited Katavi National Park. Fourteen days, about $7,500, includes charter flights.

Flora and Fauna International is a conservation group working

A group rafts on the Rufiji River through the Selous Reserve in Tanzania, one of the most untouched places in Africa. *Remote Rivers Expeditions; www.remoterivers.com.*

on several projects in Africa (stabilizing animal populations after uprisings in Liberia, for example). Their Carnivore Conservation project in the Serengeti has been responsible for vaccinating village dogs against rabies and distemper. See www.flora-fauna.org.

SOUTHERN AFRICA: BOTSWANA, ZAMBIA, ZIMBABWE, AND NAMIBIA

These four countries share boundaries in what's called the Four Corners Heartland (see www.awf.org), probably the richest game area in the world. In the center sits the mighty Victoria Falls (accessible from Zambia and Zimbabwe). The Great Kalahari Desert stretches east-west across southern Botswana into Namibia, and the true Namib Desert runs along the coast of Namibia. The differences are great: the Kalahari (San Bushmen country) is scrub desert with long gray rocky stretches; the Namib is famous for its high, sculpted dunes and orange sands.

Politically, parts of this area are unstable; but the wildlife is extremely abundant and diverse. Stories exist of elephants raiding the kitchens of camps and hyenas scrounging for snacks; one luxury camp reported finding a hippo swimming in its pool during the dry season. Going with an organized tour company is a good idea because of their knowledge of the area and its current conditions.

Botswana

Botswana has large animals—elephants, buffalo, lions—in legendary numbers, largely because of its interplay of wet and dry. Rivers and the Okavango Delta periodically swell and water the north, while the dry Kalahari Desert, which covers 80 percent of the country, depends on occasional pools. Migratory birds gather by the thousands, including some not often seen elsewhere. Such animals as zebras have their own migratory routes between wet and dry, and wildlife corridors permit passage between the country's five national parks and game reserves.

Chobe National Park

The huge number of elephants—estimated to be close to 120,000—are thought to descend from Africa's original elephant population. They are different than elephants seen on other parts of the continent. They are bigger, have smaller tusks, and are much more expressive: visitors remark on their loud trumpeting and interaction with each other. They gather along the banks of the Chobe River by the thousands to drink and play. During the heavy winter rains from January to March, they migrate each year about 120 miles from the northeast part of the park to the southeast.

Chobe National Park—Botswana's first—established in 1967, covers about 4,300 square miles and occupies the upper northwest part of the country. It has four ecosystems—savannah, forest, swamp, and marsh—dominated by the Chobe River. Game viewing can be spectacular in the dry season, May to November; you can take boat trips along the Chobe River at that time.

In the Savuti marsh area in the western part of the park, lions and spotted hyenas are so abundant you have to watch your step throughout the day and night, especially if you stay in the campsite. Beyond them, expect to see large numbers of jackals, giraffe, Burchell's zebras, elands, all kinds of antelope, wildebeest, Cape buffalo by the thousands, and warthogs, in addition to elephants. Visitors say this is the best park in Africa because of the strategies so much diverse wildlife needs to survive together.

In the northwest part of the park is the Linyanti Swamp, about 550 square miles with large numbers of giraffe and antelope in the forests, elephants, zebras, and buffalo nearer the river. Roads in Linyanti are dirt and are almost impassable in the wet season when the Chobe River swells to overflowing.

Siemer & Hand Travel   750 Battery Street, Suite 300, San Francisco, California 94111. Tel: 800-451-4321 (toll-free); 415-788-4000; Fax: 415-788-4133; E-mail: travel@siemerhand.com; Website: www.siemerhand.com.

Wings Over Botswana offers a trip guided by an ornithologist who takes you to some of the 300 species of large and small, daylight and nocturnal birds, including the breeding colonies of carmine bee eaters, flashy red and black birds with turquoise heads that live in the Chobe National Park and the Moremi Game Reserve. Fourteen days, about $5,500.

Eco-Expeditions   192 Nickerson Street, No. 200, Seattle, Washington 98109. Tel: 800-628-8747 (toll-free); 206-285-4000. E-mail: zoe@zeco.com; Website: www.zeco.com.

"Ultimate Botswana" takes you by bushplane, dugout canoe, 4x4, and marshcraft through the entire country. Luxury camps, 21 days, about $14,000.

Zambia

Zambia, the birthplace of Africa's national parks, has nineteen national parks and professional guides. The former Northern

Rhodesia also has copper mines in the north near the border with the Democratic Republic of Congo. The U.S. State Department advises staying away from this border because of land mines (see travel.state.gov). Roads are not so great, and it's a good country from which to experience wildlife from a camp or a lodge within the parks. Dry season is May to November. Because the country is 4,000 to 5,000 feet high, it never feels really tropical.

Lower Zambezi National Park is home to hundreds of hippos in the Zambezi River, which you have to take into consideration when you do the park from the river. Fishermen love this place for its tiger fish, as do numerous sea eagles, hornbills, marabou storks, and Pel's fishing owl, which gather in abundance on the shores. Self-catering campsites to luxury camps are in the park; most camps in the park organize day and night game drives, canoe safaris, walking safaris, and combination canoe and walking safaris.

Chiawa Camp has a resident African hornbill named Momba, rescued from poachers, and a big playmate of the local monkeys. See: www.chiawa.com/pages/momba.htm.

South Luangwa National Park and **North Luangwa National Park** span the Luangwa River Valley in western Zambia. Not easily accessible, they are famous for being remote and wild and home to some unusual endemic species. Fly-in safaris are recommended. Of only 1,200 Thornicroft's giraffe thought to exist in the world, 700 are in South Luangwa National Park, identifiable by their redder color and lack of spots from their knees to their hoofs, making them look as if they are wearing kneesocks.

Similarly, Crawshay's zebras, which have thinner stripes; and Cookson's wildebeest, browner than their northern cousins, also inhabit South Luangwa National Park. Herds of buffalo, more than 2,000 dense, graze in North Luangwa; elephants swim the river, trunks up. Lots of crocodiles, toads, snakes, as well as vervet monkeys, baboons, numerous species of birds, butterflies, spiders, and lots of lions and leopards like these parks for their relatively few tourists.

North Luangwa cannot be entered without a licensed guide; two camps, one with thatched camps the other a tented camp, accommodate visitors.

South Luangwa has campsites and lodges outside the park, and two lodges inside. The lodges will arrange game drives and boat safaris.

Kafue National Park is a contender for the largest African national park, almost 9,000 square miles of grassland interspersed with small lakes. It is also known for having the largest number of antelope species on the continent, in its Busanga floodplain: waterbucks, pukus (horned, golden, about six feet long), greater and lesser kudus, impalas (called "bush hamburger" by some African hands), sable antelope, the elusive loner sitatungas, red lechwes by the thousands, Lichtenstein hartebeest, oribis (small red antelopes), and tsessebes (reddish antelopes with a hump and L-shaped horns). Where antelopes are, huge prides of lions, wild dogs, and especially leopards abound. In fact, leopards hunt during the day. Also look for large African Monitor lizards, civets, genets, mongoose, baboons,

A pair of bongos, a species of African antelope, meet at river's edge in the Jacksonville Zoo. *Roger Archibald*

and zorillas (a skunk-like pole cat). Four-foot-tall shoebills enjoy Kafue. You can also see the usual suspects: elephants, buffalos, and zebras. Five tented camps offer organized game drives and walks, as well as fishing and boat trips. See: www.zambiatourism.com.

The following companies run trips to the parks, some of which are flying safaris:

Mountain Travel Sobek   6420 Fairmount Avenue, El Cerrito, California 94530. Tel: 888-687-6235 (toll-free); 510-527-8100; E-mail: info@mtsobek.com; website: www.mtsobek.com.

Guerba Africa at Adventure Center   1311 63rd Street, Suite 200, Emeryville, California 84608. Tel: 800-228-8747 (toll-free); 510-654-1879; Fax: 510-654-4200; Website: www.adventure center.com.

Geographic Expeditions   2627 Lombard Street, San Francisco, California 94123. Tel: 800-777-8183 (toll-free); 415-922-0448; E-mail: info@geoex.com; Website: www.geoex.com.

Zimbabwe

Zimbabwe is blessed with an abundance of game, eleven well-maintained national parks, Victoria Falls, and the Zambezi River, popular with white-water rafters. The professionalism of its guides has been called the highest in Africa. At this writing, joblessness and threatened famine among Zimbabweans is fueling a volatile political situation, causing the U.S. State Department to issue a travel warning. The borders are dangerous because of land mines.

To date, parks are safe and well maintained, and tourist dollars can only help. Flying in is recommended, because roads are bad or non-existent. Always go with a professional guide. Best season for game viewing is June to October.

Victoria Falls National Park and **Zambezi National Park** are tiny parks with a big waterfall. Victoria Falls can be viewed from Zambia and Zimbabwe, or by crossing the bridge from Zambia into Zimbabwe. The falls are about a mile wide and cascade down for about 350 feet. In mid-April, at full water mark, the falls produce a huge spray that in the full moon creates a lunar rainbow.

Monkeys, baboons, elephants, antelopes, and lots of birds, including falcons, inhabit the surrounding area. Cruise or canoe above the falls and see hippos and elephants onshore, or fly over the falls in a helicopter or ultralight ("Flight of Angels"), for the big picture, which includes game. A huge choice of lodges along the banks of the Zambezi and regal hotels in Livingstone. Canoe trips are permitted on the gentler portions of the Zambezi.

Hwange National Park borders the Kalahari, but has abundant forest in its 9,000 square miles. Thousands, maybe tens of thousands, of elephants call this home, largely because of the sixty or so artificial waterholes that have been dug to create a perpetual presence of water, which means the animals have little need to migrate. Hwange is a premier spot for seeing some of the area's 600 species of migratory birds and good for seeing hyenas, leopards, cheetahs, Masai giraffes, black rhinos (which breed here), and wild dogs. Three camps inside the park provide armed ranger guides.

Matusadona National Park is renowned for lions and is an Intensive Protection Zone for black rhinos and babies orphaned when their mothers were killed for their horns. This 600-square-mile park at the end of Lake Kariba has lots of antelopes, buffalo, cheetahs, and crocodiles. You can take a motor yacht, which comes with a professional guide—probably the safer way of doing the lake. Within the park are several first-class camps and lodges, including the Matsudona Water Wilderness, a group of floating houseboats. Walking tours are permitted.

Mana Pools National Park, a World Heritage Site, has four pools (old lakes) in the northern part of the park, which attract lots of hippos, crocodiles, and thirsty animals such as wild dogs, elands, buffalo, and greater kudu, as well as unusual elephants, many of which have no tusks. An estimated 12,000 elephants and 16,000 buffalos live here. Visitors on walking safaris with professional guides are amazed at the proximity they have with bull elephants (less than six feet). In the eastern part of the park there are no roads, and walking and canoeing safaris are the only ones permitted.

Three- to nine-day canoe safaris are available at three levels: camping on islands in the Zambezi River; first-class safaris, which include a vehicle that follows your progress on the river and sets up mobile tented camp with shower, allowing for night game drives; and luxury safaris, which includes all of the above, plus larger tents, showers, and toilets. Accommodations in the park include ten camp-grounds, and three luxury lodges on the banks of the Zambezi. For Zambezi canoe safaris, see: www.zambezi.co.uk.

Also see: **ZamSaf Zimbabwe**   The Heights, P.O. Box 158, Kariba, Zimbabwe. Tel: 263-61-2532; E-mail: info@zambezi.com.

The following companies offer trips to southern Africa:

National Geographic Expeditions   P.O. Box 65265, Washington, D.C. 20035-5265. Tel: 888-966-8687 (toll-free); Website: www.nationalgeographic.com/ngexpeditions.

Journeys International, Inc.   107 Aprill Drive, Suite 3, Ann Arbor, Michigan 48103-1903. Tel: 800-255-8735 (toll-free); 734-665-2945; E-mail: info@journeys-intl.com; Website: www.journeys-intl.com.

Natural Habitat Adventures   2945 Center Green Court, Boulder, Colorado 80301. Tel: 800-543-8917 (toll-free); 303-449-3711; E-mail: info@nathab.com; Website: www.nathab.com.

Naturequest   30872 S. Coast Highway, Laguna Beach, California 92651. Tel: 800-369-3033 (toll-free); Fax: 949-499-0812; E-mail: naturequest@aol.com; Website: www.naturequest tours.com.

Namibia

The Namib Desert, a true desert, deeply red-orange, with star-shaped dunes (studied by dune experts), and smooth vistas that con-trast sharply with the deep blue sky, runs in a strip about 90 miles wide and 1,200 miles long down the coast of Namibia. This is great country for unusual creatures. Fogs often rest in the desert valleys, blown in from the cool Atlantic Ocean; plants like the welwitschia have learned how to drink the fog and stay alive for thousands of years, and beetles like the fog-basking beetles collect the moisture of the fog by raising their forelegs and letting drops fall into their mouths.

The Namib is thought to be the oldest desert in the world (30 million years), with dunes that continue to grow. South and east of it lies the "moonscape" Kalahari Desert, a rocky stretch of beige and gray sand covered with sparse grass. North of it is Etosha National Park, a dry salt pan for most of the year.

Etosha National Park is unique in that game live in the grasslands and forest surrounding the vast salt pan, but all the diverse species gather at the waterholes in the pan some of which are artificial, which, from July to September, the dry season, makes for easy game viewing. Once a lake, its flat dry aspect allows you to see some of Namibia's unusual species: blue wildebeest, black-faced impalas, gemsbock, desert elephants, the tiny Damara dik-dik, as well as Burchell's zebras, black rhino, jackals, and leopards, and hundreds of species of birds, pelicans, flamingos, and vultures.

Above all, keep a eye on lions in the Etosha Pan: they hunt in a style that has been compared to a rugby team's strategy, coming in from the sides and the center; and they specialize in one very fast antelope, the springbok.

Accommodations are three camps within the park, and several luxury lodges outside it. See www.namibweb.com.

Namib Naukluft National Park is composed of the orange dunes, some dry gray sands, and two rivers. Where the dunes flatten into rocky desert, ostriches and gemsbok abound. Where the desert rises to a plateau are Hartmann's mountain zebras, caracals, mongooses, and colonies of meerkats. Thousands of seabirds migrating north to the Arctic from Antarctica stop and roost along the coast. Campsites are available; several luxury lodges near Sossouvlei. Contact: reservations@iwwn.com.na.

Skeleton Coast National Park is in fact lined with skeletons of ships and whales. Fur seals gather here by the hundreds, and the park is unique worldwide for having lions that hunt the seals and take them down, despite their size differences. Jackals and brown hyenas also prowl the beach looking for dead whales and dolphins. Along the rivers that feed to the beach are huge groups of ostriches, as well as baboons, flamingos, black rhinos, and desert elephants. Accommodations include campsite, tented camp, lodge; for information contact: reservations@iwwn.com.na.

Community-Based Tourism

NACOBTA Booking and Information Office   P.O. Box 40504, 40, Tal Street, Namibia Crafts Center, 1st floor, Windhoek, Namibia. Tel: 011 (264) 061 255977; E-mail: nacobta@iafrica. com.na; Website: www.nacobta.com.na.

Namibia has an active community-based tourism effort, located in the Karas and Hardap region in the south between the Kalahari and Namib deserts. Here sheep farmers raise carakul sheep for their wool to make carpets and garments. Near Fish River Canyon and Quiver Tree Forest, several communities are training guides and developing their homes to accommodate tourists.

Discovery Initiatives   The Travel House, 51 Castle Street, Cirencester, Gloucestershire, GL7 1QD, UK. Tel: 011 (44) 01285 643333; E-mail: Enquiry@discoveryinitiatives.com; Website: www. discoveryinitiatives.com.

A pioneer tour to bring together tourists from abroad and community leaders and wildlife experts, this safari spends time on a farm that is conserving cheetahs; visits with members of the Humba, Damara, and Herero communities; sees black rhinos and desert elephants in the wild on a walking tour in the true bush west of Etosha; and overnights at a research fly camp on the Skeleton Coast. At Etosha National Park, wildlife guide and storyteller Chris Bakkus, a longtime Namibia resident, will also help you understand the unparalleled night skies. Fifteen days, about $4,700.

Join a Scientific Project

Biosphere Expeditions   Sprat's Water near Carlton Colville, The Broads National Park, Suffolk NR33 8BP UK. Tel: 011 44 1502 583085; E-mail: info@biosphere-expeditions.org; Website: www.biosphere-expeditions.org.

Cheetahs are vulnerable in Namibia; for the past few years they have been the farmers' sore problem, often sneaking into the corral to eat domestic animals. To discourage farmers from shooting them, various organizations are experimenting with compensating farmers for their livestock loss.

But the star player, the cheetah, remains unknown. No one knows exactly how many cheetahs exist in Africa, nor why they would eat cattle instead of chasing their favorite, antelopes.

Part of a larger cheetah census project, Biosphere invites volunteers of any age to join a two-week expedition focused on cheetahs. Based near the Okatumba Wildlife Research Center in central Namibia, guests drive the territory in Land Rovers, look for tracks, check box traps, capture and radio-collar cheetahs, and radio-track

A pair of young cheetahs play in Kenya. *Gary Stolz, U.S. Fish and Wildlife Service; www.fws.gov*

them. From blinds built to spy on waterholes, visitors record cheetah behavior while studying cheetahs' preferred diet: kudu, oryx,
and hartebeest. Lodging is in a comfortable tented camp with showers, toilets and good food. About $2,500.

Cheetah Conservation Fund, a group dedicted to the welfare of
the cheetah, runs a research center and museum in the middle of
the Waterberg Plateau, a refuge area for black and white rhinos, as
well as antelopes and lots of birds. It's located about thirty miles
east of Otjiwarongo. E-mail: cheetah@iafrica.com.na; Website: www.
cheetah.org.

Hot-Air Balloon Trips

Elena Travel Services   P.O. Box 3127, Windhoek, Namibia.
Tel: 011 264 61 244443; E-mail: info@namibweb.com.

They depend on the wind and the weather, but if conditions are
clear and gentle, Desert Balloon Safaris will pick you up one half
hour before sunrise at your lodge in Sossusvlei in southern Namibia,
or your hotel in Swakopmund, or your camp in Damaraland. Once
up, you travel for an hour over the dunes and desert, seeing the full
play of early morning activity. One hour and a half, about $380.

A good source of information and contacts, including day trips to
the dunes, is www.namibiaweb.com.

The following companies run trips to Namibia:

Premier Tours   217 South 20th Street, Philadelphia, Pennsylvania
19103. Tel: 800-545-1910 (toll-free); E-mail: info@premiertours.
com. Website: www.premiertours.com.

Journeys International, Inc.   107 Aprill Drive, Suite 3, Ann
Arbor, Michigan 48103-1903. Tel: 800-255-8735 (toll-free);
E-mail: info@journeys-intl.com; Website: www.journeys-intl.com.

South Africa

The most famous national park in all of southern Africa, **Kruger
National Park** wins the prize for the most species in any park in

Africa: 130 species of mammals, 468 species of birds, 114 species of reptiles, and lots more, according to the African Wildlife Foundation. Kruger National Park also attracts close to a million visitors each year, closely guided in park vehicles that adhere to well-worn paths.

Fortunately, parts of the 55-mile-wide, 220-mile-long park are unfenced, allowing game to mix with game in neighboring unfenced private reserves. Game viewing tends to be less structured in the private parks, with well-trained guides staying in touch via walkie-talkies with other guides throughout the areas and venturing off the trails to follow predator dramas into the bush. They are also less crowded.

It's all there to see, and you can stay in any of several luxury tented camps and lodges, cheaper in Kruger N.P., but well run, in all cases.

See www.krugerpark.co.za.

Sabi Sands Game Reserves: www.sabikrugerpark.co.za.

Mala Mala Game Reserve: www.malamala.com.

Elephant Safari

Kapama Reserve and Lodge   Website: www.kapama.co.za.

Located near Kruger National Park, this former cheetah breeding farm is now a rescue center for big game. This explains the presence of elephants, refugees from conflicts in Zimbabwe, now trained to take visitors on safari. Tours are given of the research station. Staying at Camp Jabulani, a collection of luxury tented camps on the reserve, provides lots of up-close and personal time with elephants; in fact you can even take a five-day elephant safari, leaving each morning to venture into the bush. Several options for lodging, range from $225 to $490 per person, double occupancy.

2

APES

CHIMPANZEES

You will probably hear chimps before you see them and when you see them they might be in the trees. Called the noisiest of all jungle creatures, chimps are us: 98.4 percent of our DNA matches theirs. Plus, chimps make and use tools to get the best last termite out of the mound. They solve problems, for example, how to crack tough nuts: wedge them between two branches, then whack them with a stone. Unlike other apes, chimps eat meat, even hunt small mammals. On occasion, they cannibalize their young, and they engage in wicked warfare. Chimps, says legendary researcher Jane Goodall, are more like human beings than they are like gorillas.

Maybe Smarter Than We Know

Jane Goodall, who has spent fifty years observing and monitoring them and putting them in focus for the rest of the world to see, believes that chimps can make thirty sounds that mean different things, can learn 100 signs of American Sign Language, love to drum on tree trunks, and can dance. Their close cousins, bonobos, which are smaller and spend more time walking upright, have demonstrated such abilities as making stone tools after watching an expert flint-knapper. A famous bonobo, Kanzi, at the University of Georgia, is on the verge of imitating human speech, his researchers believe.

No one knows for sure, but educated guesses are that there are between 20,000 and 150,000 chimps in the true tropical rainforests of equatorial Africa, from Gabon to Tanzania. These numbers are minuscule compared with the estimated million and a half that lived there a century ago. Bonobos, thought to number about 5,000, live only in the Democratic Republic of Congo (former Zaire).

All in a Chimp's Day

Endangered, despite all their noisy and active intelligence, chimps have to deal with poachers stealing their babies and selling them for bushmeat or capturing them for medical experiments, and with loggers carving huge chunks out of their habitats. At the Ngamba Island Chimpanzee Sanctuary, chimps from one to nineteen can live in peace, having been rescued from traveling circuses, private homes where they were kept as pets, and thieves ready to pop on planes at the Entebbe airport. Technically, chimps are protected by international law, and thieves are punishable.

But the solution, as Goodall sees it, is for people to understand that chimps and human beings share a common ancestor (about 5 million years ago), and today, share common understanding. At a conference on the legal status of chimps, she told a story of chasing a chimp that she thought was afraid of her through the underbrush. When the chimp turned to face her, they eyed each other for a moment, then the chimp reached out and squeezed her hand.

More people need to have compelling experiences like this, Goodall said. "People never get over it. They're changed for life."

Get Closer

Opportunities exist to spend an hour or so walking in the forest with sanctuary chimps on an island in Lake Victoria, and tracking them in the wilds of the Ugandan rainforest in the Kibale National Park, where you listen for their pant-grunts.

Uganda

Ngamba Island Chimpanzee Sanctuary

This island sanctuary is in Lake Victoria, about fifteen miles south of Entebbe, run by a consortium of African wildlife organizations. On ninety-eight acres, surrounded by an electric fence, about forty chimps live in the island rainforest, most of them rescued from bad situations, some orphaned by poachers. Visitors are invited to watch them from two overlooks as they are fed, or to stay overnight at a tented camp on the island and to participate in their bedtime feeding routines. Those who stay overnight can take an afternoon Forest Walk with the infant chimps, aged one to eight.

Chimps are very active, and will want to play by climbing on you, stealing things from your pockets, play-biting, and holding your hand as you walk along the path.

When you are not with the chimps, you will have access to all the recreational facilities of Lake Victoria, from kayaking to swimming.

Note: Because of the closeness of the encounters, all visitors are required to undergo a medical checkup to ensure all the prerequisite inoculations and no flu-like symptoms. Health cards must show proof of inoculations against measles, hepatitis A and B, meningococcal meningitis, polio, tetanus, and yellow fever, as well as indicate a negative TB test within the past six months.

You can take a half-hour speedboat or a 1½ hour traditional motor boat from Entebbe. Or take a tour with one of the following companies.

Discovery Initiatives   The Travel House, 51 Castle Street, Cirencester, Gloucestershire, GL7 1QD, UK. Tel: 011 44 01285 643333; E-mail: Enquiry@discoveryinitiatives.com; Website: www. discoveryinitiatives.com.

This trip begins with a visit to a "high quality" clinic in Kampala to ensure visitors have all inoculations. Then you head off to **Kibale National Park** to track some of its 700 chimps in the wild with park guides. In **Queen Elizabeth Park** do some habituated-chimp tracking at Kyambura Gorge; then go to Bwindi Impenetrable Forest, one of two mountain gorilla sites in the Virunga Range. Next, spend three days at Ngamba Island Chimp Sanctuary. Eleven days, about $4,000, includes lodging, meals, and international airfare from London. It also includes a donation to the Ngamba Chimpanzee Sanctuary.

Mountain Travel Sobek   6420 Fairmount Avenue, El Cerrito, California 94530. Tel: 888-687-6235 (toll-free); 510-527-8100; E-mail: info@mtsobek.com; Website: www.mtsobek.com

Visit Kibale National Park and its chimps, then go to Queen Elizabeth National Park and see 1,000 elephants and 100 species of mammals. Track chimps in Kyambura Gorge; then spend two days tracking gorillas in the Bwindi Impenetrable Forest. Thirteen days, moderate to strenuous game hikes, about $5,000.

Tanzania

Mahale Mountains National Park

Siyabona Africa   156 Long Street, Cape Town, South Africa. Tel: 27 21 424 1037; Fax: 27 21 424 1036; E-mail: reservations@siyabona.com; Website: www.siyabona.com.

South of Jane Goodall's Gombe Chimp Research Center is Mahale Mountains National Park, home to about one thousand chimps, some of which are habituated. In this dense, roadless park, surrounded by 6,000-foot mountains, researchers guide you to the place where chimps spent the previous night. You arrive and leave by boat or floatplane, but in the park, you have no choice but to walk and to stay at Greystoke Camp, a luxury tented camp and to be among the chimps. Bill Gates vacationed here. This four-day trek includes a dhow trip on Lake Tanganyika, the longest fresh-water lake in the world—and the deepest, after Lake Baikal. Open January to March and June to October. Four days, per person, double occupancy, from $760 to $850.

Websites

The Jane Goodall Institute: www.janegoodall.org.

ChimpanZoo   The Geronimo Bldg, No. 308, 800 E. University Blvd., Tucson, Arizona 85721. Tel: 520-621-4785; Website: www. chimpanZoo.org.

ChimpanZoo is a primate research organization of the Jane Goodall Institute that observes behavior of chimps in zoos and captivity. Members train volunteers and teach data collection techniques. See also:

www.savethechimps.org.

www.chimpcollaboratory.org, the site for legal rights for chimps.

GORILLAS

Level, curious, and vulnerable, a gorilla's gaze lets us know, as George Schaller wrote (*The Mountain Gorilla*, 1963), "that the gorilla still lives within us." Whatever the transcendent magic is, gorillas are able to establish a link. Those who experience it are often moved to tears. No other animal in the wild establishes such intimacy, perhaps because gorillas, unlike chimps, convey an otherworldly calm.

Of the three species of gorilla, most Eastern Lowland gorillas are in zoos; and several thousand Western Lowland gorillas inhabit the dense jungles of Cameroun, Gabon, and the Central African Republic; all are subject to the problems at the human interface. Of the 1,200 Western Lowland gorillas, which live in a national park in Congo Republic, for example, 800 were recently killed in an Ebola epidemic.

Bushtracks Expeditions   P.O. Box 4163, Menlo Park, California 94026. Tel: 800-995-8689 (toll-free); 650-326-8689; Fax: 650-463-0925; E-mail: Website: www.bushtracks.com.

Western Lowland gorillas might remind you of King Kong: the silverbacks are extremely huge. Traveling by private air to access national parks in Central African Republic and Congo Republic that are rarely visited by any tourists, you join up with Pygmy trackers who will take you on foot through true tropical rainforest to the gorillas. At a salt lick you will be able to watch forest elephants, forest buffalo, and flocks of gray parrots. Then take a dugout canoe through gorilla territory in Congo. Eleven days, includes all internal travel by private air, about $9,000.

USA Adventure Center   1311 63rd Street, Suite 200, Emeryville, California 94608. Tel: 800-227-8747 (toll-free); 510-654-1879; Fax: 510-654-4200; E-mail: ex@adventurecenter.com; Website: www.adventurecenter.com.

Working in conjunction with a local forest preservation group in Gabon, this trip takes you by train from Libreville to a wildlife reserve with some 5,000 Western Lowland gorillas. Then traveling on foot, in dugouts, and 4-WD go deeper into the rainforest to the Mikongo Primate Research Center. Eight days, about $2,500.

A silverback lowland gorilla shows his muscle at the New Orleans Zoo.
Roger Archibald

Mountain Gorillas

Mountain gorillas are so endangered, researchers know most of them by name. Located almost exclusively around the volcanic Virunga Range that straddles Democratic Republic of Congo, Rwanda, and Uganda, Mountain gorillas range tenuously between family farms, poachers, leopards, and traps set for antelope—and all of this in areas that have been hard hit by genocidal wars and the atrocities of mindless rebel groups.

In nearby Democratic Republic of Congo, tens of thousands of refugees, forced into a national park, squeezed gorillas' range. Congolese coltan mines eat holes in their habitats. A couple of years ago, European Space Agency satellites began monitoring the area to figure out how bad the habitat degradation is.

Time for Tourists to Step In

Tourists come, despite the danger, drawn to find the jewels in the forest, as if the danger is a kind of payment for the special privilege. Armed rangers usually accompany groups in Rwanda and Uganda. For those researchers who complain that ecotourism is destructive because guides cut viewing paths through gorilla habitat and tourists bring disease, conservationists argue that bringing in tourists is good for the local economy because it offers an alternative to poaching; it's good for the gorillas because it brings attention to their problems; and it's good for tourists who have the experience of a lifetime.

Rwanda

On the slopes of extinct volcanoes in the Parc National des Volcans, you hear branches being snapped and the sound of chewing when you are close. Gorillas' odor has been described as a pungent mix of wild and barnyard. A silverback might pound his chest or stomp the ground or even make a mock attack, before turning back. But they are gentle herbivores, smaller and fewer than their western cousins, interacting with grunts and squeals, perennially seeking or noshing leaves and shoots.

Gorilla Rules

Guides imitate gorilla vocalization by clearing their throats in a guttural bark. Because they are habituated to people, these gorillas show no fear. Twenty-four feet is the closest you are allowed to go—for the health of the gorillas, which are highly susceptible to human bacteria and viruses. If you sneeze or cough, you must cover your mouth—that's a rule. Visitors are encouraged not to stare or point, as this agitates gorillas. Nevertheless, gentle and curious, gorillas might come closer to you to peer into your eyes. The hour that you are officially allowed to spend goes quickly.

Karisoke Research Station, Parc des Volcans

In Rwanda, you can visit the Karisoke Research Station begun by Dian Fossey in 1966, which served as her home until 1985 when she was murdered (*Gorillas in the Mist*). Her grave is nearby, next to those of her gorillas.

The Parc National des Volcans is the protected home of about 350 mountain gorillas. About six feet tall and weighing an average 400 pounds, these gorillas have long black fur to compensate for cool mountain temperatures. They were not discovered by Europeans until 1903; their behavior has been the subject of research for fewer than forty years.

Trained park rangers lead small groups up into the montane forests, where gorilla troops usually gather in the leafy clearings to eat the vegetation. Four troops of various sizes live here, usually consisting of one silverback, a few females, and their young. Gorillas eat, lie around, play, interact, and rest during the day, usually centered around the silverback, who is very much in control. Toward sundown, they build sleeping nests in trees or on the ground.

Be prepared for the height: the mountains range between 8,000 and 15,000 feet. Depending on the season and its fruits, gorillas move over a ten- to fifteen-square-mile home range.

Park fees are $275 a day. The beginning of the rainy season, October and November, are good months to see gorillas. In the dry season, June to September, they range farther for food; in the rainy season, December to May, it's just too wet. The following compa-nies offer guided trips to see mountain gorillas in Rwanda:

Premier Tours   217 South 20th Street, Philadelphia, Pennsylvania 19103. Tel: 800-545-1910 (toll-free); E-mail: info@ premiertours.com; Website: www.premiertours.com.

. This company has guides experienced in all three gorilla coun-tries: Uganda, Rwanda, and Congo. They arrange six- and eight-day trips to Uganda and Rwanda, with the option of three gorilla treks. To arrange a custom trip, call 800-545-1910, ext. 414, or email: bobb@premiertours.com.

African Wildlife Foundation   Craig Sholley. Tel: 888-4WILD-LIFE [494-3543] (toll-free); E-mail: csholley@awf.org; Website: www.awf.org.

This combo chimp/gorilla trip begins in Uganda with a visit to the Ngamba Chimp Sanctuary, then goes to Kibale National Park (700 chimps) and the Bwindi Impenetrable Forest, where you spend three days with the gorillas, before going to the Parc des Volcans gorillas in Rwanda. Fourteen days, about $8,800 (includes interna-tional airfare from New York).

Uganda

Bwindi Impenetrable Forest

The Virunga Mountains stretch north into Uganda and provide a dense forest for about 350 mountain gorillas. Guides and armed park rangers lead groups through the tangled jungle until they hear the characteristic "bark" and grunts and bamboo stems being broken that signify gorillas. In an environment that is slightly lower and slightly warmer than the Parc des Volcans, the gorillas have a slightly different diet, which occasionally leads them into competi-tion with wild chimpanzees that do not inhabit Rwanda. Otherwise, the two apes tolerate one another.

This park suffered from an attack by rebels in 1997 when eight tourists were killed. Since then Ugandan officials have increased security, and curiously, tourism has increased as well.

Park (gorilla) fees are about $250 a day; because they are in high demand, you should apply six months in advance. (If you go with a group, they will take care of the fees.)

In addition to the companies already mentioned, the following run tours to Bwindi:

Journeys International   107 Aprill Drive, Suite 3, Ann Arbor, Michigan 48103. Tel: 800-255-8735 (toll-free); 734-665-4407; E-mail: info@journeys-intl.com; Website: www.journeys-intl.com.

Rainbow Tours   Canon Collins House, 64 Essex Road, London N1 8LR, UK. Tel: 011 44 020 7226 1004; Fax: 44 020 7226 2621; E-mail: info@rainbowtours.co.uk; Website: www.rainbowtours. co.uk.

Websites

Mountain Gorilla Conservation Fund: www.mgcf.net.

Great Ape Alliance: www.great-apes.org.

Koko meets Robin Williams!   Koko was one of the first gorillas used in language-training research. Taught American sign language in the 1970s, she is able to communicate her thoughts and reactions, as well as a lot of love. Today Koko lives in Hawaii and stays in touch through a website: www.koko.org. Her painting accomplishments are posted for sale, as is the video made of her goofing it up with Robin Williams on a recent visit.

ORANGUTANS

Borneo

The red-haired "Man of the Forest" (*orang* is forest, *utan* is man), all 15,000 to 20,000 of them, lives in the deep true tropical jungles of

A mother orang and her baby visit Camp Leakey. Young
orangs stay with their mothers for eight years.
*Georgeanne Irvine, Orangutan Foundation International;
www.orangutan.org*

Borneo and Sumatra. They are about five feet tall and have arms
that are almost as long, used in swinging from branch to branch in
search of fruit, which they sometimes reach for hanging upside
down. One visitor to Camp Leakey, the orang research station in
the middle of Borneo where bicultural orangs and humans inter-
mingle, was trying to photograph orangs in the dense trees, when
she became separated from her group and was completely lost in
the dense jungle. Suddenly behind her was a thud, and there was
one of the orangs she had been photographing, standing inches
away. He reached out, took her trembling hand, and led her out to
a clearing and the rest of her group.

Stories like these abound around the camp, a sort of triage center
for orangs that are shot by miners or poachers or loggers, and an
orphanage for baby orangs whose mothers have been killed, and a
rehab center for orangs whose range has been cleared by loggers,
miners, or farmers. It's also a place where orangs that were reintro-

duced to the wild in the 1970s and 1980s return for occasional company and assurance. They are called "bicultural."

Begun in 1971 by Dr. Birute Mary Galdikas as the first orang research center, Camp Leakey (named after her mentor, paleontologist Louis Leakey, who also counseled Jane Goodall and Dian Fossey) is now open to visitors. Wood walkways surround it, used by both human beings and orangs. If you don't mind living in the Rimba Lodge in a swamp in the middle of a rainforest, where the only transport is boat, where spiders are the size of your hand and the shower spouts river water, you'll have a wonderful time. Orangs love it.

Research is ongoing here with American and Indonesian graduate students working on projects such as orang sign language. You can talk to people about the recent findings that orangs exhibit at least thirty-six documented cultural behaviors—habits they learn from their parents and relatives. In parts of Borneo, for example, orangs "kiss-squeak" (a really big kissing sound): sometimes they do it with leaves to amplify the sound; other times they cup their hands around their mouths to make it even louder. It seems to mean that they don't like something or someone nearby.

Like chimps, orangs are big users of tools: branches as bee-swatters, sticks to scratch their backs or get seeds out of their fruit, and big leaves to serve as ponchos in the rain. Harvard anthropologist Cheryl Knott saw one pregnant female orang cradling a bunch of leaves like an infant.

See Them While You Can

Researchers predict that orangs will be totally extinct in the wild in five to ten years. Most trips begin in Pangkalan Bun, then catch a boat upstream on a "kelotok" (repeat it fast, and you hear the motor) to Rimba Lodge across the river from the Tanjung Puting National Park. The lodge is on stilts.

Orangutan Foundation International   822 S. Wellesley Avenue, Los Angeles, California 90049. Tel: 800-ORANGUTAN

[672-6488] (toll-free); 310-207-1655; E-mail: ofi@orangutan.org; Website: www.orangutan.org.

This conservation group offers a variety of trips to Camp Leakey. Their five-day tour is a taste of the area, beginning in Pangkalan Bun then traveling upstream to the Tanjung Putung National Park. Visit the Orang Rehab Center and Camp Leakey. Five days, about $900.

For those who are above average fitness, over eighteen, and can spend six weeks working in Borneo, you can help build a new rehab area, Lamandau Reserve. Food and lodging are about $120 a week.

Discovery Initiatives   The Travel House, 51 Castle Street, Cirencester, Gloucestershire, GL7 1QD, UK. Tel: (00 44) 01285 643333; E-mail: Enquiry@discoveryinitiatives.com; Website: www. discoveryinitiatives.com.

This total-immersion, unconventional nine-day trip splits into teams that go out from Camp Leakey into the jungle, tracking and recording data on orang movements, social interaction, and individuals in the wild. Traveling by motorboat or in dugouts or on foot, you get to know orangs, the jungle, and some of the people who live nearby. A portion of tour money goes back to the Orangutan Foundation. Nine days, about $3,100.

Eco-Expeditions   192 Nickerson Street, No. 200, Seattle, Washington 98109. 800-628-8747 (toll-free); 206-285-4000; E-mail: zoe@zeco.com; Website: www.zeco.com.

This trip explores wildlife in **Mount Kinabalu National Park**, before going deeper into the true tropical rainforest of Danum Valley, home of wild orangs. Night tours enable you to see clouded leopards, red flying squirrels, and unusual and rare species such as the slow loris and tarsier (big-eyed, fuzzy nocturnal tree-dwellers). By river through the Sakua rainforest, look for primates, langurs, flying lemurs, and on the riverbanks, saltwater crocodiles. Then spend a few days upclose with orangs at the Sepilok Orangutan Rehabilitation Center. Seventeen days, about $8,000.

GIBBONS

Thailand

The fourth ape (in company with gorillas, chimps, and orangutans), gibbons are endangered generally. Native to Southeast Asia, gibbons comprise thirteen species, two of which have only twenty individuals left.

Not as flashy as their African or Bornean brothers and sisters, gibbons live in the canopy of the forests in Southeast Asia, Thailand, Sumatra, and the Malay Peninsula. They swing with their

A mother white-cheeked gibbon and her infant live at the Gibbon Conservation Center, where volunteers are invited to help at feeding time. This species gives birth to one infant at a time; it will stay with its mother for a year and a half. Once free-ranging in southeast Asia, almost all gibbons are now endangered. *J. Zuckerman, www.gibboncenter.org*

long arms from branch to branch faster than anything else in the upper forest. They also win the Olympic prize for the longest leap of any brachiating primate: thirty feet.

Called "lesser apes," including the siamang with its inflatable throat sac (to amplify its voice), they range over fifty acres, looking for fruit, flowers, insects, birds, anything tasty to eat. At night gibbons sleep sitting up in the fork of a tree and greet the dawn with a half hour of hooting that can be heard for three or four miles. It means: This is where I'm having breakfast; enemies keep their distance, please. They mate for life and keep their kids around until they are about seven years old.

Gibbons, like all apes, are being pushed off their territory by people when they are not being hunted to serve as pets.

Ecovolunteers   website: www.ecovolunteer.org. You can also book with **Wildwings**, 577 Fishponds Rd., Fishponds, Bristol BS16 3AF, UK. Tel: 011 44 0117 9658 333; Fax: 0117 9375681; E-mail: wildinfo@wildwings.co.uk; Website: www.wildwings.co.uk.

If you are interested in getting to know the white-handed gibbon, common in Thailand, then sign on with the Gibbon Sanctuary on Phuket Island, Thailand. Here in the Khao Phra Thaeur National Park, volunteers are invited to work in a gibbon rescue and rehabilitation center for gibbons that have been in failed home situations or hurt in the wilds. The object is to reintroduce them to the wild, but not all are able to reach that level.

Work is eight hours a day, six days a week and consists of preparing food and repairing things that need to be refurbished in the sanctuary. On some days you will observe individual gibbons, noting every nuance of their behavior. On other days you will greet tourists. You will not be asked to handle the gibbons. Lodging is in a bungalow in a small village. Three weeks minimum, about $1,500.

International Center for Gibbon Studies   P.O. Box 800249, Santa Clarita, California 91380. Tel: 661-296-2737; E-mail: gibboncntr@aol.com; Website: www.gibboncenter.org.

The Gibbon Conservation Center, a member of the American Zoo and Aquarium Association (AZA), runs a captive breeding and behaviorial study program for six of the most endangered species. You will learn how to be a keen animal observer when you become a volunteer. Work with 40 gibbons, including the rare moloch gibbon, of which there are only 300 in the wild. All gibbons live in pairs as they would in the wild, and they are housed in spacious outdoor cages.

You can volunteer at various levels: primate keeper, center assistant (maintain the grounds, do observations and library research), and clerical assistant (do observations, fund-raising, and word processing). The primate keeper oversees the animals' feeding, does observations, and lots of other tasks. This job is physically strenuous because gibbons are strong and never still.

You must be eighteen, in good health, and have all your inoculations, including TB and hepatitis B. About $50 a week for residents of one month. Day volunteers are asked to commit to two days a month.

The Center gives educational tours to groups of fifteen or more at various levels of interest, from college to elementary school. Call to reserve. About $9 adults, $8 seniors and teens, $6 children ages two to twelve. To protect the gibbons, all visitors must be in good health and expect to dip the soles of their shoes in disinfectant on entering. For volunteering information call 303-584-0371; E-mail: gibbonvolunteer@earthlink.net.

Websites

For the latest research on gibbons in the wild: www.gibbons.de. This is the site of gibbon researcher Dr. Thomas Geissmann.

3

ELEPHANTS

AFRICA'S LARGEST MAMMAL

Somehow, elephants manage to tiptoe so quietly through the bush that they can send a startled game drive into reverse when they suddenly materialize from behind a stand of trees. In fact, the only sound you might hear is the unmistakable sound of passing gas. A source of jokes among those who work in the bush, elephant flatulence is the natural result of their 350-pound daily diet of grass and leaves, much of it undigested fiber.

Beyond that, being in the presence of an elephant inspires awe, that the largest land mammal, provided it is not threatened, is so mild-mannered. Recent research suggests that elephants are family oriented, heavily into compassion.

Odd Relatives

Early elephants, which inhabited just about everywhere (except Australia and New Zealand) looked a little like tapirs. Cousins of mammoths, elephants are related to species that look nothing like them: the manatee (aquatic Barneys) and the hyrax (which resemble a mean squirrel without a tail). A resident of the earth for at least 50 million years, elephants grew like Topsy, perfecting columnar legs and padded feet, and an upper lip, or trunk, long enough to take leaves from a twenty-foot tree, sensitive enough to detect smells several miles away, and precise enough to pick up a tiny seed pod.

For Want of a Dentist

Elephants' life span depends on their teeth. Their diet demands lots of grinding, and new molars grow as they are needed until an elephant is sixty years old. When the last set of molars wears out, an elephant is on its own in the wild, unable to chew and facing starvation.

Historically, Asian elephants were helpers and haulers; Alexander the Great's men brought them back to Greece. Hannibal used African elephants on his famous trek across the Alps. Although elephants have been clocked racing at twenty-five miles an hour, they are generally slow. Elephant-back safaris move through the bush at about two miles an hour, even more slowly if it is hot.

A Loyal Sisterhood

For psychologist Cynthia Moss, who began studying elephant social structure in Kenya's Amboseli National Park in the 1970s, elephants are spookily sophisticated. She identified more than fifty elephant families, each with five levels of community and social interaction. The gals stick together, with the matriarchs (usually the grandmothers) calling the daily shots, because their elephant memory—for seasonal water holes, food sources, and dangerous places and creatures—has so much in it.

Babies are few and far between: after an almost two-year gestation period, single calves are born separated by four to five years, and they don't reach reproductive age until they are fourteen years old. For these reasons, the females in the herd families continuously guard the young elephants. They are indulged, forgiven, and savagely protected. Moss and her assistants gave most of the Amboseli elephants names like Maud, Mary, Evelyn, and Ellen. The bulls, on the other hand, identified earlier by a (male) British researcher, are known as M-16, K-5, and so on (see Cynthia Moss, *Elephant Memories*, 1998).

Bulls are huge loners for the most part. When their testosterone is high, and they are in *musth*, their temporal glands (at the temples) drip down the sides of their heads, exuding a pungent odor, and they are ready to mate or take on any adversary, from other elephants to

Few elephants get through the day without a lot of play. This one is playing with his food at the Los Angeles Zoo. *Roger Archibald*

Land Rovers. Tracking down female herds, a bull sniffs each female until he finds one in heat, then mates. Researcher Katy Payne, from the Cornell University Bioacoustics Research Progam, recorded a mating with a female in heat that took a total of forty-five seconds.

Not all bulls are alike. Cynthia Moss's favorite bull elephant, M-22, which she named Dionysus, stood out from the rest of the crowd by his good manners, including, Moss noted, stroking the face of his chosen female before mounting her.

What You Can't Hear

Researchers Joyce Poole, Payne, and Moss are all studying the rumbles, trumpetings, and mumbles of elephant communication—but especially the rumbles—which Payne described as trembling through her body like the extreme low notes of an organ playing Bach: she felt them rather than heard them. Based on her research with whale communication, Payne, who is currently working with Forest Elephants in the Central African Republic, recorded a herd of Amboseli elephants in 1987, then played it speeded up. What came through was a series of sounds at 5 hertz (Hz), far lower than human hearing (20 Hz is the lowest).

The low frequency infrasound waves, Payne reasoned, were able to pass through any obstacles in the bush and across the savannah to travel a distance of four miles and stay in touch with other families for news and information on water and food conditions and poachers in other parts of the savannah. Cynthia Moss, funded by a Macarthur grant, is currently studying the rumbles of Amboseli elephants.

Trunks Are Fun

The original water babies of Africa, elephants use their trunks as snorkels to cross rivers in southern Africa. They also use them when they play at deep waterholes, wallowing in the mud, blowing water on themselves and at each other. Katy Payne described coming upon a scene at a waterhole in Zimbabwe where she was unable to distinguish tangled legs from trunks, as a whole herd of elephants played, half submerged, while on the shore, three elephant calves had devised a form of leap-frog, with the last leaper landing in the water. (See Katy Payne, *Silent Thunder*, 1998.)

Elephant Problems

When Ernest Hemingway aimed his guns at wildlife in the early 1920s, several hundred thousand elephants occupied East Africa. In the 1970s and 1980s, conflicts with people and environmental problems began to reduce their numbers. The worst were (and are) ivory poachers, who used AK-47s and chainsaws to cut off the tusks and killed elephants by the thousands.

Throughout the 1970s severe drought dried up the vegetation

that elephants eat and turned their water holes to dust bowls (they drink more than twenty gallons of water per day). Angry farmers took aim when hungry elephants stole their crops or wiped out stores in their kitchens. Plus, wars made villagers homeless and hungry and forced them to render elephants into bushmeat. Land mines buried at borders blew up under elephants' feet. These have all contributed to altering elephants' lifestyles. Today all three species—the African, the Asiatic, and the Forest elephant—are threatened or endangered. The Asiatic elephant is endangered; fewer than 25,000 exist in India, what's left after a few decades of poaching and loss of habitat.

In 1979 there were an estimated 1.3 million elephants in all of Africa, according to the African Wildlife Foundation (www.awf.org). Today estimates range from 300,000 to 600,000, with the under-population in East Africa in contrast to the overpopulation in southern Africa. Ten years ago, conservationists estimated that African elephants could be extinct by 2020, and put them on the endangered list. Two years ago CITES (the Convention on International Trade in Endangered Species) dropped that to "threatened." The change was largely due since the 1970s to the successful development of national parks and private reserves, which provide protection, food, water, and habitat for elephants and other wild animals. Now governments impose severe punishment on poachers, and some rangers shoot to kill poachers.

Locking the Cupboards

But farmers and elephants still compete for space. Off the park range, all wild animals are in danger. Tanzanian Alfred Kikoti, a researcher with the African Wildlife Foundation, leads a team that is working to do geographic information system (GIS) transects of elephant migration paths of some of the 1,500 Kilimanjaro-area elephants. He is also identifying hotspots—conflict areas where farmers and elephants come together—and is working on ways in which they can be encouraged to live together. Kikoti has discovered that sometimes simple things, such as flashlights placed around conflict areas, work to divert elephants from crops and water storage tanks.

Who Are Elephants?

Like lions, elephants help each other when help is needed. In her several years of research, Katy Payne noted that there is enormous variation in individuals; like us, she said, they can be both compassionate and brutal. A lot of their behavior is mystifying: she once witnessed a young adult male try fifty-seven times to make a dead calf stand up.

Researcher Joyce Poole found that female elephants have a lot more infrasonic chatter going on than males. If studying their vocalizations has taught her anything, she said in a speech given in 2001, it is how much elephants value their family and friends. "Over and over again," she said, "elephants use vocalizations to tell one another how much they are valued and how important their contribution is."

Websites

For updates from Amboseli, see the site of the Cynthia Moss's African Elephant Conservation Trust, www.elephanttrust.org.

For elephant sounds, see Katy Payne: www.birds.cornell.edu/brp/elephant.

Join Leonardo Di Caprio in a campaign against ivory poachers: www.ifaw.org.

See also www.awf.org, the African Wildlife Foundation.

CITES: www.cites.org.

www.savetheelephants.com.

4

LIONS

COMPLEX CATS

"To the list of inert noble gases, including krypton, argon, and neon, we would add lion," wrote behaviorial researchers Craig Packer and Anne E. Pusey in *Scientific American*, May 1997. "Lions are supremely adept at doing nothing." What started out as a short project to investigate lion social structure stretched over several years to accommodate lions' rest periods.

Part of a study of lions since 1966 in Serengeti National Park, Tanzania, Wildlife Conservation International researchers Packer and Pusey found that lions are far more complex than even the *Lion King* suggested: in addition to being masters of the art of lazing around, they pick cooperation over competition every time.

In some areas of southern Africa, researchers have discovered that female lions approach a speeding prey in a U-shaped ambush, from behind and from the sides. In the Serengeti, on the other hand, lionesses often hunt alone if the prey is easy or small, such as antelopes or wildebeest on migration, but will join a group ambush if the prey is large or difficult, such as a Cape buffalo. Lionesses will not join a sister if she is an adept lone hunter, but they will rise to the occasion if their sister is a bumbler who misses every time.

Packer and Pusey discovered that generating and protecting the young—lions' ticket to survival—is the main driver in their cooperation. Groups of either related or nonrelated males join a pride, or society of related females. Often one or two lions, either the health-

52

iest or the youngest, will mate with all the females, a situation that does not cause conflict with their brothers, which readily patrol and protect the territorial borders at night from other invading males.

The females with cubs form a creche, or child care cooperative, in which cubs nurse from all nursing mothers, and the mothers look after each others' cubs. Packer and Pusey found that the amount of milk in a nursing mother depended not on the number of babies she had, but on how much food she had to eat. So a hunting lioness, often away on business trips, as it were, depended on her sisters for her children's welfare.

Every two to three years, however, roaming bands of males invade to upset the resident males and take over the pride. Bloody battles often ensue. If the new invaders are successful, they might also kill the youths of the previous males in the pride. Females also fight to the death if their hunting territory, den, or waterholes are invaded by other female lions.

Join a Scientific Project

Discovery Initiatives   The Travel House, 51 Castle Street, Cirencester, Gloucestershire, GL7 1QD, UK. Tel: 011 44 01285 643333; E-mail: Enquiry@discoveryinitiatives.com; Website: www.discoveryinitiatives.com.

Do your part for lions from the air and on the ground. Part of a long-term study by two wildlife biologists working in conjunction with the Botswana Department of Wildlife and National Parks to identify lion activity in the Okavango, the Botswana Lion Survey is conducted by researchers from off-road vehicles and low-flying aircraft who seek and track members of lion prides that have been tagged. Volunteers and researchers also do counts along the road of herbivores, such as Cape buffalo, and take fixed-point pictures from the plane to monitor vegetation changes. Best of all, you will become familiar with each lion and be able to identify it whenever you see it. If time and conditions permit, you might track lions from the ground.

Staying at a comfortable camp with safari tents with adjoining private facilities, you are well briefed, learn to do transects and aerial surveys, then spend five days on three-hour twice-a-day flyovers. The plane is a six-seater Cessna that flies about eighty-five miles an hour at an altitude of about 300 feet. Back at camp, coordinate data.

Downtime you can take a mokoro trip and experience zebra, greater kudu, impala, plus saddlebill storks, and many other species in abundance. Twelve days, from about £2,000 ($3,500) to £4,200 ($6,300), depending on the season; includes airfare from London.

PERSECUTED PREDATORS: LAIKIPIA LIONS

Aside from other lions, their only predators are human beings, with guns and poisons that are hard to reckon with. In Kenya, many new villages with corrals of livestock in the middle of lions' usual hunting ranges have had a tremendous impact on lion population. With diminished numbers, lions have undergone a personality change: normally a daylight hunter living openly in the savannah, the Laikipia lions have taken to hunting only at night and are rarely seen.

In the Laikipia Project, in conjunction with Wildlife Conservation International, in the district of Laikipia, northern Kenya, Laurence Frank has been studying the effects on the social units of lions that are regularly killed by angry farmers. Calling lions "persecuted predators," he hopes to find ways in which human beings and lions living close together can work out a manageable situation.

The lions' skittishness has made research next to impossible: to dart them in order to take DNA and blood samples and attach radio collars, researchers had to set snares at the lions' kill sites and catch them when they returned to eat. Twice-monthly aerial transects allow Frank and his assistants to track the more than seventy collared lions. But lab data do not indicate how many cubs have lost their natural mothers, or how the pride survives without male protection. To get this information, Frank and his assistants have to crawl through dense bush and spy undetected, they hope, on the lions.

Because it is easier to get to people than the lions, Frank and his assistants are working on helping the Masai build predator-proof corrals—ones whose walls lions can't leap over—even if the new corrals represent a complete break with Masai building tradition. Commercial ranches, which contain many livestock, have found they are willing to absorb a few lion attacks as an annual cost of doing business.

Worth More Alive

If it can be sold to both the provider and the tourist as an attractive alternative, ecotourism does wonders for animals. Conservation groups are training local people as nature guides who will interpret lions to tourists. They also help them create tourist-friendly bed-and-breakfasts and gift shops to provide income that will not only compensate for the loss of an occasional sheep or a goat, but raise the lions' value as something worth preserving. (See: www.awf.org for the Laikipia Predator Project.)

MAN-EATERS? TSAVO LIONS

A century ago, word spread that workers on an East African train-building project were being hunted and eaten in their beds by maneater lions (see the 1996 film *The Ghost and the Darkness* with Michael Douglas and Val Kilmer). Most of those lions were ultimately taken down by lion hunters. A century later, their descendants, recently absolved of their ancestors' crimes (see Philip Caputo, *Ghosts of Tsavo*, 2002), have become what some researchers believe is a subspecies, created when the few survivors took to a wary lifestyle, hunting by night and rarely being seen, a fate that might await the Laikipia lions.

Survivors of the great drought of 1970, today the lions of Tsavo are healthy, hefty, and maneless, physically different from their relatives in other parts of Kenya. They are also socially different, with only one male per pride. Like their Laikipia cousins, they suffer from being squeezed off their range by local farmers.

Join a Scientific Project

Earthwatch   3 Clock Tower Place, Suite 100, Box 75, Maynard, Massachusetts 01754-0075. Tel: 800-776-0188 (toll-free); 978-461-0081; Fax: 978-461-2332; E-mail: info@earthwatch.org; Website: www.earthwatch.org.

To help find out more about these intriguing lions, you can join researchers Bruce Patterson, Samuel Kasiki, and Roland Kays who are studying Tsavo lions' social systems. Because they are nocturnal hunters, you have a choice of searching for them from vehicles on one of three teams: early evening, late night, and early morning, during which you can also check out which prey they catch successfully and where the prey lives. Photograph them and analyze the photos to identify their whisker patterns. Sleep during the day at a luxury tent camp with solar-powered hot water and electricity. Two weeks, about $3,000.

ASIATIC LIONS: A CASE STUDY

Lions once roamed most of the world, including North America during the last Ice Age. Hunted for bounty by Romans on the fringes of the Empire, lions moved south into Africa and east into India.

Today few Asian lions remain, all of them in the forested Sasan Gir Lion Sanctuary in the northwestern state of Gujurat, India. Smaller than African lions, males have shorter manes, thicker coats, and characteristic tufts of fur on their elbows and longer fur on their bellies and tail tips. Their prides consist of two females. Only about 300 exist—a bonanza given their sad story.

About 100 years ago in the Gir area, a small community of people with livestock coexisted with the lions in the Gir Lion Sanctuary, because lions had enough room to range for prey and water to drink. In 1960, the newly formed state government leveled much of the forest and created hydroelectric projects that diverted water and introduced new settlements near the area. The result was no more hunting range and very little water for the lions, and no more grazing area for the cattle.

The government's solution was to open the lion sanctuary as a grazing area for the cattle and buffalo of herdsmen in the area. The lions thought they had died and gone to heaven. Unfortunately, that's exactly what happened: entire lion prides were poisoned by angry herdsmen until dangerously few lions remained.

In 1972, the Sasan Gir Lion Sanctuary was begun, today patrolled by 800 park rangers, who keep out illegal trespassers and keep waterholes full. Lion prey is abundant, and the lions are healthy as long as they stay within the 1,000-acre park. A few Maldhari herdsmen still coexist in the sanctuary, selling their dairy products in nearby towns.

It's a happy ending except for the edge of the sanctuary, on the north and south of the park, where smaller communities of lion prides have settled in. Their future is guarded. The sanctuary can't support many more than 300 lions, and constant run-ins with farmers outside the park spells ultimate doom for the expanded group of lions. (See David Quammen, *Monster of God*, 2003, for more on Sasan Gir Lion Sanctuary.)

Rangers will guide you around the park in Jeeps, from mid-October until spring. Or take a tour with:

Tiger Trails, Ltd.   Dale Cottage, Calderbridge, Cumbria, CA20 1DN, UK. Tel:/Fax: 011 44 1946 841495; E-mail: tigertrails@ sawai.freeserve.co.uk; Website: www.tigertrails.co.uk.

Researchers have found that lions spend a huge amount of time relaxing, like this magnificent beast at the Franklin Park Zoo, Boston. *Roger Archibald*

5

THE OKAVANGO DELTA

BOTSWANA

Most fish, shellfish, and amphibians spend their infancies in wetlands; and serious reptiles, such as crocodiles, live in the reeds on the banks.

The Okavango is a wetland, but a weird one. Called a large desert oasis, the delta is the end point of the Okavango River, which flows south from Angola then turns east into Botswana where it collects seasonally into a lake in the northwest corner of the country. Then it forms fingers that disappear into the yellow sands of the Kalahari Desert. It once flowed into a lake called Makgadikgadi in Bushman country in central Botswana, until earthquakes diverted the river, and the lake dried up. Today it is considered to be the largest and most important landlocked wetland, about 12,000 miles of networked canals, dotted with palm-tree islands, lined with papyrus reeds, and scattered with woodlands and savannah.

From life around the delta, you get a sense of easy African pace. The rainy season starts in October and lasts until April or May, but the waters of the Okavango River don't swell in Botswana until December and won't complete the flow until July, two months into the dry season.

Wildlife follows the water but waits for the peak season. Around May game take advantage of the settled delta and long gray days without rain, and they will hang around until the Delta begins to dry out and the rains being again in October.

On the other hand, birds prefer the rainy season for the abundant flora and appear in abundance from December to May.

The Okavango Delta has all the game usually ascribed to Africa, with especially large herds of elephant. But because the land is so varied—swamps, seasonal grasslands, and savannah—it attracts a wide array of mammals, from wild dogs to water buffalo, hippos, and the rare sitatunga, a small member of the same family as bongos. Nile crocodiles love the papyrus rushes in the swampy areas where they lay their eggs and tenderly look after their young, confident at the top of the food chain. Biologists agree that most species, especially the large number of spiders, scorpions, plants, and fish, are yet to be classified.

How to Relate

Getting around in a wetland is best accomplished by dugout canoe, or *mokoro*, which holds two passengers and a poler who will pole you through the shallow water. The Okavango Polers Trust is a coalition of polers who provide trips and bush camping (see www.okavango-delta.net).

If you are a confident and experienced rider, horseback is an excellent alternative, remembering that the game you see up close and personal is wild and unpredictable: you might have to sprint.

Another way is by elephant-back, in a way the best, because elephants provide an ideal vantage point, and they know the area.

Lodging

On the east side of the delta is the **Moremi Game Reserve**, which is well stocked with lodges, some of them luxury. Since Moremi is sandwiched between the Okavango Delta and Chobe National Park, it's a convenient place to stay.

Island Safari   E-mail: info@island-safari.com; Website: www.
island-safari.com.

This is a company that operates in Botswana, taking care of
details, placing you in the lodging of your desire, and providing
local naturalist poler guides. Island Safari offers a variety of organized tours as well, from a Hemingway Nostalgia tour for about
$4,000 to five nights in the Okavango with camping along the
Mokoro Trail for less than $1,000.

By Elephantback

Botswana lodging tends to be expensive. The premier is Abu Camp,
safari tents with teak appointments, antique sleigh or four-poster
beds and copper bathtubs, about $1,000 per person per night.

Abu is Arabic for "everything to do with elephants." Members
of a resident herd of five adults and seven juvenile elephants will
take you on a slow and thrillingly elevated ride through the delta to
see game on dawn and sunset rides, or on all-day excursions. When
you are not riding the elephants, you can watch them graze and
play in the waterholes near camp. See Website: abucamp.island-
safari.com.

By Horseback

Naturequest   PMB 185, 30872 South Coast Highway, Laguna
Beach, California 92651-8162. Tel: 800-369-3033 (toll-free);
949-499-9561; E-mail: info@naturequesttours.com; Website:
www.naturequesttours.com.

Staying at the Macatoo Horse Camp, with a stable of twenty-six
well-trained horses that can be ridden either English or Western
saddle, you ride out each day after dawn and coffee or tea in camp,
and explore the Okavango. Tours are flexible and can be customized
to your needs. Some include two nights at Fly Camp, located near
the Kalahari, which is a collection of treehouses (complete with
facilities) overlooking a hippo pool.

You must be a good rider and be able to prove you can canter for ten minutes straight comfortably. Nine days, about $3,000.

In the Delta

For a down-and-dirty experience of Okavango Delta life, with real wild beasts rummaging about at night and never far away during the day, try the following—the only lodges in the actual delta. From both, you can join naturalist guides/polers on night safaris along the ever-changing channels of the Mokoro Trail in the Moremi Game Reserve, stopping at various palm-studded islands to camp overnight. Both of the following are reached only by taking light aircraft from Maun, the nearest airport. The season lasts from July to October.

Oddballs is a basic camp built on a raised platform with six-by-six-foot domed tents, with showers and toilets in separate units. It has a community dining area and lounge with hammocks, a real African-war-stories bartender and bar, and a provisions store. The dining area overlooks the Boro River. It averages about $150 a night.

Gunn's Safari Camp, located in the delta across from Chief's Island, a sort of reserve unto itself, with both prey (water buffalo and hippos) and predators (lions and leopards), has seven luxury tents with adjoining toilets and showers as well as electricity. It also has a separate honeymoon chalet. Birders love this place. About $250 to $350 per person per night.

(See www.okavango-delta.net/lodges&.htm for a good list of the whole area.)

Community-Based Tourism

Okavango Polers Trust   Box 24, Seronga, Botswana. Tel: 011 (267) 676 861; Fax: 011 (267) 676 851; Website: www.duke.edu/~sas21/autobotswana/opt/.

This coalition of polers and native guides offers an alternative to expensive lodging. They provide the mokoro, guide, and camp-grounds; you bring camping gear, tent, and your own food, which you can buy from a shop in the village of Seronga or from villagers who sell food (baked goods, local specialties) from their houses.

Take a plane from Maun to Seronga and sign up for anything from one to fourteen days in the delta. Three days including guide, mokoro, bush camp, and Mbiroba Camp, about 305 pula—or U.S.$60 per person.

Join a Scientific Project

Crocodiles

Earthwatch   3 Clock Tower Place, Suite 100, Box 75, Maynard, Massachusetts 01754-0075. Tel: 800-776-0188 (toll-free); 978-461-0081; Fax: 978-461-2332; E-mail: info@earthwatch.org; Website: www.earthwatch.org.

Crocodiles of the Okavango allows anyone interested in these ancient reptiles to get to know them better. Working with a South African researcher who hopes to understand where Nile crocodiles, some of which can be formidable predators, fit in relation to villagers (are villagers ever attacked?) and how much they suffer from poaching (how many crocodiles are there, anyway?).

In a day shift that begins at dawn, you visit the papyrus swamps and collect crocodiles caught overnight in traps to weigh and tag them. Members of the night shift travel along the canals by boat, do a count of the ones they see (red eyes that pop up out of the water), and capture smaller ones to measure and tag.

Camp is basic, with latrines and showers and a cook. June to November, about $2,500.

6

OCEANS

PLANET OCEAN

Check any map: the Blue Planet is blue for a good reason: oceans comprise 145 million square miles on Earth, compared with only 57 million square miles of green and tan land. Half the population of the United States lives on the coasts, as close to the ocean as they can get, and more than a third of the entire population of the world lives within 40 miles of the ocean.

Nevertheless, as oceanographers like to point out, we know more about the surface of the moon than we do about the ocean. Scientists from fifty countries currently participating in the first census of ocean species have found more than 210,000 life forms in the sea, a number they expect will double by 2010, their target date. (Website: www.come.org/come.htm.)

The Coast Is the Place to Be

What we do know is that ocean animals—fish, mollusks, mammals—live near coasts, on coral reefs and seamounts, and in the very deep ocean, especially near hydrothermal vents, way below the light needed for photosynthesis. The familiar species that depend on sunlight for their life disappear about 800 feet down. Below is the realm of the giant squid. But huge acres of the ocean are apparently empty, crossed like ocean freighters by cruising large mammals and fish and sea turtles.

The average ocean depth is two and a half miles, with dips in the valleys between mountain ranges as much as seven miles; this is a lot of real estate for tiny bioluminescent creatures that live here—eating each other—and large creatures like the megamouth shark that browse with their mouths open to collect whatever there is to eat, mostly carcasses fallen from above. Deep sea corals, small and brown, but alive, also feed on dead things.

Ocean creatures may be hard to see, but everything that swims in the ocean emits some sort of sound, from low grunts to squeaky chirps. Volcanoes periodically explode and tremble throughout the deep ocean, sounds that travel about 3,000 miles an hour underwater. Add the terrific booms of lightning strikes in the tropical oceans, and the constant rumbling of earthquakes along the active midocean ridges, and you get the picture that sometimes, at least, the ocean is

Among the huge variety of creatures that live in the dark warmth of a hydrothermal vent in the Gulf of Mexico is this spider crab, accompanied by worms and mussels. *I. MacDonald, OAR/National Undersea Research Program, Texas A&M University; www.photolib.noaa.gov*

a fairly noisy place. For a sample of sounds and some fascinating research, see oceanexplorer.noaa.gov; www.oceanlink.island.net; www. pmel.noaa.gov; www.animalvoice.com.

The Vents

Marine biologists were astonished to find thriving colonies of life in a place in the ocean off the Galapagos Islands where a tiny volcanic fissure was spewing hot minerals and creating the perfect recipe for life and species of animals that had never been seen before. That was in 1977, and the beginning of explorations in all the oceans that have since found hundreds of hydrothermal vents—so-called because the otherwise 34-degree-Fahrenheit water around the smoking vent is heated to as much as 750 degrees Fahrenheit.

Since then, deep ocean explorers have found that these vents, located a third of a mile down, teem with microbes that thrive without sunlight in super-hot water, breathing the iron found around fissures in the submarine earth and excreting magnetite. These completely alien life forms live among magnetite beds dated to 3.2 billion years ago, remnants of their ancestors that suggest they were the first life on Earth.

The vent chimneys are constantly growing, as the heated earth spews forth underwater geysers as high as those in Yellowstone National Park, and stretch over areas about 200 yards long. The so-called Lost City Vent beneath the Atlantic Ocean several hundred miles east of Bermuda has colorful cooled mineral chimneys more than 150 feet tall. The chimneys eventually topple over, but the vents are not new: some are 30,000 years old!

Lots of completely adapted animals gather at the smoking vents, blind and albino, and stranger than anything in the atmospheric levels we are used to, such as ten-foot giant tube worms, mouthless, stomachless, but inhabited by several species of bacteria that do all the work. Blind shrimp, tiny bleached clams, beds of mussels, spaghetti worms, and lots of bacteria thrive in the super-hot, chemically charged water that allows them to synthesize carbon and communicate by electrical current. Scientists are beginning to think they are looking at the earliest life on Earth, and maybe at the life forms that will survive us all.

Pacific Vents off the Mexican Coast

Nine Degrees North

Deep Ocean Expeditions   64b Sunninghill Avenue, Burradoo NSW 2576, Australia. Fax: 011 61 2 48623013; E-mail: info@deepoceanexpeditions.com; Website: www.deepocean expeditions.com.

If you read Jules Verne's books with a certain amount of envy, you now can take a trip that even he would have envied. In a submersible that is tested for 20,000 feet under the sea, join a pilot and take a companion and dive deep to see the hydrothermal vents located at 9 degrees north of the equator in the Pacific Ocean. They are only 8,600 feet down, and in waters that are full of fish, dolphins, and whales, which you will pass as you descend into the darkness.

The *MIR-I* and *-II* submersibles, twenty-five feet long and eleven feet wide, are lowered into the water with a crane from the deck of the Russian research ship *Akademik Kheldysh*, staffed by Russian Academy scientists from the P.P. Shirshov Institute. Also on board are former U.S. Navy submarine captains.

The dive at 100 feet a minute takes about two hours. You need to be nimble enough to get into the craft, and not claustrophobic, because the excursion lasts about ten to twelve hours.

As you reach the bottom, lights go on, and you see the brilliant stage of architectural mineral formations amid billows of black and white smoke, with strange creatures going about their business. Keep a lookout for Dumbo, a creature with eight legs, huge ears, and beautiful blue eyes. From your porthole, you can take pictures to your heart's content.

Because of the duration and nature of the trip, there are some health concerns: divers must have healthy lungs and hearts, and no diabetes, asthma, obesity, or anxiety. See a full list of requirements at www.deepoceanexpeditions.com.

Twelve days, from Acapulco, about $24,000—$5,000 if you do not make the descent. Comfortable lodging aboard the *Akademik Kheldysh*, with lots of lectures and video presentations, and good food.

Vents from Home

For a virtual expedition, join divers in submersibles from the Woods Hole Oceanographic Institution: www.divediscover.whoi.edu.

7

FISH

Get closer to fish without catching or eating them.

GREAT SARDINE MIGRATION, SOUTH AFRICA

SEAL Expeditions Sea Air Land   Tel: 011 27 (82) 253-5678; E-mail: nic@sealexpeditions.com; Website: www.sealexpeditions.com.

Incredible Adventures   6604 Midnight Pass Road, Sarasota, Florida 34242. Tel: 800-644-7382 (toll-free); E-mail: info@incredible-adventures.com; Website: www.incredible-adventures.com.

Why Run with the Bulls When You Can Run with the Sardines?

Sardines' place on the food chain is right down there with the most important Little Fish. Big Fish are sure to follow.

Once a year off the Indian Ocean coast of South Africa south of Durban, millions of sardines migrate north in the Natal Sardine Run. They cling to a northbound current close to shore, feeding on tons of plankton, "like choreographed ballerinas performing perfect parabolas," according to Nic, director of SEAL. Likened to the Great Wildebeest Migration on the Serengeti Plain, this amazing migration snakes its way north from May until July, when what are left of the sardines migrate back south in November. In 2002, the sardine march was so big it was visible from space.

In pods of 3,000 to 5,000, as many as 20,000 common dolphins join the sardine group, which measures about 9 miles long, 2 miles wide, and 120 feet deep. They are joined by thousands of bottlenose dolphins, leaping and strategizing to make the sardines form into a bait ball for easy eating.

Once the ball is formed, tens of thousands of gannets (sea birds) begin their attack both above and below the water's surface. Below the ball and the activity of the dolphins, copper sharks cruise slowly, occasionally rising to take a big bite out of the ball. Hundreds of Cape seals swim into it, barking and biting; then come a pod of Bryde's whales. As the migration proceeds north, the beaches are packed with fishermen, netting as many sardines as they can to sell as bait or to send to the packers.

This trip is restricted to advanced divers, although if you do not want to dive, you can ride in the open boat (no toilet facilities). The procedure is to get information radioed in from a microlight, motor to the sardines, dive in for five or ten minutes, get back in the boat, motor to get ahead of the crowd in the water, dive in and wait. Great for photographers. You will have luxury beachfront accommodations. You will need them. Fourteen days, includes lodging and dive boat, about $3,000 for both divers and non-divers.

Sharks

Give sharks their due: they are among the most perfectly adapted creatures in the sea. Sinuous, with no bones to impede their action and double rows of razor-sharp teeth that automatically grow back when needed, sharks eat what they want even if they seem to make a lot of mistakes in the process.

Most researchers say sharks really do not like human meat and will quickly release a human after a taste. That, however, is better for the shark than the chewed victim. Don't get caught between shark and chum. Sharks do attack metal objects, like boats and cages, and researchers suspect sharks are attracted to electric fields, including the bioelectric fields that human beings give off. If it gives any comfort, you are more likely to survive a shark attack than an alligator attack, according to the International Shark Attack File (www.flmnh.ufl.edu/fish).

At least 350 shark species are known, some of them really mysterious, like the megamouth, sighted only seventeen times. It's large and quiet and seems to live several hundred feet below surface. Some sharks have extraordinary and peculiar adaptations, like the hammerhead; others match the colors of the rocks they swim near or resemble other fish, like catfish.

The most exciting species to divers are the great white sharks because they are huge—twenty feet long, and famous—thanks to Hollywood.

South Africa

Great Whites

Dive in a Cage in The ocean

Discovery Initiatives   The Travel House, 51 Castle Street, Circencester, Gloucestershire, GL7 1QD, UK. Tel: 011 44 01285 643333; Fax: 44 01285 885888; E-mail: enquiry@discovery initiatives.com; Website: www.discoveryinitiatives.com.

The greatest congregation of great white sharks in the world is in the cold channel between the two islands that comprise Dyer Island in the South African Atlantic. Called Shark Alley, it is about 900 feet long and 450 feet wide. Sharks are chockablock here because they eat seals unfortunate enough to go for a swim; in one day researchers were able to tag eighteen individual great whites.

On this expedition run by the South African White Shark Conservation, Education, and Exploration Society, you stay in Cape Town and make daily forays of approximately eight hours to the Dyer straits, where you join researchers in a small boat or in the cage from which you will collect data on and tag individual sharks—photographing, filming, and recording them.

Back on land, you help wash the boats and get the gear ready for the next day before dinner and discussion. If you want to live, breathe, and immerse yourself in sharkville, this is for you.

Twelve days, June to October, about U.S.$2,000, plus international airfare. Includes lodging, food, boats, lectures, and educational materials.

California and Mexico

Incredible Adventures   Tel: 800-644-7382 (toll-free); 941-346-2603; Fax: 941-346-2488. E-mail: info@incredible-adventures.com. Website: www.incredible-adventures.com

Captain Lawrence Groth was among the first to run daily charters to photograph sharks from a cage in the cool waters off San Francisco. Recently, he helped write guidelines for the best way to dive with sharks without disturbing them in their National Marine Sanctuary, the Gulf of Farallons.

Leaving at 6 A.M. in the thirty-two-foot *Patriot*, shark divers can expect to spend about ten hours on the boat or in the cage about four feet below the surface. Some of the largest great white sharks swim here—up to twenty feet long, which attracts many filmmakers and photographers.

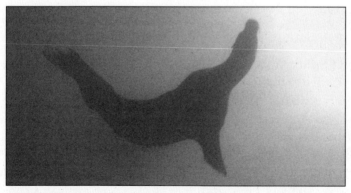

Nothing stimulates a great white's appetite more than the silhouette of a plump sea lion, like this one in the Monterey Bay National Marine Sanctuary. *National Oceanographic and Atmospheric Administration; www.photolib.noaa.gov*

Don't be surprised if you come away with more respect for the shark in its natural feeding ground: those who have watched them remark on their slow and relaxed style and the gentle way they eat the seals and sea lions with which they share the waters.

September 15 to November 15, about twelve hours altogether, includes lunch, tank hookup (you do not need to be a certified diver): $975.

Live-Aboard

Isla Guadalupe

Leave San Diego, motor through the night on a ninety-six-foot range diving and tuna fishing boat with fifteen 2-diver cabins. Have breakfast after dawn, then go into the cage. The water is warm and clear in Isla Guadalupe, and the sharks are great white sub-adults, twelve to sixteen feet long. You will be able to dive day and night for three days.

August to November. Five days, lodging, food, cage, about $2,300. You must have your card proving you have open water scuba qualification to use the cage.

Florída

In an Aquaríum Tank

The Florida Aquarium   701 Channelside Drive, Tampa, Florida 33602. Tel: 800-353-4741 (toll-free); 813-273-4000; Website: http://wahoo.flaquarium.org; or www.flaquarium.net.

Thirty minutes in an aquarium tank swimming with the sharks can be enough for some folks. After an initial preparation, a dive master accompanies two divers in a cage on the descent into the tank. Once acclimated, the cage door opens, and there's nothing between you and the sharks. The dive master maintains constant monitoring and carries a "shark wand."

The entire program is ninety minutes. $150—includes souvenir

The International Shark Attack File offers guidelines for swimming with sharks (here condensed):

- Swim in a group. Sharks like lone swimmers.
- Stay close to shore.
- Don't swim after sundown.
- Don't go in the water if you are bleeding.
- Don't wear shiny jewelry, contrasting colored clothing, or bright colors.
- Don't swim near live-bait fishermen.
- Don't swim near sandbars, sewage drainage, or in murky waters.
- Don't swim if you know sharks are there.

photos and a T-shirt. You must be Scuba certified and at least fifteen years old.

Some species are endangered because they have been overfished for herbal remedies, aphrodisiacs, and longevity pills.

Mexico: Baja California

Whale Sharks

Baja AirVentures Tel: 800-221-9283 (toll-free); E-mail: bajaair@cox.net; Website: www.bajaairventures.com.

The largest fish in the sea is the whale shark, a big chunk of underwater monster, some forty to sixty feet long with a mouth more than five feet wide. Not to worry. If your breathing rate increases 100 percent when you see one underwater, remind yourself that they are gentle and "harmless plankton eaters," cruising the surface to eat. And they are endangered, on top of that. Be informed, however, that harmless plankton eaters, like mantas and whale fish, simply open their vast mouths and scoop as they cruise. *Their* eyes may be closed, but keep *yours* open, as that mouth is very big.

In the Sea of Cortez, in Baja California, Baja AirVentures flies you from San Diego in a private plane to the remote La Unica Wilderness Retreat. Stay in seaside bungalows and spend the days snorkeling and looking for sea turtles, dolphins, and mantas, some of the marine life that love this area. Whale sharks do, too, and if they choose to swim with you—and you might see a whole group of them, a rare sight—you will have an astounding experience. Also watch for some members of the ten species of whales that inhabit the same waters. Four or six days, relaxed, small groups.

Price includes air from San Diego, all-inclusive resort. Six days, about $1,600; four days, about $1,200.

8

CORAL REEFS

AN OCEAN HOME

Sponges, mollusks, octopi, sea stars, sea turtles, sea horses, algae, anemones, shrimp, and more than a third of the world's fish species—most of them a dazzling collection of hot pinks, yellows, blues, and dizzying stripes—gather on sunlit coral reefs to eat and breed in the otherwise desolate wasteland of the ocean. These outposts of high-density real estate have the same meaning to a traveling fish as a mall does to a family after six hours on an interstate. Called underwater rainforests, coral reefs are bustling hubs of different species, from the algae that give coral polyps their color to the sharks that eat the little fish.

The Dark Side

Watch your back when you dive or snorkel coral reefs: not every species is friendly. Female sharks come here to lay eggs; tiger sharks hang out around reefs and the coast. In Australian waters, keep a keen eye for the deadly irukandji jellyfish, the size of a thumbnail; and the blue-ringed octopus, the size of a big gum ball when it is rolled up, no more than four inches with tentacles out. Their stings are subtle and fatal.

Inveterate divers always search for new and undiscovered reefs, but the two they can rely on for variety, excitement, and beauty

Jellyfish of all kinds congregate at coral reefs. Some—like these—have a seriously poisonous sting. *Roger Archibald*

are the Great Barrier Reef in Australia; and the slightly smaller Belize reef.

Australia

A World Heritage Site, the Great Barrier Reef is "the only living organism visible from space," according to the World Wildlife Foundation.

More than 1,200 miles long, this spectacular Pacific reef is actually an archipelago of 2,900 separate coral reefs strung together along the northeast coast of Australia on the Coral Sea. It is home to Pacific hard and soft corals—those with brilliant colors and shapes like waving fans or small forests of purple trees or beds of tiny flowers, and no exterior skeleton. The reef has lots of cavities and shelters for everything from big blue parrotfish to tiny butterfly fish. The forty-mile-wide warm and shallow lagoon separates the reef from the coast, a collection of long sandy beaches, vast stretches of seagrass meadows, and mangroves.

Dive with an Ichthyologist

American Museum of Natural History   Discovery Tours, Central Park West at 79th Street, New York, New York 10024-5192. Tel: 800-462-8687 (toll-free); 212-769-5700; Fax: 212-769-5755; Website: www.discoverytours.org.

Accompanied by an ichthyologist, who will explain life on the reef, this tour cruises aboard the small ship *Coral Princess II* to the remote Outer Ribbon Reefs on which you can make two dives a day, and look for some of the fish that disguise themselves, like cuttlefish, to keep from being eaten.

The final days of the trip are spent on land exploring wildlife in the Daintree Rainforest, where the lakes harbor giant eels, and the rivers are home to crocodiles. Ten days, about $5,000 to $6,500, depending on berth.

For general information, see: www.barrierreefaustralia.com.

Pacific Reefs

Society Expeditions   2001 Western Avenue, Suite 300, Seattle, Washington 98121. Tel: 800-548-8669 (toll-free); 206-728-9400; E-mail: info@societyexpeditions.com; Website: www.society expeditions.com.

The Great Barrier Reef is just one coral reef in the Pacific area. Stretching along the Marquesas, Society, Cook, Fiji, and Tonga island chains, the Pacific is strewn with sandy coral atolls and fringe reefs that extend outward in emerald seas from empty beaches. Society Expeditions has been running Pacific trips for a few decades on the *World Discoverer*, which cruises at a leisurely pace between islands. On board, naturalists offer lectures as well as visual presentations. Zodiacs take you over the reef where you can snorkel and scuba. Eighteen days, about $6,000 to $8,000 and more, depending on berth.

The **Waikiki Aquarium** (waquarium.otted.hawaii.edu/class/travel.html) sponsors a Family Science trip to a South Pacific reef each year. In the past, these trips, accompanied by marine biologists, have visited the Midway Atoll National Wildlife Refuge and Christmas Island Atoll in Kiribati. Sign on for updates with Mark Heckman; Tel: 808-923-9741; E-mail: mheckman@hawaii.edu.

Belize

The Belize Barrier Reef, which protects the Belize coast from the assaults of stormy seas, is a collection of more than 200 cays, or islands, some tiny with a single coconut palm, others lush with sea grape and tangled underwater mangrove roots. A World Heritage Site, the Belize Caribbean Reef is composed of hard coral, which is the architectural result of coral polyps, the tiny animal that secretes calcium carbonate as an external skeleton that builds reefs like small cities. Just as colorful and busy as a soft coral reef, hard coral is "bleached" only after the algae that color the coral polyps are eaten away by fish (which would be eaten themselves in a healthy ecosystem). It takes a healthy reef about 1,000 years to grow sixty feet. The Belize Reef stretches for 140 to 180 miles.

Kayak the Belize Reef

Island Expeditions Company   1574 Gulf Road, No. 156, Point Roberts, Washington 98281. Tel: 800-667-1630 (toll-free); 604-452-3212 (international); Fax: 604-452-3433; E-mail: info@island expeditions.com; Website: www.islandexpeditions.com.

Island Expeditions Company, which specializes in trips to the Belize Reef, organizes numerous kayak expeditions along the reef. Fifty-five miles off Belize City is Half Moon Cay and Lighthouse Reef, the farthest point of the Belize Barrier Reef. In the middle of its atoll is the Blue Hole, discovered by Jacques Cousteau, a perfectly round 1,000 feet across and more than 400 feet deep.

Traveling each day between five and ten miles to the best wilderness snorkel sites where you stop and explore, you return each night to base camp at Half Moon Cay, and comfortable tents and hammocks where you hunker down like a shipwrecked pirate.

Eight days, with five on the Lighthouse Reef islands and four at a lodge on the mainland, about $2,000. Includes kayak and tent gear, all meals. This trip is operated in conjunction with the Belize Audubon Society.

Dive and Research

Oceanic Society   Fort Mason Center, San Francisco, California 94123. Tel: 800-326-7491 (toll-free); E-mail: info@oceanic-society.org; Website: www.oceanic-society.org.

The Belize Reef includes three atolls, which are circular reefs. The largest, Turneffe Atoll, has never been studied, and local conservation groups have no record of what species live there or of how well the reef is doing.

Funded by the National Geographic Society and the Ford Motor Foundation, in cooperation with Belizean agencies, the Oceanic Society has set up a field station on Blackbird Caye, adjacent to Turneffe Atoll. Their mandate is to identify what different species live there and how they create a community. The information will provide a baseline on the current health of the reef.

This is a chance to spend a week living in a beachfront cabana (with private bath), learning how to do underwater transects with a video, and taking still pictures of members of each fish and coral species. On four-hour daily dives, you will become very familiar with the atoll and learn a lot of research techniques as well.

Seven days (November to April), about $1,900, plus international airfare. Divers must be certified.

Egypt

Red Sea Coral Reef

If you could fly north along the Rift Valley from Kenya to its most northerly limit in the Middle East, you would dip into the sea off the coast of Egypt and experience one of the most dramatic reefs in the world. Composed of hard coral, the Red Sea Reef extends from the Sinai Peninsula to Yemen. Underwater, its colorful collection of reef habitats includes walls with drops of 300 meters and a blue hole. More than 2,000 species of fish live here, as well as several species of dolphins. Because it rarely rains, the waters are superclear.

You can stay at numerous places along the Egyptian coast (or at the famous Sharm el Sheik resort on the tip of the Sinai Peninsula). One accommodating place is Hurghada, where the Sahara meets the sea, and near particularly rich sections of the reef off the Gif-tung Islands. Now being developed into a very active resort, it still maintains its flavor as a small Egyptian city. Numerous companies provide not only scuba air, equipment, and courses (for about $250 to $350), but also live-aboard trips that allow you to dive as much as you want and can afford (about Euros 40 to 60 a day). Or you can snorkel from the beaches.

On the beach, you can rent an Arabic-style tent and stay a few feet from the sea or check into an intercontinental luxury hotel (five-star hotel, about Euros 100 to 125 a day). The big attractions, Luxor and Cairo, are not far away; also interesting are some remnants of ancient Roman outposts in the desert. Jeeps are easily rented.

For a virtual tour of some of the reef attractions, see: www.virtourist.com. To visit the city site log on to www.hurghada.com. For info, email: hurghada@hurghada.com.

Florida

The Flower Garden Banks

Full Moon in August

The Flower Garden Banks National Marine Sanctuary 1200 Briarcrest, Suite 4000, Bryan, Texas 77802. Tel: 979-846-5942; Fax: 979-846-5959; E-mail: shelley.dupuy@noaa.gov; Website: flowergarden.noaa.gov.

Located 100 miles from land in the middle of the Gulf of Mexico, two unusual underwater "salt domes" have spawned a deep-water coral reef so rich and big, it is called the Flower Garden Banks. Every year on the eighth day after the full moon in August, a huge cloud of "snow" seemed to rise from the sunken gardens. Divers identified the snow as millions of fertilized eggs from various residents of the reef, shot up and out to the moon to be carried by the tide to the most fertile places to settle.

It was not until the 1960s that divers from the Houston Museum of Natural Science discovered what fishermen had been saying for decades: that somewhere out there in the Gulf were huge gardens of corals. Divers were surprised to discover that the reef was massive and supported by an ancient drowned reef, a few million years old.

Now a National Marine Sanctuary, the Flower Garden Banks are the most northern coral reef in the United States. The reef crest contains about 350 acres spread over more than forty-one square nautical miles.

Because the reef is more than sixty feet beneath the surface, you need to scuba dive to see the glowing corals and tiny Caribbean reef fish. Only a few charter operators know where it is, because it is a protected sanctuary. For a list-in-progress, see: flowergarden.noaa. gov/about/getthere.html.

Click on their Virtual Dive site if you can't make it to the Bank.

More on the National Marine Sanctuary Program at www. sanctuaries.nos.noaa.gov.

The Pacific, Atlantic, and Caribbean Coasts

Research with Fishwatchers

The Reef Environmental Education Foundation   P.O. Box 246, Key Largo, Florida 33037. Tel: 305-852-0030; E-mail: reefhq@reef.org; Website: www.reef.org. Dive Reservations. Tel: 888-363-3345 (toll-free); E-mail: reef@diveres.com.

The Reef Environmental Education Foundation invites certified divers to dive and identify fish. Data will be contributed to the Living Reef Project, a database of reef invertebrates available on the website to anyone interested in doing research.

Field surveys are usually Sunday to Friday throughout the year and are conducted on coasts in the Pacific, the Atlantic, and the Caribbean.

The best part is that you combine research with a vacation. If you have a "life list" of fish, this is a good chance to add to it. Researchers teach the standard survey method, and you dive at least twice a day.

Lodging is varied, sometimes luxurious, and always comfortable. Price ranges from $1,000 to $2,000, based on double occupancy and includes food. This is a nonprofit and eligible for some tax deductions.

Reef Fish in the Tank

The Florida Aquarium   701 Channelside Drive, Tampa, Florida 33602. Tel: 813-367-4005; Website: wahoo.flaquarium.org; www.flaquarium.net.

The Florida Aquarium offers a chance to swim in the coral reef tank with schools of *Nemo*-bright reef fish. The sixty-minute program includes instruction in the supplied–air snorkeling equipment (carry a small air tank on your back) and thirty minutes in the fish tank.

Swim with the Fishes adventure is for anyone over the age of six and an excellent way to learn about the complexity of the coral reef. Kids six, seven, and eight must be accompanied by an adult. $75 includes aquarium admission.

Coral Farms

A recent study of Caribbean shallow-water, hard-coral reefs revealed that 80 percent of the reefs had disappeared since the 1970s. Rising sea surface temperatures, unidentified "viruses," and overfishing over the past few years have disrupted the marine harmony of many reefs and produced acres of bleached coral.

These, plus anchor hits and pollution from ships and shore, have left some reefs in a sorry state. Especially serious off the coast of Florida, bleaching has affected as much as 10 percent of reefs around the world.

Two aquariums sponsor exhibits on growing corals, which are the poster child of underwater ecosystem health. Under the right laboratory conditions, coral can be farmed by growing tiny tips as small as one-half inch collected in the ocean. Some coral grows as much as seven inches a year.

Caribbean Corals

The Florida Aquarium   701 Channelside Drive, Tampa, Florida 33602. Tel: 800-353-4741 (toll-free); 813-273-4000; Website: wahoo.flaquarium.org; www.flaquarium.net.

An exhibit explains how coral is grown. Coral grown here is actually reintroduced to the reef.

For a live webcam underwater view of coral reef life near the Dry Tortugas off Florida, connect to: www.noaa.gov/seakeys. The SEA-KEYS Program is a monitoring system that provides daily automated network data of the Caribbean reefs. It is run by the National Oceanic and Atmospheric Administration (NOAA) and the Florida Institute of Oceanography.

Pacific Corals

Waikiki Aquarium   University of Hawaii-Manoa, 2777 Kalakaua Avenue, Honolulu, Hawaii 96815. Tel: 808-923-9741; Fax: 808-923-1771; Website: www.waquarium.otted.hawaii.edu.

This program was the first coral farm and supplies other aquariums and private vendors with Pacific corals. Check their website for the ingredients for a coral farm, if you want to grow your own.

Click on Live Cameras to see the corals in the research tank, which is a colony begun in 1990 from a tiny animal from Fiji.

Fossil Coral

Windley Key Fossil Reef Geological State Park   P.O. Box 1052, Islamorada, Florida 33036. Tel: 305-664-2540; Website: www.windleykey.com.

Florida State Parks Information Center: Tel: 850-245-2157.

To get a sense of how long coral reefs have flourished, visit this cross section of ancient eight-foot-tall coral. Originally discovered by railroad baron Henry Flagler who quarried much of it ("Key Largo limestone"), the reef is now preserved in a state park.

The Fossil Reef is located on Windley Key at Mile Marker 85.5.

Check out the coral reefs at the **Monterey Bay Aquarium** in Monterey, California at www.mbayaq.org.

For more on coral reefs, visit www.Coralreef.noaa.gov.

For a map of coral reefs with clickable hotspots, log on to www.reefrelief.org.

A silvery school of small-mouth grunts weaves through branches of elkhorn coral in the Florida Keys National Marine Sanctuary. *Paige Gill, Florida Keys National Marine Sanctuary, www. photolib.noaa.gov*

9

SEA TURTLES

CREATURES OF THE SEA

These ancient creatures of the sea suffer greatly in the simple course of a day: fishermen haul them in in nets, sell their shells, market their meat for food, or squeeze the oil from their bodies for medicines or fuel. If the turtles are lucky enough to find a dark, empty beach to lay eggs, their eggs are in danger of being collected and sold as aphrodisiacs or eaten by alligators. Plus, because they eat jellyfish, turtles are more liable than other fish to swallow plastic bags or mylar balloons, or strangle on plastic six-pack holders.

What researchers know about turtle lifestyles is that they are global migrators but never forget where they call home. This is the beach where they were hatched and where they will leave a deposit of eggs, even though it might be 20 years later and a few thousand miles away from where they feed. Turtles have been around for 200 million years, and habits are hard to break.

Killing sea turtles to sell their parts is illegal, and some species are officially threatened or endangered. A few organizations do what they can to spread the word on how to protect turtle habitats and nests, and they offer experiences to participate in turtle egg–laying.

Costa Rica

Caribbean Conservation Corporation   4424 NW 13th Street, Suite A1, Gainesville, Florida 32609. Tel: 352-373-6441; E-mail: ccc@cccturtle.org; Website: www.cccturtle.org.

The Caribbean Conservation Corporation has been engaged in researching and protecting sea turtles for more than forty-five years. On the black sand beaches of Tortuguero, Costa Rica, large populations of green and leatherback turtles come to lay their eggs. Among the most decimated of species, the turtles are studied by researchers at the John H. Phipps Tortuguero Biological Field Station.

Working at night in four-hour shifts, you will help tag and measure females after they dig holes and as they deposit hundreds of eggs. Some turtles are huge: leatherbacks can weigh up to 2,000 pounds. You have to work quickly, because the turtles return to the sea when they are finished. During day shifts, participants walk the beach and keep count on the eggs.

One week about $1,400; two weeks, about $1,850; three weeks, about $2,200. Fee includes two nights' hotel in San Jose, lodging at the field station, and all meals and ground and boat transportation. No prior knowledge is required.

Mexico

Natural Habitat Adventures   2945 Center Green Court, Suite H, Boulder, Colorado 80301-9539. Tel: 800-543-8917 (toll-free); Website: www.nathab.com.

Olive Ridley turtles lay their eggs in only four places around the world. One of the nesting sites is on a beach at Mazunte in Mexico, on the Pacific coast, where thousands of Olive Ridley turtles gather from July to October to lay eggs.

Accompanied by a naturalist from La Escobilla Turtle Camp, you become familiar with all aspects of this amazing event and help patrol the beach to monitor the hatchlings. Stay in an ecolodge on the beach. Five days, about $2,000.

Rescue and Rehabilitation

Mote Marine Laboratory   Sea Turtle Conservation and Research, 1600 Ken Thompson Parkway, Sarasota, Florida 34236. Tel: 941-388-4331; Website: www.mote.org.

One problem with turtle life in Florida is that human beings have built on the beach. When turtle hatchlings break out of their shells and dig their way out of the sandy pit, they head toward any light they think is the ocean. If they see a light in the window of a beach house, instinct will lead them there, away from the sea, and into the jaws of a raccoon, coyote, or family dog.

Hatchlings have a hard time, generally. Once in the sea, just about every fish is bigger than they are and hungry for a bite. If they make it to adulthood, they are subject to being hit by a motorboat or infected with an alien virus. Many of them are beached in a sorry state.

In Sarasota, Florida, the Mote Marine Laboratory runs the Turtle Conservation and Research Program, which monitors turtle activity among a huge population of loggerheads on the west coast of Florida, and rescues sick or injured turtles.

Hang Tough, a green sea turtle, was spotted floating in the sea with a fish hook in its eye. When it was finally rescued, veterinarians at the Mote Laboratory found it also had a skull fracture from a blow that also destroyed the optic nerves in the other eye. Blind and near death, Hang Tough survived, thanks to some dedicated caretakers in the Mote Marine Laboratory. It is now in permanent and happy residence at the aquarium. Volunteer to help monitor turtles on the beach, or adopt a sea turtle.

Clearwater Marine Aquarium   249 Windward Passage, Clearwater, Florida 33767. Tel: 888-239-9414 (toll-free); 727-441-1790; Fax: 727-442-9466; Website: www.cmaquarium.org.

Several species of sea turtle swim in the Gulf of Mexico: loggerhead, green, hawksbill, Kemp's Ridley, and leatherback. All species but the loggerheads are endangered. Many of them are injured by boats, are ill with a virus, or need minor surgery to restore their health.

When they beach on Pinellas County beaches, biologists from the Clearwater Marine Aquarium rescue and rehabilitate the sick and injured. In cases where damage is irreparable, the turtles are given a home in the aquarium.

Anyone twelve and above can be "Biologist for a Day" and work alongside a biologist who, among many duties, will feed the sea turtles. Join in and help staff from the aquarium monitor the many sea turtle nests along the beaches beginning in April.

The Clearwater Aquarium also sponsors programs to assist beached and ill whales, dolphins, and sea otters. Volunteers are welcome to help in their many marine programs.

Sea Turtle Rehab

Marine Science Center   100 Lighthouse Drive, Ponce Inlet, Florida. Tel: 386-304-5545; Website: www.marinesciencecenter.com.

Near Daytona on the Atlantic coast of Florida, visit the sea turtle rehabilitation center.

Many beach hotels and motels in Florida do what they can to protect eggs and turtles and encourage their guests to do the same. See www.flausa.com

10

TIDE POOLS AND COASTAL EXPEDITIONS

LIFE AT LOW TIDE

When the tide goes out, the tiny pools left on the rocks and beach teem with life: tiny fiddler crabs, periwinkles, barnacles, limpets, even baby starfish. Biologically timed to predict the tides, they spend low tide hunting for food and high tide tucked away in their rocky refuges. Low tide is also a great time to see animals and birds, from seals to bears to eagles (depending on the area), as they take advantage of an easy meal.

Canada

Bay of Fundy

Fundy Hiking and Nature Tours   18 Beach Street, St. Martins, New Brunswick, Canada EOG 2Z0. Tel: 800-563-8639 (toll-free); 506-833-2534; Fax: 506-833-1112; E-mail: nature@fundy.net; Website: user.fundy.net

The most extreme tides in the world are in the Bay of Fundy, where high tide rhythmically thunders over underwater ledges, and low tide rages breathlessly down the slopes of rocky beaches.

Rushing in between New Brunswick and Nova Scotia, the Fundy tide rises forty-five feet every twelve hours; when the moon is new or full, the pull increases to sixty.

All of this back-and-forth has created huge towers of eroded rock on the shore, and exposed thousands of fossils, some dating to the Precambrian, which was when anything alive lived in the sea, at least 600 million years ago.

Puffins and eagles are some of the species that dine on the abundant and robust tidal pool marine life. Out of the sea, seals clamber up to the ledges; in the tossing waters, whales of several species feed on the rich plankton.

Put all of this together with some very comfortable lodges and expert guides, and you can spend seven days immersed in the coasts

Horseshoe crabs—even with clams on their backs—mate by the hundreds during the spring in shallow water near shore in North America and Southeast Asia. Then they lay their eggs in the sand. *Roger Archibald*

and tidepools of Nova Scotia and New Brunswick. Hike winding trails along windy cliffs, follow ancient paths into green and mossy forests, and paddle the Shubenacadie River, where the Fundy tide surges with six-foot waves when the moon is full.

Mexico: Baja California

The Intercultural Center for the Study of Deserts and Oceans Puerto Penasco, Sonora, Mexico. *In the United States:* P.O. Box 44208, Tucson, Arizona 85733-4208. Tel: 520-320-5473; E-mail: info@cedointercultural.org. *In Mexico:* Apartado Postal No. 53, Puerto Penasco, Sonora, Mexico 83550. Tel: 638 382-01-13; E-mail: info@cedointercultural.org; Website: www.cedo intercultural.org

At a conjunction of the Upper Gulf of California and the Colorado River Delta, and the Pinacante and Gran Desierto de Altar in Sonora, Mexico, is CEDO, the Center for the Study of Deserts and Oceans. This area is preferred by whales, sea lions, seals, mantas, and unusual fish.

Families are invited to enjoy this spectacular stretch and participate in dune hikes, coastal wetland treks, and tidepool explorations accompanied by expert guides at the CEDO Environmental Science Center in Puerto Penasco, Sonora.

For teenagers fourteen to eighteen, try the Marine Biology Field Camp, for four days of exploration in the intertidal zone, bunking at the CEDO field station, about $350.

For kids ten to thirteen, CEDO offers a Wet Feet Ocean Camp, with three days of field trips and hands-on activities, about $350.

Tidepool Explorations: Two hours, $15 adults; $10 kids. Kayak Capers: around coast, includes lunch, guides, and rental (must be eighteen). Six hours: $85 nonmembers. **Estero Excursions**: coastal wetland exploration, three hours: $20 adults; $10 kids. Destination Dunes: five-hour hike, $40, includes lunch. Pinacate Peregrination: all-day geology tour of Pinacate Biosphere Reserve, $65 includes lunch.

Alaska

Kachemak Bay

Center for Alaskan Coastal Studies   P.O. Box 2225, Homer, Alaska 99603. Tel: 907-235-6667; Fax: 907-235-6668; E-mail: cacs@xyz.net; Website: www.akcoastalstudies.org.

Jakolof Ferry Service reservations   Tel: 907-235-2376; Website: www.jakolofferryservice.com.

Kayak tour reservations: Tel: 800-770-6126 (toll-free); Website: www.homerkayaking.com.

Extreme low tides and rocky beaches at the Peterson Bay Field Station in Alaska's Kachemak Bay, across from Homer on the southern coast, provide amazing opportunities to examine and photograph a variety of marine animals and birds, from starfish and chitons, to puffins and eagles, to black and grizzly bears that sniff out a diet of shellfish. The forest wilderness adds a dark mystery, as do bogs, and some prehistoric archaeological traces.

Combine a hike with a guided kayak coastal tour, and an overnight in a six-bunk yurt (bring your own sleeping bag). The beaches are reached by a ferry from Homer. Bring food, and dress warmly. Day tours: adults: $80 to $90; kids under 12: $50 to $60.

Maine

Kayak Tide Pool to Tide Pool

Maine Island Kayak Company & The Ocean School   Peaks Island, Maine. Tel: 800-796-2372 (toll-free); E-mail: info@maine islandkayak.com; Website: www.maineislandkayak.com.

Maine has more miles of coast than California. Its surging tides rush into hundreds of inlets etched into the shore and swirl around more than 2,000 coastal islands. Add extensive conservancies, and you can feel as if you are the first person to land on shore.

On this point-to-point camping kayak trip between Lubec and

the Schoodic Peninsula, you can negotiate the coastal tides, often in mysterious fog, and learn to listen to seabirds telling you where the tide left something interesting. Five days, bring your own pad and sleeping bag. About $900, includes food, boat, and guide. Expect to see whales too.

Websites

Find the latest research at two premier sites: Woods Hole Oceanographic Institution (www.whoi.edu) and Scripps Institution of Oceanography (www.sio.ucsd.edu).

Check www.seaweb.org for the latest news concerning the ocean.

For everything you could want to know about fish, ever: www.fishbase.org.

What is the ocean without Jacques Cousteau? The father of oceanic awareness generated several projects that continue all aspects of ocean research and conservation. The Cousteau Society is a membership organization that will keep you in touch. See www.cousteau.org.

"People protect what they love," Cousteau said.

11

WHALES AND DOLPHINS

WHALES

Whales are curious, and they will frankly stare at you, rising from the depths, squeezing next to your boat and snorting as they look the situation over. Then before you can snap a picture of the gigantic eye, they are gone, and seconds later, several yards away, a tail breaks the surface before disappearing into the depths.

Scientists did not begin significant investigations into whale biology and behavior until the 1970s, with the Marine Mammal Protection Act of 1972 that outlawed killing or harassing whales. New discoveries come regularly.

A recent find of stone and ivory harpoon points in a dead bowhead whale in the Arctic Circle baffled modern-day Inupiat Eskimo whale hunters who had never seen them before. No surprise: the points were dated to sometime before 1870. How old do whales live to be, exactly? Later laboratory analysis at Scripps Institution of Oceanography of other bowhead whales harpooned by the Inupiat revealed that all were more than 100, and one was 200 years old.

Scientists' initial reaction when they dived with whales was how elegantly graceful they are, despite their size, and the gentle curiosity with which they approach human beings, despite our dreadful history with them. Whales are still hunted, but illegally, after the 1984 international edict outlawing further slaughter of the mammals that supported whole industries around the world.

Underwater Chatter

Touching them seems to be as much a thrill for them as for us: one researcher said a gray whale's whole body "trembled" when she placed her hand on it. If you listen carefully and dive just below the surface around whales, or use a waterproof microphone and amplifier, you can hear singing, especially from humpbacks during mating season. Killer whales sound like underwater seagulls; belugas bleat and moo; sperm whales click; and blue whales moan deeply, a sound likened to the horn of an eighteen-wheeler cruising down the highway.

Scientists have identified numerous whale dialects that can extend over 1,000 miles. Southern Pacific whales speak a different dialect from those in the northern Atlantic; individual pods, or family groups, develop their own ways of communicating things within the family. Whales also use sonar, or echolocation, to identify the area and judge distances.

Some spy-hop—stick their heads up to eye level and swivel like a periscope, or breach—leap completely up and out of the ocean. Most often, whales flash their flukes or tails before they dive, or slap the surface of the water several times with a lot of ocean commotion.

Orcas, or killer whales, the beautiful black-and-white *Free Willy* mammals, known for their keen hunting instincts, sometimes fly out of the water and skim along the surface. They also swim upside down.

Whales are friendly and gentle, generally. Technically, for the safety of you and the animal alike, there should be at least 100 yards between you. Whales set the rules, however; photographers on small-boat cruises often find they don't need a zoom lens, kayakers experience close encounters that defy description.

Keep Moving

Perpetual migrators, whales cover huge distances and never stay in one place long, plying the waters either above or below the equator, sucking in the abundant plankton population. You can find northern hemisphere humpbacks feeding in the summer around Alaska and the Bering Strait, and off Greenland, Norway, Nova Scotia, and New England (especially around the Stellwegen Banks off Boston, Massachusetts, and in the ocean off the Saguenay River in Maine).

Whales head south in the winter to breed in the Pacific around Japan, Hawaii, off Baja California, and in the Atlantic, in the Caribbean (especially in the Silver Banks off the Dominican Republic).

In the southern hemisphere, humpbacks feed in the waters off Patagonia, Antarctica, and South Africa in the Atlantic and Southern Ocean; and then they fan out north to breed in areas off Africa and Australia and islands in the South Pacific.

With humpbacks are often a few other species, such as minke, fin, sei, sometimes blue, or northern or southern right whales.

How to Connect

You have a lot of options to understand whales. From every port where whales are known to breed or feed, you can find whale watch trips that will take you offshore to see them for a few hours, while an onboard naturalist explains their activities. Large cruise lines will take you on longer trips or to areas such as Antarctica, where many whale species gather to feed. Many companies sponsor kayak trips; some encourage you to swim with whales. A research trip allows you to get more closely involved.

Alaska

Humpbacks Research

Intersea Foundation, Inc.   P.O. Box 1106, Carmel Valley, California 93924. Tel: 831-659-5807; Fax: 831-659-5821; E-mail: info@intersea.org; Website: www.intersea.org.

Off Alaska, you can see pods of six or seven humpbacks engage in a coordinated blowing of air bubbles on the surface, called bubble netting. As choreographed as the Rockettes, the whales organize a bed of krill or herd a school of herring, corraling them to the surface where they become netted by the bubbles, ready to be eaten. As the whales leap for their catch, red-necked phalaropes fly in and dart among the bubbles and help themselves to the krill.

All of this was first documented by Cynthia D'Vincent and her researchers at Intersea Research Foundation off the coast of southeast Alaska several years ago. D'Vincent's researchers also recorded humpbacks singing a song unique to the Alaskan summer feeding ritual.

You can join the nonprofit Intersea on a small cruising yacht off southeast Alaska in July and August and participate in the collection of information about the humpbacks. Are the same whales back from the southern breeding grounds? Have they changed their song? Passengers help take video footage, film, and still photos, as well as record the ocean song. The veteran researchers who accompany the trip know most of the whales by name and give lots of information. Seven days, about $2,400 to $2,500, single berth or suite.

Canada: The St. Lawrence

Blue Whales Research

Mingan Island Cetacean Study   285 rue Green, St. Lambert, Quebec, Canada J4P 1T3. Voice mail/Fax: 450-465-9176; E-mail: Richard Sears at rsblues@polysoft.com; Website www.rorqual.com.

Blue whales, not only the largest animal in the ocean, but the largest animal on Earth, and maybe the largest animal *ever*, can reach lengths of 110 feet. Their hearts are the size of an SUV. Their large size, however, has been their undoing. Some researchers speculate that as much as 95 percent of their global population wound up as whale oil. Blue whales are now endangered and protected.

These are *rorqual* whales, which is a Norwegian word that describes the folds of skin under their lower jar that swells and enables them to eat like a pelican. They eat four to six tons of krill and fish a day, cruising feeding grounds, sucking in seawater and krill, and straining the krill through their baleen.

The Mingan Island Cetacean Study (MICS) researchers who were the first to do long-term studies of blue whales, identified and photographed 410 individuals in the North Atlantic. On the West Coast, MICS identified 310 individuals in the Sea of Cortez that were then identified as the same whales that migrated to summer feeding areas off the coast of California. This was the first migratory pattern of blue whales established in the Pacific.

In the Atlantic, blue whales join humpbacks, fin, and minke whales and gather in the summer in the waters from Greenland to the Gulf of St. Lawrence, which blue whales particularly like. Slow movers, the blues rise to the surface and blow a spout of air as much as forty feet high. Underwater, they are among the *loudest* animals on Earth: their low grunts register 180 decibels.

In groups of no more than six people, volunteers are invited to join in the ongoing research of blue whales in the Gulf of St. Lawrence, led by principal investigator Richard Sears. In the Mingan Archipelago National Park Reserve/Anticosti Island Region off Quebec, MICS is actively involved in collecting data on blue whales' vocalizations (some of which have extreme low frequency, at 10 Hz); doing skin biopsies to determine individuals' gender and DNA; analyzing blubber for toxins like pesticides; as well as understanding more about their feeding and migration patterns and social behavior.

You will observe and do research with biologists for six to eight hours on the water in a twenty-four-foot inflatable boat with a reinforced hull. Dolphins, seals, and numerous other whale species will check you out. On land, you will be able to work in the lab. Nights will find you safe in bed in a private room in a B&B or motel in Longue Pointe de Mingan. Begin the day with a hearty breakfast ashore, have lunch on board, and dinner in local restaurants. Minimum stay is one week, about $1,900 Can.; two weeks, about $3,500

Can. Single supplement, $140 Can. a week. No prior knowledge is required; Sears and his assistants will provide training.

Washington

Orca Research in Puget Sound

Center for Whale Research   P.O. Box 1577, Friday Harbor, Washington 98250. Tel: 360-378-5835; Fax: 360-378-5954; E-mail: orcasurv@rockisland.com; Website: www.whaleresearch.com.

Earthwatch   3 Clock Tower Place, Suite 100, Box 75, Maynard, Massachusetts 01754-0075. Tel: 800-776-0188 (toll-free); 978-461-0081; Fax: 978-461-2332; E-mail: info@earthwatch.org; Website: www.earthwatch.org.

Researcher Ken Balcomb at the Center for Whale Research has

An orca, or killer whale, spy-hops to see what's around. *NOAA; www.photolib.noaa.gov*

been studying orcas or killer whales (which are really dolphins) in Puget Sound since 1976. Attracted by salmon (which they love to eat), the orcas form a more or less stable population of a few generations of the same family, which Balcomb and his assistants have photographed and documented over the years. The population increased from sixty-eight in 1976 to ninety-one in 1992, but has been steadily dropping since then.

Balcomb would like to know why. He would also like to be able to isolate subtler factors in the environment (for example, the increased presence of small motorboats or underwater sounds) that might affect their overall health. From new data, he can begin to chart their birth and death rates.

You can join Balcomb at his Center for Whale Research on an Earthwatch expedition. Working from small boats you track orca pods; photograph them with high-speed black-and-white 35-mm film; record their vocalizations; and note weather conditions and the presence of other boats. Onshore, you will do lab work, maintain the boats, and cook.

Resident pods of orcas are also known to travel in search of more or better food. In the past few years, the salmon population in Puget Sound has thinned out. Are orcas looking far afield for new food? For veterans of previous whale studies, you can be part of a mobile sea team, venturing out from Puget Sound to track the orcas' travels.

Ten days, June to December, about $2,200, includes dormitory or private room at the rustic lodge that houses the Center for Whale Research, and meals.

The Azores

Deep Sea Whales: Sperm Whales

Cruise with Sperm Whales

Lindblad Expeditions   720 Fifth Avenue, New York, New York 10019. Tel: 800-397-3348 (toll-free); E-mail: explore@expeditions. com; Website: www.expeditions.com.

Plunk in the middle of the Atlantic Ocean, the Azores archipelago is a magnificent collection of ocean-ruled volcanic islands whose rich soil and steep hills are full of flowers, birds, and vineyards. Part of Portugal, the Azores was once a center of the whaling industry. The whaling is finished, but several species of whales still cruise the ocean not far from shore.

From the deck of the small ship M.S. *Endeavor* in the middle of the Atlantic Ocean on the edge of the Continental Shelf, you might see a sixteen-foot blow. That is a sperm whale, the largest toothed whale in the ocean and the one usually depicted in early whaling pictures, with a huge square head. If you are lucky, you will see twenty or more together, either a pod of females or young males. Sperm whales eat the giant squid that inhabit waters about 3,000 feet down. Older huge loner males make extremely deep and long dives, possibly as much as two miles.

Onboard naturalists explain the whales' habits, and Welsh historian David Barnes leads tours on land, with visits to some remnants of the whaling industry. Nine days, about $3,000 to $6,000, depending on berth.

Togo

Humpbacks in the Bight of Benin

Dreamweaver Travel Company   1185 River Drive, River Falls, Wisconsin 54022. Tel: 715-425-1037; E-mail: dudley@dream weavertravel.net; Website: www.dreamweavertravel.net.

The West African country of Togo, tucked between Ghana and Benin, is about the width of a good beach, and that's where you will catch a whale-watch trip with a local captain who knows where the migrating humpbacks are. Onshore, guides will introduce you to elders, musicians, dancers, and some of the craftspeople who weave the famous Togan cloth. If the whales and dolphins are having a slow day, the captain has gear aboard to fish for yellow-fin tuna. Seven days, about $1,800.

Antarctica

Humpback and Minke in the Ice

Lindblad Expeditions   720 Fifth Avenue, New York, New York
10019. Tel: 800-397-3348 (toll-free). E-mail: explore@expeditions.
com; Website: www.expeditions.com.

In the Antarctic whale tails and spouts are a common sight, along
with penguins, the elegant emperor, the tiny adelie, the noisy
gentoo, and the ones with the chinstrap, all of which huddle by the
dozens, or dive for fish. Kayak among the whales in two-person
floats, if you wish. Lindblad also follows the whales to the sub-
Antarctic islands, which have even more species of penguins. Travel
on the naturalist-guided research ship *Endeavor*. Lindblad has been
taking people to Antarctica for more than three decades. Fifteen to
twenty-five nights, from about $8,000 to $13,000.

National Geographic Expeditions   P.O. Box 65265,
Washington, D.C. 20035-5265. Tel: 888-966-8687; Website: www.
nationalgeographic.com/ngexpeditions.

Join photographer Gordon Wiltsie on a trip from Ushuaia,
Argentina, to the Antarctic Peninsula, looking for leopard (crab-
eater) seals; penguins, including rockhopper and king; blue-eyed
shags; and whales. Zodiacs and kayaks take you to shore for a walk
among the penguins. Sixteen days on the research ship *Endeavor*,
from about $10,000 to $17,000.

Russia

Sea of Okhotsk

Zegrahm Expeditions   192 Nickerson Street, No. 200, Seattle,
Washington 98109. Tel: 800-628-8747 (toll-free); 206-285-4000;
E-mail: zoe@zeco.com; Website: www.zeco.com.

Tourists are new here, and none of the millions of seabirds, or
hundreds of seals or grizzlies onshore, or the hundreds of hump-

Where whales are, seals are not far behind. A spotted seal waits on shore. *Captain Budd Christman, NOAA Corps; www.photolib.noaa.gov*

backs, minkes, bowheads, and orcas in the sea appear ever to have been looked at. In this sea off Siberia, surrounded by the Kamchatka Peninsula and the chain of islands that become Japan, explore on the small ship *Clipper Odyssey*. Fourteen days, about $7,500.

Kayak with Whales

Inveterate whale watchers say the best way to view whales is from a kayak. For one thing, your body is sensitive to every move in the water from the kayak, and you gain a full appreciation of the size and the intelligence of whales, sea lions, seals, and dolphins who will be both curious and respectful of you and your space.

A few words of advice about kayaking near whales. Michael Kundu, director and founder of Project SeaWolf, a nonprofit ocean study organization, says:

- Never interfere when whales are feeding, breeding, or nursing.
- Know what the whales are doing when you are around them.
- Try to stay at least 100 yards away.
- If one comes toward you, maintain a passive parallel course. Whales are frightened by head-on approaches.
- Never startle a whale. If you see a pod ahead of you that you want to photograph, make a lot of noise as you advance toward it. (Kundu says he sings or talks loud, or keeps his paddle sculling below the surface.)
- Respect their busy schedule. Feeding whales spend 65 percent of their time getting food or eating it. The rest of their time they relax and have social interactions. Kundu says, "There is no spare time in their itinerary to avoid kayakers."

British Columbia

Gray Whales

Sea Quest Expeditions   Tel: 888-589-4253 (toll-free); 360-378-5767; E-mail: orca@sea-quest-kayak.com; Website: www.sea-quest-kayak.com/bc.htm.

The nooks and crannies of the British Columbian coast are spectacularly beautiful and the coastal sea is full of gray whales and orcas. On land, Cape Caution is a huge rainforest (note: it rains a *lot* here) of ancient tall evergreens where bear, moose, and bald eagles live in abundance. If you get tired of watching the large population of gray whales, paddle over to the resident orca pod, which are there to eat the fish; or to the visiting humpbacks, which make lazy dives after they scoop up krill.

These gray whales are migrating from Baja Mexico to the Bering Strait, thought to be one of the longest ocean hauls for whales. In fact, individual gray whales are believed to travel close to 500,000 miles over a lifetime. Grays are baleen whales, but they feed on the bottom by lying on one side and scooping up organisms as well as mud, which clouds the water when they surface and filter out the edible food.

This area, which also has twelve-foot tides and huge tide pools, is made for kayaking. Sea Quest Expeditions provides guides knowledgeable about kayaking, cooking, the area, *and* whales, birds, and land mammals. Most guides have degrees in biology or natural science.

In new sturdy tandem kayaks (no Eskimo rolls), you paddle between camps where you sleep in two-person tents, enjoying the wild scenery and the possibility for exploration that presents itself at every turn.

No prior knowledge of kayaking is necessary (although it helps to be in fairly good shape in your upper body). Seven days, June to September, about $1,100, includes all necessary gear and food. Families with kids at least twelve years old are welcome.

Alaska

Humpbacks, Minke, and Orcas from a Kayak

Alaska Discovery   5310 Glacier Highway, Juneau, Alaska 99801. Tel: 800-586-1911 (toll-free); 907-780-6226; Fax: 907-780-4220;

E-mail: info@akdiscovery.com; Website: www.mtsobek.com. (Alaska Discovery is a member of the MTSobek family.)

On this nine-day tour in southeast Alaska, spend the days kayaking among whales, sea lions, and seals; and several nights at a former lighthouse, where you can go clamming for steamer clams and enjoy the sauna in the evening. Then kayak to explore other inlets, and stay at Alaskan lodges along the way, before taking a charter boat to the center for Alaskan Coastal Studies in Kachemak Bay and a beach tour at the minus-tide. You have the option of hiking the forest trails. Nine days, includes lodging, kayaks, food, about $3,700.

Swim with Whales

This is one of the more cathartic experiences you can have in the ocean: the sheer awe of being next to a giant and the thrilling realization that although it could, it will not harm you. Being in the same place and time with a whale makes you aware of the creature's innate dignity and your own vulnerability.

South Pacific

Vava'u, Kingdom of Tonga

Whale Swim Adventures   For more information, in the United States, contact Deb. Tel: 503-699-5869; E-mail: Deb@whaleswim. com. For more information on the tour listed, contact Rae Gill (in New Zealand). Tel: 011 (64) 09 372 7073; E-mail: rae@whale swim.com.

About 450 humpbacks, fat and fresh from feeding in Antarctica, migrate from August to October to the warm South Pacific waters around the islands of Tonga. The King of Tonga has a royal seat in the capital city of Nukualofa on the largest island in the archipelago. Vava'u is one of the smallest and most beautiful of the islands, with white coral beaches in aquamarine waters.

Whales are there to breed and give birth to calves, but Tongan captains have an uncanny intuition of where to find them. When whales surface, you slip quietly into the water, snorkel, view, and maybe swim alongside a mother and her calf.

This tour requires you to be a confident and fit snorkeler and swimmer.

Ten-night "flexible" tour, about $2,200 to $3,000 Aus. ($1,650 to $2,200 U.S.), depending on accommodation, which ranges from a "backpacker's lodge" to a resort hotel on the beach. The flexibility is built around the whales, but there are many things to explore in Tonga, especially the sweet and friendly people and the fine art of doing nothing.

Dominican Republic

Silver Banks

The Divine Dolphin   21444 Marana, Mission Viejo, California 92692. Tel: 305-443-0222; Website: www.cyberark.com/dolphin/whale.htm.

Afficionados of animal communication know Penelope Smith, author of several books on animal telepathic communication. Smith leads tours to the Silver Banks each winter when humpbacks gather to breed (sometimes aggressively) and to calve. This trip is a live-aboard licensed by the Dominican Republic Whale Commission and runs according to international rules of non-harassment.

Anchoring on the banks allows you to ride in smaller boats closer to the whales where you are able to observe, listen to their vibrant songs, and snorkel near females and babes. Plus, you have the important added insights of Penelope Smith, gifted with the ability to read their thoughts. Seven days aboard, includes all meals; about $2,500.

Another company that does live-aboard whale trips on the Silver Banks, seven days, about $2,500: **Journeys of Discovery**   Website: www.ajourneyofdiscovery.com/whale.htm.

Rescue and Protection

The International Fund for Animal Welfare (IFAW)   P.O. Box 193, Yarmouth Port, Massachusetts 02675. Tel: 800-932-4329 (toll-free); 508-744-2000; Fax: 508-744-2009; E-mail: info@ifaw.org; Website: www.ifaw.org.

Whales and dolphins range around the world, and their protection has to be international. This global conservation organization protects marine mammals and their habitats and mounts rescue operations when they are in distress. Hunting whales is still legal in some countries; read IFAW member actor Pierce Brosnan's articulate and passionate words against hunting whales. See www.ifaw.org/actionforwhales.

For links to whale sites and for information on adopting a whale, log on to WhaleNet at whale.wheelock.edu

DOLPHINS

The Bahamas

Atlantic Dolphins

For all we know, wild dolphins are running tours to swim with human beings. Known for their intelligence, the sophisticated ones from numerous species know all the tricks to win your heart.

When wild dolphins choose to swim with you, consider it a special privilege. They fit you in to their tight schedule of hunting fish, swimming in the vortex of boats' wakes, playing, mating, checking out new places, and the thousand other things dolphins do.

When they do come by your boat dolphins might engage swimmers in spins and games. You hear them even before you get in the water, clicking and chirping in a high-pitched tone. Being with them is pure tonic if you are tired, overworked, or otherwise out of joint, because these ancient creatures not only tolerate us but take sympathy on us. Some serious work is being conducted at various places between captive dolphins and autistic and sick children. Twisting and
~~.. playing and leaping with wild dolphins can change your life.

Many tours exist to swim with wild dolphins, all from a boat. On some you stay in landside accommodations; on others you never leave the boat. What follows is just a sampling.

Liveaboard

NatureQuest PMB 185, 30872 South Coast Highway, Laguna Beach, California 92651. Tel: 800-369-3033 (toll-free); 949-499-9561; Fax: 949-499-0812; E-mail: natureqst@aol.com; Website: www.naturequesttours.com.

From this live-aboard cruise, you will be able to snorkel and swim as much as you want. Dolphins come by sometimes three times a day and stay for an hour. An onboard naturalist acts as an intermediary.

Seven days, includes food and berth on a ninety-foot catamaran, about $1,400. Bring your own snorkeling equipment; NatureQuest recommends a wet suit.

Hawaii

Pacific Dolphins: Naturalist Day Cruise

Pacific Whale Foundation   Eco Adventures, 300 Ma'alaea Road, Waikiki, Hawaii 96793. To reserve places on the dolphin cruise, which leaves from Maui: Tel: 800-942-5311 (toll-free); E-mail: reservations@pacificwhale.org ; Website: www.pacificwhale.org.

The Pacific Whale Foundation has been studying the athletic Pacific dolphins for so long they have created dossiers on individuals. Researchers photograph, monitor, and document family members of spinner, bottlenose, and pantropical spotted dolphins. They attach suction-cup devices that record diving depths and study their peregrinations, family structures, and where they call home.

On board the *Ocean Odyssey* catamaran (fueled by recycled cooking oils), you have numerous vantage points for viewing dolphins as you cruise past Molokini and Lana'i, as well as hot showers to use after you snorkel the Molokini crater reef with naturalists.

The Pacific Whale Foundation suggests you keep an eye open for:

- Leaps: One dolphin in a fast-moving group suddenly leaps into the air, sometimes tail-over-head, landing on its back.

- Tail Slaps: One dolphin in a slow-moving group will slap the surface of the water with its tail, often for 20 or more times.

- Body Slaps: One dolphin in a slow-moving group rises and slaps its body against the surface of the water.

- Spinning: One dolphin leaps as much as 6 feet above the water and rotates its body in a complete spin four times in one second.

- Bow Riding: What you most often see: a group of dolphins riding the bow or stern wave apparently for the sheer fun of it.

- Caressing: Two dolphins occasionally ride belly to belly or caress each other with a pectoral fin or run their teeth along a part of another dolphin without hurting it.

- Play Behavior: Dolphins love to play with things they can toss around, like seaweed, and sometimes seem to get up a full game of tag.

Naturalists aboard keep you informed on the latest research on the dolphins. You might want to adopt one at the end of the trip.

Daily cruises, May to December. Leaves Maui at 8:30 A.M., returns at 3:00 P.M. Adults: about $75; kids seven to twelve: $15. Includes onboard barbecue lunch.

Greece

Research Dolphins

Whale and Dolphin Conservation Society (WDCS)   Brookfield House, 38 St. Paul Street, Chippenham, Wiltshire SN15 1LY, UK. Tel: 011 (44) 1249 449500; Fax: (44) 1249 449501; E-mail: info@wdcs.org; Website: www.wdcs.org.

In the clear emerald Ionian Sea, join members of the Tethys Research Institute on a long-term project to examine two species of endangered dolphins, the common bottlenose and the short-beaked common dolphin. Each day from the field station on the luxuriant island of Kalamos, you motor into the bay in a reinforced inflatable looking for dolphins. When they appear, you photograph their dorsal fins to identify them; and every six minutes, note their behavior, interaction with others in the pod, their GPS position, and route. If they are feeding, you collect fish scales on the surface to identify their prey.

One week, includes room and board and time to relax on the sandy beach, about 650 Euros.

For more on ocean mammals, see www.ocean.com.

Sea World Orlando and **Sea World San Diego** are two excellent resources for all things relating to the oceans. Overnight Adventure Camps for kids with and without their parents are designed to answer all those questions kids might have about animals. Teachers can download teacher guides. Website: www.sea world.org. In Orlando, email: education@seaworld.org; in San Diego, swc.education@seaworld.org.

12

THE PANTANAL

BRAZIL

The largest wetland in the world covers some 60,000 square miles plunk in the middle of South America, mostly in Brazil, with a few square miles extending into Paraguay and Bolivia. The RAMSAR international convention, which was convened in 1971 to identify wetlands around the world that might be threatened, created a list of about 1,350 Wetlands of International Importance. This is one of its superstars.

Most of it is flooded in the middle of its summer, October to March (it is between 15 and 20 degrees below the equator), when heavy rains create an inland sea. In diversity of species, only Africa comes close, but the Pantanal wins hands down in species size. Nothing in this part of South America is small.

Despite the fact that the Portuguese named it *Pantanal*—"swamp," the Pantanal is in fact a wetland, because from June to October it dries out enough to host giant anteaters, giant armadillos, capybaras (the world's largest rodent), and South America's largest land mammal, the mysterious tapir. Endangered giant river otters play in the pools and canals. Even the world's largest parrot, the magnificent indigo blue hyacinth macaw, extinct just about everywhere else, lives here in the treetops in loud and busy flocks.

And those are just the big species. Jaguars love this place (some say there are more than ever), as do howler monkeys, maned wolves, possum, foxes that eat crabs, and huge flocks of more than 600

Related to horses and unchanged from their Ice Age ancestors, tapirs are about five to six feet long and have a tapered snout. Shy, they often lie submerged in water for long periods of time. *Roger Archibald*

species of birds—from long-legged spoonbills and Jabiru storks, to ducks, numerous toucans, and rheas, South America's version of the ostrich.

CAIMAN

Taking advantage of the 250 species of fish are caiman. These slightly smaller alligators, left over from the Cretaceous, have developed lots of smarts living in the Pantanal.

They lie about like logs during the day, then hunt fish by night, slipping into the water after sunset and lining up to form a barricade of open-mouthed caiman smiles to catch schools of little fish, which they nail loudly with their sharp teeth. More than fifty species of reptiles live here, including anacondas, most of them slightly smaller than the behemoths that are pulled from mud holes on TV nature channels, but not to be petted: they eat humans, too.

Of 3 million people who live in the Pantanal in small towns or the larger city of Cuiaba, more than half are fourth- or fifth-generation cattle ranchers who move their herds to the dry areas in the wet season. Many others work the seasonal harvests of the cash crop soybean fields.

Until about twenty years ago before hunting caiman was regulated by national and international laws, caiman skin products were in high demand, and caiman became a threatened species. The laws are loosely enforced, however. When poachers—many of them out-of-work farm laborers—persisted, cattle ranchers banded together to counteract poachers and protect the caiman, and without a big fanfare, got into the ecotourism business. Many have converted their ranches or *fazendas*, into lodges, while maintaining their cattle. Poaching is still a problem, but not as bad as 1985 when 500,000 animals were slaughtered—caiman, jaguars, wolves, and snakes—for their skins.

Animals Versus Soybeans

The Pantanal has other problems, too: animals' habitats are polluted by pesticide runoff from the soybean farms and by the canal building that diverts some of the wetland water. Whenever habitat is affected, it is bad news for many species. (See www.pantanal.org.)

A Pantanal National Park and three private reserves have been nominated as a World Heritage Site.

How to Get There

To get to the Pantanal, fly to Cuiaba from Rio or take the bus from Sao Paulo in the dry season (September to October are least buggy), then drive south along the Transpantaneira, a raised-dirt highway,

Jaguars love the Pantanal for its wild pigs. *Roger Archibald*

which travels for about ninety miles through the various ecosystems in Pantanal forests, savannahs, and isolated swamps. Astounding wildlife is everywhere. Car rental agencies exist in the Cuiaba airport, but they do not rent 4-WD vehicles, which you will need in the shoulder seasons. In the wet season, October to March, you have to fly to Campo Grande in the center of the Pantanal; the Transpantaneira is paved from there.

Lodging

Numerous ranches offer lodging and hearty food and a taste of life in the Brazilian tropics of the 1920s, which is when most of the ranches were built. Some have pools, all have warm water and flush toilets, and most arrange tours by boat or canoe or land vehicle, or night walking tours with a naturalist. Expect a rustic lifestyle and zillions of mosquitoes. Often many Pantanal species live right around the fazenda. Average price for three days is between $500 and $600. Try www.amazontravel.com.

Fazenda Rio Negro   R. Eduardo S. Pereira, 1550-Sala 16 V. Rosa, Campo Grande, MS 79020-170 Brazil. Tel/Fax: 011 55-67-751-5191; E-mail: rionegro@conservation.org.br; Website: www.fazendarionegro.com.br.

A working fazenda, now owned by Conservation International and run by local folk is the Fazenda Rio Negro, about an hour's flight from Campo Grande. A field station for scientists, including Earthwatch volunteers, the Fazenda has been a tourist lodge for about twelve years and offers informed guides, boats, fishing gear, a *pata-choca* (former military vehicle), and horses on which to explore. Food is regional and delicious; the pace is relaxed; the lodge has lots of hammocks on the porch.

Join A Scientific Project

Earthwatch   3 Clock Tower Place, Suite 100, Box 75, Maynard, Massachusetts 01754-0075. Tel: 800-776-0188 (toll-free); 978-461-0081; Fax: 978-461-2332; E-mail: info@earthwatch.org; Website: www.earthwatch.org

On this project in the Pantanal, you can join any of five or six scientists from June to November doing things such as setting up mist nets to band migratory birds, radio-tracking white-lipped peccaries, monitoring animals at field stations, and installing camera traps to photograph jaguars. Open to anyone over sixteen. Lodging is at the

Fazenda Rio Negro; transport is in 4-WD, on horseback, or in boats. Eleven days, about $2,200.

Focus Tours, Inc.   103 Moya Road, Santa Fe, New Mexico 85708-8360. Tel: 505-466-4688; Fax: 505-466-4689; E-mail: focustours@aol.com; Website: www.focustours.com.

Douglas Trent is an ecologist who has worked in Brazil for more than twenty years. English-speaking guides provide checklists for all the species you might see, along with a spotting scope, tape recorder, and microphone (to get closer to distant mammals or birds), as well as a powerful spotlight for night viewing. Lodging is in fazendas. All tours can be custom designed; Focus Tours will also take care of arrangements if you want to travel independently.

Eco-Expeditions   192 Nickerson Street, No. 200, Seattle, Washington 98109. Tel: 800-628-8747 (toll-free); 206-285-4000; E-mail: zoe@zeco.com; Website: www.zeco.com.

This experienced company offers four days in the Pantanal, and includes trips through the Caratinga Biological Station and Caraca Natural Park, located in reserves in the Brazilian Atlantic rainforest, and home to the world's rarest primates, including the wooly spider monkey. This is followed by two days in the Serra de Canastra National Park, which has the world's largest collection of giant anteaters and their preferred diet—termites living in giant mounds. After the Pantanal, visit Iguassu Falls, a series of amazing rushing waterfalls (two and a half miles wide) at the border with Argentina. Lodging is in monasteries, Best Western lodges, and local hotels. One of the two guides is a medical doctor; both are experienced naturalists. Fifteen days, about $6,500.

13

Rain Forests

Rain Forest = Jungle

Somewhere along the line, the word *rain forest* replaced the word *jungle*, maybe because it seems easier to talk about the political problems of the rain forest, rather than the jungle. But Tarzan did not swing in the rain forest, and King Kong was definitely born in the jungle, and a jungle experience is what you will have when you go to the rain forest.

Breathless

Dense, thick with foliage and trees draped with vines, and fig trees with person-high roots, humid, hard to walk through, deafening at night with the songs of frogs and insects, and filled with mystery and mosquitoes, the jungle obscures and deceives your senses. Rains in the wet season make it sometimes impossible to see, smell, or even sense a predator within arm's reach. Snakes droop from trees or hide in the underbrush. Big mammals check you out from behind leafy screens.

Sometimes it is just quiet, and you are sure someone is behind you. "I had to acknowledge a feeling of strong forces in Cockscomb," wrote researcher Alan Rabinowitz of the jungle in southern Belize. "Maybe nothing supernatural," he said, "just the intense energy flux in the jungle coming from the never-ending battles of life and death."

Where People Fit

The true tropical rain forest, or jungle, stretches around the globe along the equator and to 10 degrees above and below it. Truly wild places on Earth exist in areas where harsh climate has precluded human population, such as the Poles, and where local wildlife are super-adapted, such as penguins and polar bears; or in parts of the ocean, where not only ships but fish and mammals are few and far between.

But the rain forest has been co-inhabited forever by many wild creatures and a few human beings. Both the Yanamomo in Venezuela and Pygmies in Africa—star jungle dwellers—learned a long time ago to fit in to the jungle infrastructure, where they learn to hunt and not be hunted, avoid what's dangerous or venomous, and identify antidotes for mishaps. They have learned that predators, like jaguars or lions, have life habits that must be understood and respected.

THE AMAZON

Lots of rivers snake through the true tropical rain forests in Central America, Asia, and Africa, but the premier tropical (and easily visitable) river is the Amazon in South America. This mighty river, which begins in the Peruvian Andes at the confluence of the Ucayali and the Maranon rivers, and travels across the entire continent to exit in the Atlantic Ocean in Brazil, is 4,200 miles long, 40 miles across at its widest (which accommodates ocean-going vessels), and no more than a narrow stream in some of its numerous tributaries. Its warmth and humidity make it truly a tropical river, which swells from December through May because of Andes' snow melt and rains; and shrinks from June to November.

The river is rich in species, from more than 2,000 species of fish and pink and gray dolphins, and at least 60 species of reptiles, particularly caiman and the giant anaconda, a quiet and compellingly long (between eighteen and thirty feet) carnivore that lives hidden in the plants along the shore. Birds are everywhere, migrating and permanent residents, including the endangered and rare hoatzin, a bird with a permanent bad-hair day and the only bird that eats leaves—sometimes so many it can't lift its body to fly.

Entomologists, especially beetle and ant specialists, adore the Amazon rainforest floor because of its abundant diversity of species. Butterflies are everywhere, especially the signature blue morphos. Jaguars like to fish the banks of the Amazon, catching caiman. They are also good swimmers, and if they prefer the opposite bank, they will jump in and paddle across.

The endangered pink river dolphin is neither pink nor particularly like ocean dolphins. Its nose is long and thin, and its many teeth are made for grinding and tearing. It is timid and doesn't move around much; spotting solitary ones or pairs of pink dolphins idling beneath the surface is not unusual.

The small (four- to six-foot) endangered grey dolphin lives in the Amazon, as well as on the coasts, but it is more lively, possibly to keep away from villagers who believe its eyes are love charms.

PERU

On the stretch of the Amazon and its tributaries that flow to the Brazilian border, a relatively virgin rain forest crowds the banks. Most trips start in Iquitos, an old river port, where there is an airport about an hour's flight from Lima.

Less visited by tourists who spend more time on the river in Manaus, Brazil, this area has lots of jungle reserves and ways to explore them: most villages are accessible only by river, and you can chug steadily along the riverbanks in a river boat; kayak, swim, and stay in lodges deep in the jungle; and enjoy the longest canopy walkway in the world—and several smaller ones as well.

To get the full experience, some companies recommend staying at least a week. That way, you become friends with the birds and small animals that hang around the lodge or camp, and they get to know you. You can also work out detentes with the insects who were there first.

The Two-Tiered Jungle

A few years ago when biologists realized a whole other rain forest was taking place in the treetops, they devised cranes, ropes and pulleys, and even blimps to get them up there. When fearless biologists came back full of stories, the travel industry seized on some of their leftover gear and built new and safe ways in which to access the canopy.

People in city apartments flee to the roof for a breath of air and quiet, but jungle creatures race to the treetops to get in on the action. Some biologists believe that more than 50 percent of rain-forest species live here, hundreds of feet above the jungle floor. Then there are the species that live in the space in between: ant specialist E.O. Wilson found forty-two species of ant living on *one* Amazon rain-forest tree. What is certain is that there are at least two rain forests: one with narrow paths with twisted roots, teeming with plants with huge leaves striving for a ray of sun; and one above, full of exotic insects being sought by brachiating primates and scores of species of flashy birds.

Now strewn throughout the rain forests around the world, tourists can find observation towers, suspension bridges, and ropes-and-harness rappelling systems called *ziplines* that get them up and carry them from high platform to platform. They are safe, some are more thrilling than others, and they can be a good way to spend an afternoon or a full day to get the entire experience of a rain forest.

The longest jungle bridge in the world is the Amazon Canopy Walkway in the Peruvian Amazon, 115 feet up, a third of a mile long, and easy for all to access. The highest one in the Amazon—a platform 140 feet high—is on a private biological reserve on a tributary of the Brazilian Amazon on Juma Lake (see below). To get an idea of the zipline experience, rent *Medicine Man* (1991) with Sean Connery.

Reserva Comunal de Tamshiyacu-Tahuayo

Amazonia Expeditions   10305 Riverburn Drive, Tampa, Florida 33647. Tel: 800-262-9669 (toll-free); Fax: 813-907-8475; E-mail: Paul.Beaver@gte.net; Website: www.perujungle.com.

From Iquitos, Amazonia Expeditions speeds you in a boat first up the Amazon, then up the smaller Tahuayo River to the Tamshiyacu-Tahuayo Reserve where you pull up to dock at the Tahuayo Lodge, an award winner from Peru's Department of Industry and Tourism and on one of *Conde Nast Traveler*'s Best Places to Stay. There are fifteen cabins, and a screened lodge with a laboratory and a library. Food and purified water are good and safe. Light is from kerosene lamps; the toilets are flushable, thanks to a septic system.

This jungle reserve, south of Iquitos on the river, is an oasis left over from the last Ice Age. It managed to keep its trees, and therefore its species, many of which exist nowhere else on Earth, such as the red-faced uakari monkey, that has long red fur and looks surprisingly like an orangutan. In fact, this reserve has the largest number of primate species of any park in the world.

Each day you and native naturalists travel the reserve or the river at your own pace in search of species, whatever your interest. You can canoe, track jaguar, fish, or swim in a blackwater lake with pink dolphins. Legislated as a reserve by the Peruvian government in 1991, the park encourages local villagers to limit the game they kill.

Expect to see a variety: pygmy marmosets, hoatzin birds, tree frogs, electric eels, unusual beetles, leaf hoppers, parakeets, anteaters, giant sloths, caiman, jaguars, and lots more.

The Zipline

You can explore the treetop canopy of ancient growth forests with a zipline, the longest one in the Amazon region. This safe system hoists you up in a rappeller's harness to a wooden platform 100 feet above the forest floor where you are attached by a carabiner to a zipline on which you can travel from tree platform to tree platform, at your own speed. You can stop to take pictures, investigate the totally different ecosystems of the treetops, or gaze in wonder at the spectacle below.

Seven days, includes everything except international airfare, about $1,300. Amazonia Expeditions can also provide a special guide for preteenage children.

Sucusarí Reserve

Amazon Explorama Lodges   P.O. Box 446, Iquitos, Peru.
Tel: 800-707-5275 (toll-free, U.S.); Fax: 51 94 25 2533; E-mail:
amazon@explorama.com; Website: www.explorama.com.

Off the Napo River, a tributary that runs northwest from the
Amazon about 100 miles from Iquitos, is a stream called the
Sucusari; it has a reserve that protects an ancient rain forest so dense
with species that some scientists refer to it as the Biodiversity Capital of the World.

Amazon Explorama Lodges is run by a coalition of former teachers who began in 1964 to buy acres of virgin rainforest next to the
lodges they developed. Since then, their group has become a non-
governmental organization called CONAPAC, which is responsible
for six major reserves in the Peruvian Amazon rainforest. They have
established ReNuPeRu Ethnobotanical Garden, where a local
shaman raises plants used in medicines. The coalition gives support
to local river village schools, which you can visit, and trains local
teachers. The Sucusari Reserve is 50 percent reforested, to replace
trees cut down by loggers or by villagers seeking more farmland.

For tourists, Explorama Lodges offers Amazon-river-style
thatched roofed huts, with meals cooked outdoors over an open
hearth. Lights are kerosene lamps. The ExplorNapo Lodge also has
a hammock house and screened dining room.

Traveling with native bilingual guides, you explore the forest by
day and take river excursions by night, looking for caiman. The
schedule is kept flexible and depends on a variety of factors from
weather to river and trail conditions.

Five days includes the transport from Iquitos, Explorama Lodge
on the Yanamono Stream, ExplorNapo, and the **Amazon Canopy
Walkway**. Guides, excursions, meals, lodges, about $1,150.

Pacaya-Samiria Reserve: By Riverboat

La Amatista is the kind of transport boat you would expect to see on
any river in the tropics. An expanded version of the *African Queen*, it
is green, three-tiered—with life preservers hung from the openwork

railings—and cruises at a slow but deliberate speed. But it is also air conditioned, has hot showers, and serves an impressive banquet. On this comfortable twenty-nine-passenger riverboat, you travel from Iquitos up the Rio Ucayali to the **Pacaya-Samiria Reserve**, largely flooded from December to May, where you take small boats then hike to see monkeys, parrots, as well as the dolphins. From a small boat at night you will see caimans. Swim in the Rio Tapiche, and walk on the **San Regis Canopy Walkway**.

International Expeditions, Inc.   One Environs Park, Helena, Alabama 35080-7200. Tel: 800-633-4734 (toll-free); E-mail: nature@ietravel.com; Website: www.internationalexpeditions.com.

Nine days, includes airfare from Miami, about $3,000 to $3,500, depending on the season. This company has designed several different trips to the Amazon. Ask about their Amazon Kids' Program, a nine-day family voyage, adults, about $3,000; kids under sixteen, about $2,600.

American Museum of Natural History   Discovery Tours, Central Park West at 79th Street, New York, New York 10024. Tel: 800-462-8687 (toll-free); 212-769-5700; Fax: 212-769-5755; Website: www.discoverytours.org.

Travel aboard *La Amatista* with a specialist in the poison dart frog to the Pacaya Samiria Reserve. The AMNH also offers special family trips in June. Nine days, about $4,000; children fourteen and under, about $3,400.

Join a Scientific Project

Amazon Basin Jungle Between Tambopata and Manu Areas

Biosphere Expeditions   Sprat's Water near Carlton Colville, The Broads National Park, Suffolk NR33 8BP UK. Tel: +44 1502 583085; E-mail: info@biosphere-expeditions.org; Website: www.biosphere-expeditions.org.

A proboscis monkey, identifiable by its long nose and unique to the jungle coasts of Borneo, joins his troop at sunset on the riverbank on the way to Camp Leakey. *Georgeanne Irvine, Orangutan Foundation International; www.orangutan.org*

East northeast of Cusco is an area soon to become a conservation area. Before that happens, however, biologists must make an inventory of what species thrive there and what their ecosystems are. To do this, local biologists have set up a rapid assessment program (RAP), which sends teams into often uncharted areas to do quick surveys of representative segments—in this case, clay licks visited by macaws and such mammals as collared peccary, ocelots, howler monkeys, capuchin monkeys, and spider monkeys.

For this project, volunteers are needed. Biosphere Expeditions organizes groups of volunteers who can join for two weeks to several weeks, if they wish, helping to catalog species in this virgin area. Biosphere emphasizes that volunteers are not expected to have specialized knowledge, be athletes, or have a desire for a military encampment. Lodging is always comfortable, in this case, a lodge with hot water showers and toilets, plus a good cook.

Volunteers split into teams and do various duties each day such as walking transects and cataloging the animals they see, checking the video cameras set up on the clay licks (clay provides minerals to cleanse any toxins otherwise in the diet), sitting in blinds and identifying the birds and the mammals that pass by, and identifying tracks on paths. Two weeks, about $1,700.

BRAZIL

Río Juma

Condor Journeys and Adventures   2 Ferry Bank, Colintraive, Argyll PA22 3AR, UK. Tel: +44 (0) 1700 841 318; Fax: +44 (0) 1700 841 398; E-mail: sanielle@condorjourneys-adventures.com; Website: www.condorjourneys-adventures.com.

To understand more about how some Brazilian Amazon dwellers live, you can join a group that goes deep into the jungle about four hours by boat out of Manaus, on the tributary Rio Juma, home of the Cablocos. Condor Journeys provides experienced naturalist guides and organizes several trips that begin and end at the Amazon Floating Lodge on Juma Lake, located among 100 acres of private biological reserve, most of which you can see from the 140-foot platform.

Their Jungle Safari begins with a jungle survival briefing and meeting with some descendants of the indigenous Cablocos. Then you paddle for three days in canoes down the numerous tributaries and streams that network the jungle, setting up hammock camps at night. This is a good chance to experience the jungle firsthand.

Back at Floating Lodge, you can take showers, have a "survivor's cocktail," and sort out your experience. Six days, airport to airport, about $1,000.

Fishing the Río Negro

Amazon Fishing Trips   E-mail: Jack McNamara, Jack@Amazon fishingtrips.com; Website: www.amazonfishingtrips.com.

The Rio Negro heads northwest from the Amazon River in Manaus, a popular rainforest tourist center in Brazil. The Rio Negro is a spectacular river that travelers fall in love with; it has white sand beaches and abundant flowers, coffee-colored water, practically no mosquitoes, and maybe more than 1,000 species of fish, many of which are exported to aquarium shops around the world. You will see pink dolphins, giant river otters, parrots, king-fishers, macaws, and monkeys.

Amazon Fishing Trips flies out of Manaus to a point on the Upper Rio Negro where you join a two-tiered river boat (eat meals prepared by a cook and sleep on hammocks). You have a choice of spending eight days fishing (eat what you catch, or catch and release) for peacock bass or other Amazon fish. Eight days, about $3,000.

Or you can take a tropical aquarium fish-in-nature tour and snorkel and swim in a remote part of the jungle river among dwarf cichlids, pike cichlids, tetras, and angel fish. This trip also includes a hike across a wetland to a bamboo forest growing out of clear water with hundreds of other species of tropical aquarium fish. Add, if you want, a day or two fishing for peacock bass and night fishing with spears. Twelve days, about $2,600.

Websites

For rain forest issues, see www.rainforestweb.org. For ecotourism information, see www.ecotourism.org.

14

JAGUARS

GOLDEN EYES

Jaguars have clear golden eyes that seem to be lit from within. Those who live near jungles say that they feel themselves melt when a jaguar looks at them.

But jaguars are very hard to see.

In dense jungle from Mexico to Argentina, jaguars slip in and out of view. Unlike other cats, they hunt both day and night on all terrains. They eat fish and caimans as much as avocados and capybaras, and their preferred diet is the white lipped peccary—a hefty wild pig. Jaguars roar loudly, and their urine gives off a powerful signatory odor. These, plus their spoor, are often the only way you know they are around. Truly cool cats, they watch from trees, hidden in the leaves, or spy from blinds in the dense forest.

For the most part jaguars seem to find human beings tedious. Staffan Widstrand writing in *BBC Wildlife* described an encounter from a boat in the Pantanal in Brazil. The jaguar, which had just eaten, lunged toward the boat in a mock attack before walking away with an indifferent toss of its head. "With belly full and the tip of his tail flicking," Widstrand said, "he projected an image of intelligence and elegance, combined with raw brutal power. A split second later, he was gone, engulfed by the forest, leaving me more hooked on jaguars than ever."

Cool and Elusive Cats

Jaguars are members of the *Panthera* family, smaller, chunky Western Hemisphere cousins of the Big Guys—lions, tigers, and leopards. (Florida panthers, cougars, and mountain lions are members of the *Puma* family.) Powerfully built, more than six feet long, about 150 to 300 pounds, gold with black spots (although a surprising number seem to be pure black), jaguars live either in harmony with, or completely indifferent to, human beings. Mayans and some other native people believe these beautiful and relatively unknown cats are spiritual representatives of deities; in most tribes it is taboo to kill them.

Poachers don't have the same rules, however. No one knows how many jaguars exist, although until they were protected by international law, about 15,000 jaguars a year became coats.

Jaguar's Generous Cousins

Wildlife Conservation, aided by a grant from Jaguar North America, the automobile company, is working with biologists to establish a safe wildlife corridor from Mexico to the Amazon and beyond where jaguars may wander freely to find mates and avoid guns from poachers and farmers. (See www.savethejaguar.com.)

In the Central and South American rainforests, the bioindicator is the jaguar. (Bioindicators are the living creatures that act as canaries in the mineshaft of the ecosystem. When the bioindicators are happy, everybody's happy.) In the past few years, jaguars have been helping themselves to cattle in the Pantanal, the vast wetland in central Brazil. Ranchers, reluctant to kill them, nevertheless have to make the choice between livelihood and respect for wildlife. But if jaguars eat cattle, it means that something is missing from their diet in the wild; in this case it is the peccary—a wild pig and a staple of a jaguar diet—whose habitat has been diminished and changed by farming and logging. Local witnesses have seen jaguars walk past grazing cattle, completely indifferent to them. Jaguars are not dedicated killers; they are simply carnivores looking for a meal.

Spying on Their Secret Lives

Still, so much remains to be known about the cat. Researchers believe their range is somewhere between 2 and 200 square miles, for example. Alan Rabinowitz recounts the story of being stopped in a truck in southern Belize while a pair of jaguars went through a mating ritual on the dirt road in front of them, completely indifferent to the truck. Do they mate for life? At certain times of the year? No one has ever photographed a mother with newborn cubs. To cast light on some of their secrets, biologists are setting up trip-wire cameras, triggered by movement, throughout the Central and South American rainforests.

Maybe because they are so hard to know, researchers who try to walk away from jaguars find they are happier spending their lives saving them.

Jungle Preserves

Trouble in the rainforest comes only when outside logging companies with major construction units do mega-collections of wood or strip areas for cash crops like soybeans, or when increased local populations demand bigger home farms. In all cases, more trees are slashed and fields burned to make way for human interests. This affects animals—especially big ones that eat little ones—that need a big range to hunt for food, like jaguars. They don't have a say at the bargaining tables in the jungle, but they *are* represented by rainforest conservation groups.

The result is the establishment of jungle preserves for wildlife that is in danger of becoming homeless. Jungle preserves make certain areas off-limits for human interests; they encourage the development of tourism, or nature- or eco-tourism, an industry whose representatives engage local folk as guides and train them to be innkeepers to offer hospitality to strangers interested in experiencing the jungle. Many international travel companies hire local guides and use local lodges, or they donate some of their profit to local conservation groups. The operative word here is "green."

Guides Are Necessary

Fortunately, local guides are plentiful and willing to share a knowledge of their home and how they coexist with wild animals, which
they know a lot about. If you choose to travel alone, you will definitely need a guide, unless you grew up in the jungle. Governments
that maintain ministries of tourism often keep lists. If you have
never had anything like a jungle experience before, take advantage
of an experienced company and travel with a small group and naturalist guides.

BELIZE

Belize Audubon Society   29 Regent Street, Box 1001, Belize
City. Tel: 02-77369; Website: www.belizeaudubon.org.
   Only one country has a reserve specially designated for jaguars,
where they are currently collared and monitored and protected from
poachers: Cockscomb Jaguar Reserve in Belize.
   Established by Wildlife Conservation International as the first
jaguar reserve in the world in the **Cockscomb Basin Wildlife
Sanctuary**, Cockscomb Jaguar Reserve consists of more than 150
square miles, a good range for the estimated 200 jaguars that hunt
lots of resident peccaries. It also houses puma, ocelots (which look
like a much smaller jaguar), howler monkeys, Baird's tapirs (Belize's
national animal), armadillo, and jaguarundis (a twenty-pound red
or dark brown cat that hunts rodents)—plus about 300 species of
very colorful tropical birds.
   If you hike, be aware that fer-de-lance snakes enjoy this jungle.
For a terrific account of Cockscomb, with all of its species, see
Jaguar (1986), written by Alan Rabinowitz, a naturalist from the
New York Zoological Society whose study of jaguars led to the
establishment of the Jaguar Reserve. The fer-de-lance is a player in
Belize, hard to see and super deadly.
   You can stay at the Cockscomb Basin Wildlife Sanctuary camp-
ground or cabins, which have water and bathing facilities. To take a

tour with a park ranger, make arrangements in advance at the Belize Audubon Society.

Island Expeditions Company   1574 Gulf Road, No. 156, Point Roberts, Washington 98281. Tel: 800-667-1630 (toll-free); 604-452-3212 (international); Fax: 604-452-3433; E-mail: info@islandexpeditions.com; Website: www.islandexpeditions.com

Island Expeditions has been taking travelers to Belize for more than a decade. Their Coral Jaguar Expedition spends four days in Cockscomb, traveling by two-person inflatable river kayaks that allow you to enter the sanctuary quietly. Steep limestone cliffs line parts of the river, which jaguars climb with superb agility.

You will also cross a few rapids and pools and come to put-in spots for hiking trails. Nights are spent camping. If you are going to see jaguar, this will be the way. Eleven days, about $1,900.

Check the weather before you go. Cockscomb is in southern Belize, which is liable to flood during heavy rains.

COSTA RICA

Another place where biologists from the Wildlife Conservation International are concentrating on jaguars is at the Sirena Biological Station in the Corcovado National Park, Costa Rica. Located on the Pacific Ocean on the Osa Peninsula in the southwest of the country, Corcovado covers about 160 square miles of dense, roadless jungle. Various hiking trails, however, take you through eight lush ecosystems, from mangroves and swamps to montane forests. Camping is available at the four biological stations, and Sirena has a lodge as well for a few dollars a night. Ideally, Costa Rica will establish a protected jaguar jungle reserve, part of the corridor from Central to South America.

Will you see jaguars? You might; more likely you will see scarlet macaws, the famous quetzals, and wild pigs. Bear in mind that tides

are often very high (no beach on the coastal trail), and rains wipe
out forest trails. Also, grunting and routing wild pigs have short
tempers on trail paths.

Costa Rica Expeditions   Dept. 235, 1601 NW 97th Avenue,
Unit C-101, Miami, Florida 33172. Tel: 305-599-8828;
In San Jose: Apartado 6941-1000, San Jose, Costa Rica. Tel: 011-
506-257-0766; Fax from the U.S.: 800-886-2609; E-mail: ecotour@
expeditions.co.cr; Website: www.costaricaexpeditions.com.

The best way to arrive is by boat, which you can catch from
Drake Bay. Or go with a guide and small group with Costa Rica
Expeditions, a veteran San Jose company. They provide flexible airport pickup, transport to Corcovado, lodging in their Corcovado
Lodge Tent Camp on Playa Carate, the beach near the trailhead for
the twenty-five-mile Park coastal hike, and a bilingual guide. Three
days, about $700; each child under sixteen, about $50.

Also check out the following companies which run longer trips to
Costa Rica.

Backroads   801 Cedar Street, Berkeley, California 94710-1800.
Tel: 800-462-2848 (toll-free); 510-527-1555; E-mail: info@
backroads.com; Website: www.backroads.com.

This company offers walking and hiking tours with naturalist
guides of Corcovado.

American Safari Cruises   19101 36th Avenue West, Suite 201,
Lynnwood, Washington 98036. Tel: 888-862-8881 (toll-free);
425-776-8889; E-mail: sales@amsafari.com; Website: www.
amsafari.com.

Small-yacht natural history tours of the entire country.

Horizontes Nature Tours   Apartado 1780-1002, San Jose,
Costa Rica. Tel: 506-222-2022; Fax: 506-255-4513; E-mail:
info@horizontes.com; Website: www.horizontes.com.

In business for 3 decades, this company custom designs trips
accompanied by naturalists.

Zoo

To spend time with jaguars, visit the new, multi-million-dollar Range of the Jaguar exhibit at the Jacksonville (Florida) Zoo. In a wide range that can hold twelve jaguars, four are currently in residence, along with other rainforest species, such as anaconda. Call 904-757-4463; or visit their Website: www.jaxzoo.org.

A jaguar shows its teeth among the ruins in the New Orleans Zoo. Their natural range extends from Mexico to Argentina. *Roger Archibald*

15

ISLANDS

UNIQUE SPECIES

All islands develop unique genetic and cultural patterns. Isolation does its thing over time. Some islands were isolated and left untouched by the last Ice Age and are excellent examples of places that have encouraged evolutionary genius: species that have adapted so well that they occur nowhere else on Earth. Other islands have been chosen as home by roving species that meet by the hundreds of thousands at certain times of the year.

Madagascar, a large island about 300 miles off the coast of Mozambique in the Indian Ocean, was isolated when the ancient landmass of Gondwana split apart. It has every terrain from open grasslands to dense rainforest, and of the 200,000 species cataloged there, 150,000 occur nowhere else.

The Galapagos, a collection of more than sixty islands in the Pacific Ocean located both above and below the equator, supports so many species with unique adaptations that biologists look on it as a dream laboratory.

The Seychelles, a remote archipelago in the Indian Ocean, has more than twenty unique bird species and is a busy breeding place of the rare and endangered giant land tortoise.

Newfoundland, in the Atlantic Ocean halfway between the North and South Poles, has only one endemic species, the most southerly herd of caribou. But it has millions of migrating seabirds, no predators, plentiful food, and a tiny population of human beings.

MADAGASCAR

A long time ago, when all the continents were joined into one giant Pangaea, Madagascar, India, and Antarctica were all part of the same land. They separated several million years ago, and unless they could swim or fly long distances, the species that were endemic stayed and cultivated all the little idiosyncrasies it takes to exist in one's neck of the woods.

About 2,000 years ago sea people from Malaysia and Indonesia drifted into Madagascar, and over time they interbred with Arabs who arrived in ships like Sinbad, and Africans who came to trade and stayed. The French colonized the place in 1896 and left behind a tradition of small hotels with impeccable service, and the language currently spoken with foreigners. Today the population is about 16 million and growing, spread over an area twice the size of Arizona, which has almost the same population.

About eighteen tribes are spread throughout the island. Most worship their ancestors, hold colorful funeral ceremonies, and speak a language whose roots seem to be in Borneo. The inhabitants have many taboos, both local and national, which a good guide will help you with since many concern the cutting of plants and rituals around the abundant wildlife. Their world-class music is celebrated through-out the year in music festivals. But don't go in February: that is cyclone season, and nothing protects Madagascar from ocean storms.

Lemurs

The lemurs, for which the island is famous, are full Madagascan. They are so well adapted, biologists are still finding new species. In 1990 not only the world's smallest lemur but also the world's small-est *mammal* was found here, the pygmy dwarf lemur, smaller than a tiny mouse. It takes its place next to the world's largest lemur, the short-tailed, black-faced indri, which Malagasies believe is descended from the common ancestor of man and lemurs. Each indri has its unique voice, and pairs (they mate for life) sit in trees, sending out eerie calls. Several calling to each other through the forest constitute an ethereal chorus.

A family of ring-tailed lemurs socialize at the Jacksonville Zoo. Lemurs are endemic to Madagascar. *Roger Archibald*

In the mountainous Mantadia National Park, not far from the capital city of Antananarivo, you might hear the staccato hiccups of sifakas communicating across the jungle. Like the indri, sifakas are prosimians, but more closely resemble gibbons, which they rival in superb tree swinging. The aye-aye, a unique rainforest nocturnal prosimian, looks like a bat with big eyes and ears; it has evolved a spooky long thin middle finger with a sharp nail with which it punctures holes in the skins of fruit, then scoops out the fruit within. Aye-ayes are endangered because Malagasies consider them to be an unlucky omen and kill them on sight.

Lemurs in general are curious and show little fear of people. The playful ring-tailed lemur, which spends more time on the ground, begins the day by socializing and eating. Then, when the sun is high, lemurs gather in a group, turn their faces upward, spread their legs and, hands on their thighs, catch a few rays.

In the twenty or so national parks and private and marine reserves scattered through the island, wonders abound. Madagascar is reputed to have about 250 bird species, 155 frog species, and half the entire world's chameleon species. Chameleons, in brilliant colors, are everywhere, ranging in size from about a half inch to two feet.

If you are lucky, you will see three unique species, known only here, all members of the same family as civets: the falanouc, a small, mongoose-like creature that inhabits the rainforest and eats earthworms and slugs; the fanaloka, which looks like a fox with spots, lives in dense woods, and hunts rats and frogs at night; and the more intimidating fossa, the island's only carnivore, a brown, solid-muscled creature with sharp teeth and webbed feet and a long tail twice its body length. The fossa looks like a cross between a cat and a dog, according to some, or a cross between a small puma and a fox, according to others. Whatever, it lives in trees and hunts at night by stalking and leaping. It eats other mammals, including lemurs, and is known as "Big Cat."

With sharp eyes you might spot a species of tenrec, a small animal that looks like a cross between a shrew and a hedgehog, or in the **Ankarana National Park**, crocodiles that live underground.

Baobab trees grow hugely tall; some of the eight species look like inflated sea anemones. Orchids are some of the 10,000 endemic species of plants growing wild and abundant. After the wonders on land, dive or snorkel the unblemished coral reef or visit a beach on one of the uninhabited islands.

The following companies know Madagascar well; many engage Malagasies as guides.

Eco-Expeditions   192 Nickerson Street, No. 200, Seattle, Washington 98109. Tel: 800-628-8747 (toll-free); 206-285-4000; E-mail: zoe@zeco.com; Website: www.zeco.com.

Tours run in November and March/April, dry seasons. Eighteen days, includes the Seychelles, about $9,200. Also includes airfare within Madagascar.

Remote River Expeditions
P.O. Box 544, Boulder, Colorado
80306. Tel: 800-558-1088 (toll-
free); E-mail: gary@remoterivers.
com; Website: www.remote
rivers.com.

This trip combines national
parks, swimming, and snorkeling,
with an eight-night camping and
hiking river trip up the Mangoky
River. A 4-WD awaits you at the
end. Experienced guides are Malagasies who know the rivers by
heart. Fourteen days, includes hotel, meals, about $3,500.

Rafting the Mangoky River in Madagascar is slow enough for you to
see some incredible species that
you will not see elsewhere. *Remote
River Expeditions, www.remote
rivers.com*

Journeys International   107 Aprill Drive, Suite 3, Ann Arbor,
Michigan 48103. Tel: 800-255-8735 (toll-free); 734-665-4407;
E-mail: info@journeys-intl.com; Website: www.journeys-intl.com.

This company has been taking travelers to Madagascar since
1989 and has established good relations with many local guides.
They will customize trips according to your interests. Nine days,
about $3,000.

Rainbow Tours   Canon Collins House, 64 Essex Road, London
N1 8LR, UK. Tel: 011 44 020 7226 1004; Fax: 44 020 7226 2621;
E-mail: info@rainbowtours.co.uk; Website: www.rainbowtours.co.uk.

Although they specialize in custom tours, Rainbow runs regular
tours during the best seasons in April, September, and November.
National parks and private reserves are their specialty. Fourteen to
seventeen days, about £3,000 to £3,200 (about U.S.$4,500 to $4,600).

Blue Chameleon Ventures   P.O. Box 643, Alva, Florida 33920.
Tel: 239-728-2390. E-mail: bill@bluechameleon.org; Website:
www.bluechameleon.org.

Bill Love specializes in tours to find chameleons. Twenty-one days, about $6,900.

THE GALAPAGOS

After British naturalist Charles Darwin visited the archipelago in 1835, he wrote in *On the Origin of Species* that in the Galapagos, a person could see "the first appearance of new beings on this earth."

He was referring to a number of species, but especially to the thirteen species of finches that have evolved in the islands, their beaks adapted to the size of the seeds on which they depend for their livelihood. The differences lie in the size of their tiny beaks, but the significance is great: creatures either compete for the same resources or share them, or, as in the case of the finches, find other resources and develop entirely different species. Whereas other bird species on the Galapagos compete or coexist, the finches spread out over different islands in search of food and went back to the drawing board with their beaks. And Darwin's finches became the poster children for species adaptative radiation.

Straddling the equator in the Pacific Ocean, about 600 miles west of Ecuador, the Galapagos archipelago, about a dozen large and more than fifty small islands, is inhabited by bird and reptile species that originally came from somewhere, but no one knows when. Some of the birds might have been storm-driven there; other species might have hitched rides with sailors from South America on prehistoric trips as early as a millennium ago. Some birds have been there long enough to develop into species that are endemic; flightless cormorants, for example, occur nowhere else. Galapagos reptiles have probably been residents for a long time: researchers tracking mitochondrial DNA in the giant tortoise recently discovered that one of the tortoise species on the island of Isabela was the only species of tortoise that survived the Alcedo volcano on the island—100,000 years ago.

No Fear

The most amazing thing about animals in the Galapagos is their complete lack of fear and their abundant curiosity about people. That's because no land mammals have ever lived there that would prey on birds or reptiles. Bruce Stutz of the American Museum of Natural History said that the revelation of the Galapagos experience is the realization that "you don't matter." Animals don't run. "On the Galapagos, you're an apparition, a fly on the wall, another creature," he said. If you want to experience life on Earth in harmony with animals, this is the place. Darwin's famous finches will leap up and stare through the other end of your lens as you take a picture.

The Galapagos and the Seychelles are the last homes of grass-eating giant tortoises, like this one in the Galapagos. *Paul Guther, U.S. Fish and Wildlife Service; www.fsw.gov*

In the 1500s, the Spanish named the islands the Galapagos, which means *tortoises*. The famous giant tortoises, up to four feet long with huge domed carapaces, lumber along like their large Cretaceous ancestors and fearlessly roam the fields in herds, grazing on grass and plants. Despite their size, giant tortoises are hard to see, except on Santa Cruz at the Charles Darwin Research Station, where rangers are carefully raising tortoises to keep the hatchlings from being eaten by rats or cats, before reintroducing them to the wild.

Galapagos National Park

More than 10,000 people call the islands home, mostly fisher families who live in Puerta Ayora on Santa Cruz who are interested in getting into the hotel/cruise boat business. But of the 3,000 square miles that comprise the Galapagos, 97 percent is the Galapagos National Park, staffed by Ecuadorean naturalist-guides. Ecotourism reigns: what comes in must go out, all trash must be carefully separated, and tourists must stay on paths, never touch or feed an animal, and go nowhere without a park guide, whose route depends on what species are not be disturbed because of current breeding or nesting. No lodging is allowed in the park.

The volcanic origins of the islands create some fantastic lava towers, deep lakes, and mountains high enough to sustain a cloud forest (on Santa Cruz), which is home to hawk-like short-eared owls that hunt by day. The coastal beaches of Isabela (the largest island) and Fernandina teem with scaly marine iguanas, which look like science fiction monsters, as well as land iguanas and tortoises, and rose (not pink) flamingos. Above the equator, the tiny island of Genovesa is crowded with tropic birds, doves, and breeding frigate birds; blue-footed boobies, red-footed boobies, and masked boobies—all with big feet and puzzled expressions; and shearwaters, sleek brown noddies, stormy petrels, and short-eared owls. On Espanola, the most southerly island, huge albatross—with eleven-foot wingspans—actually stop their long wandering ocean voyages long enough to breed in April and stay to December to nurture their young.

Oceanic Galapagos

The ocean surrounding the Galapagos is crammed to the gills with species. Because the islands sit on the equator they are surrounded by both the cold Humboldt Current, which comes up from Antarctica, then flows west along the equator, and the warm Panama Current, which flows west from Central America. This means that in the right season you can actually see colorful tropical fish swimming with penguins. Several species of sharks, including whale sharks and hammerheads, cruise the waters. Hundreds of seals loll on the beaches with sea lions, and both will play with you if you snorkel or swim.

Straight down for several thousand meters is the Galapagos Rift, where more than 300 species—including twenty-five-foot tube worms—live near the hydrothermal vents, the first ones discovered in 1977.

The best way to visit the islands is by small cruise boat, on which you can sleep and eat and from which you can take smaller motorized inflatables to shore. The Galapagos are in the true tropical rainforest belt, but the waters around the islands are an extreme mixture of very cold and very warm, which is fine for snorkeling close to shore. If you dive, however, expect sharp changes in the thermoclines.

The fee for visiting the Galapagos National Park is $100 for adults, $50 for children seven to eleven. No children under seven are allowed.

Many companies sponsor tours to the Galapagos; most are members of the International Galapagos Tour Operators Association. Following are some companies that run naturalist-guided tours.

National Geographic Expeditions P.O. Box 65265, Washington, DC 20035-5265. Tel: 888-966-8687 (toll-free); Website: www.nationalgeographic.com/ngexpeditions.

From the small ships M.S. *Polaris* or the *Isabela II*, National Geographic Expeditions sponsors several islands tours, with special trips for families in July. Sylvia Earle, NOAA's former chief marine biologist, now explorer-in-residence at the National Geographic

Society, is a naturalist guide. Depending on the vessel and berth, 11 days, $3,400 to $5,800, which includes airfare from Miami.

Mountain Travel Sobek   6420 Fairmount Avenue, El Cerrito, California 94530. Tel: 888-687-6235 (toll-free); 510-527-8100; E-mail: info@mtsobek.com; Website: www.mtsobek.com.

From small motor or sailing yachts, you can further explore the islands by sea kayak or snorkeling, or swim from one of the white sand beaches. Some of their trips include dives and always lots of nature walks with experienced Ecuadorean guides. Mountain Travel Sobek has been traveling to the Galapagos for more than thirty-five years. Eleven days, about $3,400 to $3,700.

Ecoventura   Galapagos Network. Tel: 800-633-7972 (toll-free); 305-262-6264; E-mail: info@galapagosnetwork.com; Website: www.ecoventura.com.

From a sixteen-passenger dive live-aboard, the M/Y *Sky Dancer*, with two dive masters and helpful crew, you can experience the islands from above and below. Divers must be experienced and able to handle the sharp thermocline changes, currents, and "large marine life." Seven days, about $2,700 to $2,900 per person, depending on berth.

Lindblad Expeditions   720 Fifth Avenue, New York, New York 10019. Tel: 800-397-3348 (toll-free); E-mail: explore@ expeditions.com; Website: www.expeditions.com.

Access the islands from Zodiacs launched from the eighty-passenger *Polaris*, and spend time exploring with Ecuadorean naturalists, and snorkeling. Lindblad runs weekly trips throughout the year and sometimes includes professional nature photographers. Ten days, about $3,200 to $5,500, depending on berth.

Journeys International, Inc.   107 Aprill Drive, Suite 3, Ann Arbor, Michigan 48103. Tel: 800-255-8735 (toll-free); 734-665-4407; E-mail: info@journeys-intl.com; Website: www.journeys-intl.com.

Small groups, class A sailing yachts (twelve to sixteen passengers), with a naturalist, Journeys International sponsors year-round trips. Ten days, depending on berth and ship, $3,550 to $4,400.

Zegrahm Expeditions   192 Nickerson Street, No. 200, Seattle, Washington 98109. Tel: 800-628-8747 (toll-free); 206-285-4000; E-mail: zoe@zeco.com; Website: www.zeco.com.

Marine biologist Jack Grove leads two trips a year to the islands aboard the *Isabela II*. Spend ten days immersed in the islands, hiking, snorkeling, swimming. Double, about $5,800; single, about $9,700.

Natural Habitat Adventures   2945 Center Green Court, Boulder, Colorado 80301. Tel: 800-543-8917 (toll-free); 303-449-3711; E-mail: info@nathab.com; Website: www.nathab.com.

Natural Habitat small groups ride on motor and sailing yachts. They sponsor several family trips that include children seven and older. Classic tour, eleven days, about $3,000 to $5,000, depending on berth.

The Charles Darwin Foundation, Inc.   407 North Washington Street, Suite 105, Falls Church, Virginia 22046. Tel: 703-538-6833. Website: www.darwinfoundation.org.

This nonprofit membership organization promotes education and conservation in the Galapagos.

THE SEYCHELLES

The Seychelles, an archipelago of 115 islands about 1,000 miles off Africa and 130 miles northwest of Madagascar in the Indian Ocean, are worth visiting if only to see the world's largest giant land tortoise, affectionately named Esmeralda.

Esmeralda is actually a chunky 700-pound male, thought to be almost 200 years old, the lucky survivor of a shipwreck in 1880. Caught by sailors aboard the *Hirondelle* and carried for meat, Esmeralda swam to safety on Bird Island, where he lives today.

A private island about one mile wide by one and a half miles long, Bird Island has one lodge with twenty-four bungalows and a restaurant; it is distinguished, in addition to Esmeralda, by the 2 million sooty terns that visit from May to October, as well as hundreds of breeding endangered hawksbill turtles.

Bird Island is one of the many tiny coral islands filled with wildlife surprises in the southwest part of the island chain. Aldabra, a World Heritage Site, is a seventy-mile-round coral atoll, home to more than 100,000 Indian Ocean giant tortoises.

The islands of the Seychelles that were part of the original Pangaea are composed of granite, eroded over the years into strange formations. A few miles north of Aldabra, the large island of Silhouette with steep, worn granite cliffs, is a sanctuary for giant land tortoises, where they are bred for reintroduction onto the other islands in the Seychelles chain. Curieuse, a minute of a coral island, is also a giant land tortoise sanctuary. The only other place on Earth to see giant tortoises is the Galapagos Islands; this endangered species, dating from the Cretaceous period, has been protected from hunters only since the 1970s.

The second World Heritage Site in the Seychelles is the Vallee de Mai on the island of Praslin. In this dense rainforest (the Seychelles Islands are 4 degrees below the equator) lives the endemic black parrot. Palm trees, more than 100 feet tall, produce the world's largest nut, the Coco de Mer. Cinnamon trees also grow here, which, with *copal* (coconut oil) and fish, are the Seychelles' major exports.

Of the approximately 175 square miles that make up the Seychelles landmass are numerous special reserves or national parks, set aside to protect the magnificent reef fish and the twenty endemic bird species, including the brush dove and the red, cardinal-like fody (known locally as *Toq Toq*).

Most of the human population of about 80,000 live on three larger islands: Mahe, Praslin, and La Digue. English and French are both official languages, reflecting the islands' former colonizations. Now independent, the Seychellois have French, Arabic, Indian, Chinese, and African backgrounds; some might be descendants of the many pirates who once preferred the Seychelles for R&R.

Blessed with magnificent weather (a fairly constant 80 degrees Fahrenheit year-round) and rainy months only from December to January, the islands have been a destination for beach lovers and anglers for several years. Tourism, which is only thirty years old here, is, along with fishing, the chief industry, and growing. But spread over more than 540,000 ocean miles (typically it takes about thirty minutes to fly from Mahe, the largest island, to many of the others), the Seychelles have superb reefs, both coral and granitic formations that drop steeply into the ocean and attract huge numbers of tropical fish. Coral reefs, thick with fish, border all the islands, but especially the island of Desroches, 3½ miles long, where the steep underwater Desroches Drop attracts marine life from angelfish to hawksbill turtles. Aside from 7½ miles of white beaches, Desroches has a first-class resort with a dive center. Three nights, two people, about $1,000.

For more on the Seychelles, see www.sey.net; www.seychelles-online.com.

Zegrahm Expeditions 192 Nickerson Street, No. 200, Seattle, Washington 98109. Tel: 800-628-8747 (toll-free); 206-285-4000; E-mail: zoe@zeco.com; Website: www.zeco.com.

To know more about the numerous species of birds, fish, lizards, and tortoises, travel with the founder of the Nature Protection Trust of Seychelles, and director of the breeding project of the giant tortoises, Ron Gerlach. You will be able to snorkel into the seventy-mile lagoon of Aldabra, naturally riding the incoming tide along with the fish. Aldabra is the quiet home of numerous species of birds, including the Seychelles flightless rail, and more than sixty species of endemic flowers and ferns. This trip is also guided by ornithologist and nature photojournalist Greg Homel and expedition leader Tim Soper, dive master and ocean scientist from the UK. Cruise on *Le Ponant*, a three-masted sailing vessel. Ultimate Seychelles: sixteen days, about $9,500 double occupancy, includes lodging, food, lectures.

Rainbow Tours   Canon Collins House, 64 Essex Road, London
N1 8LR, UK. Tel: 011 44 020 7226 1004; Fax: 44 020 7226 2621;
E-mail: info@rainbowtours.co.uk; Website: www.rainbowtours.
co.uk.

This company specializes in custom-designed tours and special
birding tours, and will guide you to one of the world's fifty rarest
birds, the magpie robin. Guided by an expert on Seychelles birds,
you will also get to see the Seychelles sunbird, blue pigeon, bulbul,
kestrel, white-eye, and, on a night tour, the rare scops owl. Ten
days, includes airfare from London, local transport among the
islands by air and boat, and lodging, about $4,000.

NEWFOUNDLAND

Sea birds, millions and millions of them—Leach's stormy petrels,
puffins, guillemots, kittiwakes, murres, shearwaters, and skuas—
stop in their migrations either from Antarctica or the Arctic, or
come here to eat, rest, and nest. Because of Newfoundland's place
in the mouth of the St. Lawrence River, and because it experiences
both the warm waters of the Gulf Stream and the chill of icebergs
slowly drifting to extinction, and because of its sparse human population—only about 600,000 people spread over 43,000 square
miles—Newfoundland is a preferred halfway destination for birds.
Most, including bald eagles, come to eat the plentiful small fish—
capelin—that swim near shore; many come to breed and raise their
young before flying off again over the ocean. Some, such as Atlantic
puffins, eat too much to fly far. Black and white dovekies, which
summer in the Arctic, spend the winters here.

To ensure their comfort, the country has developed ecological
reserves and parks where the sea birds can gather undisturbed on
the rocky coast. Birders, photographers, and interested tourists
easily access boats that take them past the nesting areas, which are
out of bounds to foot traffic. Because there are so many birds, you
can also catch them from vantage points on land.

Newfoundland boasts the world's most southerly herd of woodland caribou, about 20,000; they live in the woods in winter, eating lichen, then actually migrate, like their northern cousins, to the coasts for summer.

A healthy population of moose that inhabit the 500-square-mile **Avalon Wilderness Reserve** are latecomers, descended from a few happy moose couples relocated from Nova Scotia and New Brunswick about 150 years ago.

Rich plankton attracts lots of humpback whales, which swim among the drifting icebergs in the eastern Iceberg Alley.

Newfoundland was the first North American landfall of the Vikings about 1,000 years ago who came looking for grapes and found terrific seafood instead. Their sparse collection of artifacts join those of the Beothuk Indians from about 1,500 years ago. Beaches are strewn with fossils, some 600 million years old.

It's a great place to sea kayak and camp on beaches, as well as catch and cook your own seafood.

Newfoundland Eco Adventures Tours   Anna Buffinga, 50 Monkstown Road, St. John's, Newfoundland, Canada A1C 3T3. Tel: 877-888-3020 (toll-free); 709-579-3977; E-mail: coastalsafari@coastalsafari.com; Website: www.coastalsafari.com.

This company will customize your tour for your special interests and provide all the gear. You can also stay in their coastal safari tent camp in Fortune Bay, with tents on wooden platforms. Seven days wilderness camping/kayaking, about Cdn$1,400.

Wildland Learning Vacations   P.O. Box 383, St. John's Newfoundland, Canada A1C5J9. Tel: 709-722-3123; E-mail: wildtour@nfld.com; Website: www.wildlands.com.

David Snow or Heather Ivany will help you construct a trip to see whales and icebergs, among other attractions. This company has won several Canadian awards for sustainable tourism.

Newfoundland has a robust tourism industry (see www.new foundland.com).

For a travel guide to Newfoundland, call 800-563-6353.

For information on ferry rides past birds from Nova Scotia, call 800-341-7981.

For ferry rides from Newfoundland to Labrador, and back, call 866-535-2567.

Natural Habitat Adventures   800-543-8917 (toll-free); 303-449-3711; Fax: 303-449-3712; E-mail: info@nathab.com; Website: www.nathab.com.

Natural Habitat, which works in conjunction with the World Wildlife Fund, runs a naturalist-guided tour to Newfoundland with comfortable hotel lodging in St. Johns and lots of short fresh-air hikes to see the birds, as well as boat trips in Newfoundland's fjords, and to see whales and icebergs. Seven days, about $3,000.

Sea birds, red-crowned cormorants and horned puffins, nest and feed on rocky crags in the Pribilof Islands and Newfoundland. *Captain Budd Christman, NOAA Corps, www.photolib.noaa.gov*

16

INSECTS

MILLIONS AND MILLIONS

Heads up! Four out of five animals on earth are worms, round nematodes burrowing through the earth, plants, people, and in the ocean. Some are microscopic.

Then there are the microbes that live with human beings: the protozoa, bacteria, and viruses that can cause trouble, and the ones we rarely think about, those tiny things with legs that live in eyebrows and wall-to-wall carpets. Some bacteria are extremophiles, pushing their limits to the max in the deepest ice of the Antarctic as well as in the super hot deep ocean vents.

But of all the living creatures on Earth beyond microbes, insects outnumber everything. Scientists already know that a million insect species exist, and they expect to find several million more. Some are direct descendants of insect families from the Cretaceous period, 100 million years ago.

Now You See Them, Now You Don't

What we do know about insects is that they are everywhere, tunneling into the earth, swarming through the air, skimming across the surface of the water. They know the territory. In fact, *swarm intelligence*, the magic that makes the whole group build nests, gather nectar, or swoop in perfect spiral ellipses, has been analyzed by engineers and biologists to find more efficient ways of building computer systems (see: Eric Bonabeau, www.antoptima.com).

Insects come in all colors, shapes, and sizes, from cockroaches the size of a hand to fairy flies you will probably *never* see. They breed fast, mutate a lot, and therefore develop sophisticated adaptations. A species of mud beetle in the Ecuadorean Amazon, for example, not only bites but injects a nasty parasite that causes paralysis in its victims, which can be anything bigger than it. The African dung beetle, which rolls its treasured elephant dung into a ball then pushes it home, maintains its straight direction guided by the position in the sky of both the sun and the moon.

Scientists call insects bioindicators; they are usually at the bottom of the food chain, which means that if they are healthy and abundant, everything above them is healthy—birds eat, seeds are scattered, the earth is fertilized.

As with mammals, the big, sometimes fuzzy charismatic insects, like tarantulas and bumble bees, get all the attention. But check them *all* out: insects are among the most interesting animals on Earth.

To get up close and personal, visit a bug farm.

BUG FARMS

Audubon Insectarium   Audubon Nature Institute, 5601 Read Boulevard, Joe W. Brown Memorial Park, New Orleans, Louisiana 70178. Tel: 800-774-7394 (toll-free); 504-246-5672; E-mail: air@auduboninstitute.org; Website: www.audubon institute.org.

More than 900,000 species of insects are available, dead and alive; some are huge and mounted, others chillingly realistic animatronics, such as a gigantic earthworm you can visit underground. Lots of interpreters available. At this lively insectarium, you can also watch a cook demonstrate recipes for some of the insects in high culinary demand in other parts of the world. Adults, about $5.00; kids, two and up, $3.00.

Philadelphia Insectarium   8046 Frankford Avenue, Philadelphia, Pennsylvania 19136. Tel: 215-338-3000; E-mail: insectarium@aol.com; Website: www.insectarium.com

Take a look at some of the eating and living habits of cockroaches and termites in exhibits conceived by a former exterminator, which show a display kitchen and bathroom crawling with things that would take over if people did not object. On other floors, get more exotic with creatures such as tarantulas and huge hissing cockroaches from Madagascar. Check out the schedule for gourmet dinner parties, featuring an all-insect menu, both exotic and all too familiar.

O. Orkin Insect Zoo   Smithsonian National Museum of Natural History, 10th Street and Constitution Avenue, NW, Washington, D.C. 20560. Tel: 202-357-2700; Websites: www.mnh.si.edu; www.orkin.com.

Pest control technicians know more than most people about their subject, and Mr. Orkin took his knowledge to Washington. Here in permanent residence is a huge collection of centipedes, millipedes, and spiders, as well as ants and tarantulas. Take a look at the fascinating house, surrounded by a picket fence, with current information on the ongoing insect activity happening there all the time, not all of which is visible. Admission is free.

Insectarium de Montreal   4581 Sherbrooke Street East, Montreal, Quebec, Canada H1X 2B2. Tel: 514-872-1400; Fax: 514-872-0662; E-mail: insectarium@ville.montreal.qc.ca; Website: www2.ville.montreal.qc.ca/insectarium.

Most dead-insect collections are the product of dedicated entomological collectors, and sometimes represent one person's life work, which is invaluable for later entomologists. The Insectarium in Montreal, Quebec, houses one of these collections. More than 140,000 plus insect specimens are available for study, with 4,000 on display.

You can also visit more than 100 live species of arthropods (spiders and scorpions). Housed in a building designed to resemble an insect, it is surrounded by seasonal gardens that attract butterflies and insects and is operated by the city of Montreal in the complex that includes the Biodome.

Adults, about $11; children five and above, about $6.

Insect Cuisine

The Bay Area Bug Eating Society (BABES)   San Francisco, California. Website: www.planetscott.com.

For those who believe the sheer number of insects combined with increasing human population can only mean that one of us will wind up eating the other, and better that we eat them first, this is a site for you. BABES caters to a collection of insect gourmets, with nutritional information, advice about procuring insects, and recipes.

Try grasshoppers in melted white chocolate, mixed with snack mix, for example, for a tasty added 14 grams of protein per 100 grams of grasshoppers.

BUTTERFLIES

Butterfly World   3600 W. Sample Road, Coconut Creek, Florida 33073. Tel: 954-977-4434; Fax: 954-977-4501; E-mail: gardens@butterflyworld.com; Website: www.butterflyworld.com.

The first butterfly farm in the United States, and the largest in the world, Butterfly World houses an average 3,000 members of fifty species of butterflies and moths from around the world. A separate exhibit illustrates their pupae in various stages of development. Opened in 1988, Butterfly World grew out of electrical engineer Ronald Boender's hobby of breeding butterflies for zoos. The colorful, informative guidebook alone is worth the trip. Also check out the Hummingbird Aviary. About $16 for adults; $11 for children three and up.

The Butterfly House   Missouri Botanical Garden, 15193 Olive Boulevard, Chesterfield, Missouri 63017. Tel: 636-530-0076; E-mail: admin2@butterflyhouse.org; Website: www.butterfly house.org.

A butterfly is only as good as the nectar it drinks. Here at the Missouri Botanical Garden, researchers identify which flowers are favored by which butterflies. A native-habitat garden in the "back-   designed to appeal to certain caterpillars. Lots of information is available if you wish to create your own butterfly farm. You can also get married here among the butterflies. Adults, $5; kids four and up, $4.

For a list of butterfly houses and farms around the world, check the list of the International Association of Butterfly Exhibitors: www.butterflyexhibitions.org.

BUTTERFLIES AND BEETLES

England

Butterflies and beetles take over fields in warm months, eating leaves and grass, and flying and eating from one place to another. Can anyone create a map of their movements?

Earthwatch Europe   267 Banbury Road, Oxford, OX2 7HT, UK. **The Volunteer Programme**   Discovery Projects. Tel: 011 44 01865-318831; Fax: 44 01865-311-381; E-mail: info@ earthwatch.org.uk; Website: www.earthwatch.org/Europe.

Earthwatch   3 Clock Tower Place, Suite 100, Box 75, Maynard, Massachusetts 01754-0075. Tel: 800-776-0188 (toll-free); 978-461-0081; Fax: 978-461-2332; E-mail: info@earthwatch.org; Website: www.earthwatch.org.

If you enjoy spending summer days and nights in the Devon countryside, and have an eye for the subtle movements of crickets and butterflies, join a team with entomologists Dr. David Skingsley and Dr. Kevin Reiling in South Devon, England, for a long weekend.

You have a choice of tracking the great green bush cricket (large but not *that* large), checking by day what it eats and by night where it is, using sound transects. You can also spend time studying the green lanes that serve as corridors for butterflies, which are among the most beautiful in Europe.

Four days, about £300 (about U.S.$450), includes a camp bed in a village hall, and food.

MONARCH MIGRATION

Mexico

Don't ask how many generations it takes to do it, since the average life span of a butterfly in summer is two to six weeks. But monarchs, the orange and black butterflies prevalent in summer in the eastern United States and Canada, migrate south and west to warmer climes in Mexico to spend the winter—whole flocks of them—clouding the skies as they travel more than 3,000 miles.

Researchers think that migrating monarchs live from August to April. But not all survive the trip; some stop to breed and die, leaving their tiny eggs in milkweed, where they take a month to develop into an adult. Fortunately for them, the caterpillars that become monarchs taste so bad that predators avoid them.

By winter, some 300 million make it to the Transvolcanic Range, near Michoacan, Mexico. Here the butterflies begin to arrive in November to settle in to winter over until spring, when they head out again and fly north. The tall fir trees of the Rosario and the Chincua monarch butterfly sanctuaries become thick with butterflies that blaze into orange when the sun warms them and they open their wings. You can actually hear the wings beating, a sound so ethereal, "your soul is shaken and your life is changed," said Carlos Gottfried, president of the Monarca A.C., a Mexican environmental group. Mexicans believe the butterflies are the reborn souls of the dead.

Most trips include the newer Piedra Herrada Butterfly Sanctuary, in a less traveled, denser part of the forest, as well as a stop at the Botanical Gardens in the historical town of Toluca. New migration centers are still being found; the first areas (now Rosario and Chincua sanctuaries) were not discovered until the 1970s.

The highest point of the Transvolcanic range is about 11,000 feet, and the butterflies cluster in the fir forest slightly below. The trip up the paths is done on easy horseback, followed by a quiet hike, the gentlest way into the sanctuaries. The temperature in winter hovers above 40 degrees Fahrenheit.

Best way to appreciate this phenomenon is to take a tour with an expert. The following companies organize tours with specialists, and local guides, and horses. Lodging is in small inns.

American Museum of Natural History   Discovery Tours, Central Park West at 79th Street, New York, New York 10024-5192. Tel: 800-462-8687 (toll-free); 212-769-5700; E-mail: discovery@amnh.org; Website: www.discoverytours.org.
Six days, about $2,600.

National Wildlife Federation Expeditions   11100 Wildlife Center Drive, Reston, Virginia 20190-5362. Tel: 800-606-9563 (toll-free); Website: www.nwf.org.
Six days, about $2,600.

Natural Habitat Adventures   2945 Center Green Court, Suite H, Boulder, Colorado 80301-9539. Tel: 800-543-8917 (toll-free); Website: www.nathab.com.
This trip is a part of the World Wildlife Foundation, which sponsors programs that compensate local loggers and landowners in order to preserve the sanctuaries. Six days, about $2,400.

TRACKING MIGRATING SPECIES

Journey North

For middle school kids, Journey North is a national networking project to track species that migrate, such as birds, manatees, and monarchs. See www.lerner.org/jnorth. This site also keeps interested people up to date on where creatures are during their migrations.

For more on early stages of butterflies, see www.whatsthiscaterpillar.com.

For a good list of insect farms, see *Let's Go Buggy! The Ultimate Family Guide to Insect Zoos and Butterfly Houses*, by Troy Corley (Corley Publications, 2002).

Websites

The Whole Enchilada

The All Species Foundation aims to speed up the classification of zillions of species on the planet by working in partnership with naturalists and field scientists around the world by bringing their new data online. Streamlining taxonomists' work by using such aids as close-up macro lenses on digital cameras, field scientists can download images of new species from the middle of the rainforest or savannah, check them against existing databases, and ultimately get a DNA readout without leaving their tent.

The site, still under development, seeks to serve as the database for all living species: www.allspecies.org. Amateurs are invited to log on and share whatever new species they think they might have found.

Spiders

For the latest classification of spiders, see Norman I. Platnik of the American Museum of Natural History, *The World Spider Catalog* at research.amnh.org/entomology/spiders/catalog81-87/index.html.

For an exhaustive list around the world, see www.arachnid.com.

Insects, etc.

A general site for all species: check the electronic zoo at www.netvet.wustl.edu/e-zoo.htm.

For a list of insect organizations, zoos, and so forth, see www.isis.vt.edu.

Also try www.eNature.com.

For some ants in California and elsewhere, see www.antweb.org.

Also try www.antcolony.org.

17

THE EVERGLADES

Technically, a wetland is a two-season grassy area saturated with
water from seasonal rains or floods for part of the year, and more or
less dry savannah with isolated pools and islands for the other part.
Some of the pools are dug by alligators to ensure a cool wet place.
Dense grass keeps a wetland from feeling squishy when you walk on
it; it is soft, like walking on a bed. Alaskan permafrost is a good
example of wetland terrain.

With so much life in them, wetlands function as food courts. All
kinds of creatures from insects to large mammals always find something to eat, often each other.

THE EVERGLADES

If the Pantanal is the world's largest wetland, and the Okavango
Delta the world's most important, the Everglades is the world's most
recognized wetland. Since 1947, when the Everglades became a
national park, it has been designated an international biosphere
reserve, a wilderness area, a World Heritage Site, as well as a wetland of international importance.

About 120 miles long by 50 miles wide, the Everglades has wet
and dry seasons but also supports mangrove and cypress swamps,
especially in the south, which is the only place in the country where
American crocodiles live. Its "sea of grass" sawgrass prairies, growing
over clear water a foot deep, is filled with nursery spe

rich algae. American alligators bask on the banks of the superclear rivers. Pinetree islands, hardwood hammocks, and swamp forest house some Florida panthers. And the waters in the Gulf of Mexico around the Ten Thousand Islands—actually clumps of mangroves too numerous to count, and maybe or maybe not 10,000—are great places to see manatees.

Water All Around

In the Everglades, rains that swell Lake Okechobee and the Kissimmee River in the north raise the water levels in the summer and move through the Everglades to the ocean. But since 1905, these water sources have been altered by levies, dams, dikes, and canals—800 miles of them by 1947—to accommodate farms, and in the 1960s, an increased sugar cane production. In the past two decades, increased water supply has been channeled to burgeoning cities, towns, and suburbs.

Over the years, water flowing through man-made channels has contributed to extreme droughts and floods in the Everglades. Until a few years ago the sawgrass water was crystal clear and phosphorus-free. But runoff from farms has introduced new chemicals, inviting what are known as invasive species—non-native plants.

Where's the Pizza?

This may not seem like a big deal. But it *is* to the insects that eat the plants, the birds that come to eat the insects, and the mammals that come to eat the birds. If you can imagine your favorite pizza place being suddenly replaced by a donut shop, you would probably go elsewhere for pizza. That's what has happened in the Everglades.

Plus Florida's attractive climate has swelled human population near the park and confused many alligators into grabbing pets or even their owners for dinner. Florida panthers, a species of the Puma family that number less than 100—most of which are collared and tracked—often are victims of hit-and-run drivers as they explore their natural territorial ranges of about 150,000 acres.

At this writing, an $8 billion project is under way to correct the irregular flow of water and restore the natural meanders to the rivers, and numerous committees are rethinking ways to manage the disrupted balance between human and animal homes.

Some native Floridians who return are shocked at the shrinkage in the Everglades—of everything, from its overall size to water levels to the numbers of annual birds.

Birds love the wetlands of the Everglades and are a fixture year-round. *Roger Archibald*

It's Still Nice

If you arrive for the first time, you will see what all the fuss is about: the Everglades is a magnificent collection of wildlife set in a vast and varied landscape filled with creatures busily going about their own business.

Everglades National Park   400001 SR 9336, Homestead, Florida 33034. Tel: 305-242-7700; Website: www.nps.gov/ever.
    The National Park Visitor Centers offer a wealth of information and informed guides at each of its locations.

Royal Palm   Tel: 305-242-7700.
    Offers ranger-led walks.

Shark Valley   Tel: 305-221-8776.
    Is neither a valley nor does it have sharks. Take a tram ride or hike the seven and a half miles along the canal (filled with alligators) to the tall lookout tower.

Flamingo   Tel: 239-695-2945.
    Offers boat excursions in Florida Bay.

Gulf Coast   Tel: 239-695-3311.
    Offers canoe or boat tours through the Ten Thousand Islands with a chance to see manatees and dolphins.

Lodging

Outside the park, you can stay at a number of motels, hotels, or camping grounds. Inside the park is only one lodge:

Flamingo Lodge   Highway 9336, Flamingo, Florida 33034. Reservations: Tel: 800-600-3813 (toll-free); 239-695-3101; E-mail: info-flamingo@xanterra.com; Website: www.flamingolodge.com.

Two nights, about $225. For the full wetland experience, ask about their "Extreme Survivalist Getaway," offered May to October. For about $70 a night, you get everything the lodge offers plus two mosquito head nets, two bottles of water, and four ounces of mosquito repellent.

If you have a large family, rent a forty-foot houseboat that sleeps eight—about $475 for two nights.

Tours

Everglades Day Safari   Tel: 888-472-3069 (toll-free); 239-472-1559; E-mail: gator@ecosafari.com; Website: www.ecosafari.com.

Captain Bob has been giving daylong Eco-Tours of the Everglades for about fifteen years. The guide is a biologist. The tour includes pickup in southwest and southeast Florida, lunch, nature walk, tram ride or boat ride—about $100; kids under twelve, about $80.

North American Canoe Tours, Inc.   107 Camellia Street, Everglades City, Florida 34139. Tel: 239-695-3299; Website: www.evergladesadventures.com.

If motorboats and breezy and noisy airboats in the wetland leave you cold, try calm canoeing through the sawgrass, camping on the pine islands. Seven nights, about $1,150.

Billie Swamp Safari Everglades Eco-Tours   Big Cypress Seminole Reservation. Tel: 800-949-6101 (toll-free); 863-983-6101; Website: www.seminoletribe.com/safari.

Native Americans, whose reservation is located on the northwest corner of the Everglades, offer trips by swamp buggy or airboat with informed Seminole guides. An authentic Seminole village gives a good insight into living in harmony with animals. Visit a café that serves frog legs and alligator tail nuggets, the Ah-Tah-Thi-Ki Museum, and a campground where you can stay in small huts called *Chickees.*

Florida panthers have their own reserve, but very few visitors are allowed. An interesting, beautiful golden cat, Florida panthers need protection as well as panthers imported from elsewhere to breed with them. Long interbred, most of the Florida cats are cross-eyed and have a unique crook in the tip of their tale. But their main problem is finding a safe place to live with a range big enough for them to hunt and not be hunted or struck by vehicles.

For information, contact the National Wildlife Refuge in Naples, Florida. Telephone 941-353-8442, or log on to www.fws.gov. Also see www.floridapanther.org.

For more information on some of Florida's endangered mammals, reptiles, and birds, see the Florida Power and Light site at www.fpl.com/environment.

To get to know Florida panthers better, visit these handsome cougars at the Caribbean Gardens, the ZOO in Naples, Florida. *Herb Boothby, Caribbean Gardens, www.napleszoo.com*

18

MANATEES

WOUNDED BARNEYS

Snorkelers who swim with manatees comment on their apparent narcolepsy: without warning, a manatee will simply drift off and drop to the seabed, face-first and fast asleep. If it's not mating season, or they are not migrating to get away from the cold, manatees eat about five hours, then sleep for ten.

As big as Barney and good natured, manatees are one of the most unusual underwater creatures around. They work in slow motion, often holding big chunks of sea grass in their mouths with their round flippers as they drift in shallow water. Three species of manatees are scattered around the world, but only the West Indian Manatee in Florida is endangered. Manatees' smaller look-alikes, the dugong, thrive on coasts in the Indian Ocean, Indonesia, and the north coast of Australia.

Florida's West Indian manatees present a special problem: hunted since prehistoric days for their skins and meat, they were federally protected in 1972, only to face new problems of the human population explosion around their quiet habitats and fast and big boats. Still operating on habits laid down several million years ago (they are related to elephants through an ancient African ancestor), the slow-moving manatee has become a wounded species.

Invisible and Slow

They average ten feet in length, weigh half a ton, and move slowly through the warm, clear spring-fed Floridian rivers in the winter. Manatees eat more than 10 percent of their body weight in sea grass each day and take frequent naps.

Their average speed is 2 to 3 miles an hour, and they often sleep on the river bottom, drifting to the surface of the water every twelve minutes or so to breathe. Because of this, manatees are subject to injury from propellers and speedboats; many of the animals bear visible scars from the hits. Stories abound about visitors seeing manatees with bleeding gashes, and rescue veterinarians often find manatees with broken ribs and collapsed lungs.

Chessie's Most Excellent Adventure

Manatees spend summers as far north as Virginia, but no farther because they cannot tolerate cold. With at least one exception. Members of the U.S. Coast Guard's Sirenia Project (www.fcsc.usgs.gov/manatees.html), which aims to create a catalog of individual life histories, photo I.D.s, and the behavior and feeding patterns of some of the 2,500 to 3,000 manatees wintering in Florida, radio-tracked a lone male manatee, Chessie, who took off into the Atlantic Ocean one August and swam as far north as Point Judith, Rhode Island. Cold waters finally turned him back toward Jacksonville, Florida, and his winter home, where he arrived three months later. How he maneuvered among the boating communities from New Jersey to Rhode Island is a mystery.

Aside from mother and baby pairs, manatees form loose communities. They show affection by "kissing" and vocalizing in squeaks and grunts. Dolphins often hang out with manatees and maybe teach them a few tricks: someone once observed five adult manatees bodysurfing on a lake, with lots of vocalizing and kissing between rides—their equivalent of whooping it up.

You can dive or snorkel around manatees, but it is generally a ___ event. Their hearing is keen, but their near vision is not. If you are very quiet, they will approach you. Sometimes manatees nuzzle swimmers with their lips, and they like to be scratched on the neck. Their pattern is to investigate swimmers, and maybe nudge them, then swim away and return. If you snorkel, stay as still as you can on the surface, and a manatee will come to you.

Local, state, and federal laws in Florida protect manatees and their habitats. The rules:

- Don't ever enter sanctuaries designated for manatees.
- Don't chase or follow a manatee.
- Don't disturb a sleeping manatee.
- Don't ever feed manatees or give them water.
- Don't harass manatees by attempting to grab or ride them.
- Don't surround a single manatee.
- Don't ever separate a calf from its mother.

Call 800-342-5367 (VHF channel 16, marine radio) to report an injured or tagged manatee.

FLORIDA

Crystal River

In winter when the air is cold, manatees crowd into the warm springs. The greatest concentration of manatees is in the Crystal River on the Gulf of Mexico coast of Florida, above St. Petersburg.

The **Crystal River National Wildlife Refuge** (http://crystalriver.fws.gov) in Crystal River, Florida, is accessible only by boat. The area is composed of several springs, including one 50-feet deep,

so the area is good for divers as well as snorkelers. Several designated sanctuaries offer protection to the manatees when they no
longer want to interact with people, and the whole refuge is monitored by rangers from the U.S. Fish and Wildlife Service.

Bird's Underwater   320 N.W. Highway 19, Crystal River,
Florida 34428. Tel: 800-771-2763 (toll-free); 352-563-2763;
Website: www.birdsunderwater.com.

Bill and Diana Oestreich, veterans of the area who have brought
media coverage to the refuge run three-hour snorkeling tours, about
$30.

Homosassa Springs

Homosassa Springs Wildlife Park   4150 S. Suncoast Boulevard,
Homosassa, Florida 34446. Tel: 352-628-2311 (recorded
information); 352-628-5343 (office). Website: www.hsswp.com.

American artist Winslow Homer spent a winter painting the
Homosassa River in 1904. This beautiful state wildlife park, about
fifteen minutes south of Crystal River, is a refuge and transition
place for injured and orphaned manatees. These manatees have
been treated at a critical care facility before they return to the wild.
They are housed in a floating observatory designed to reacclimate
them to the warm springs and which separates them from the wild
manatees that also visit. From a viewing place called the "fish bowl,"
visitors can easily observe them in the observatory, known as the
"salad bowl," so-called because of the mounds of lettuce and greens
fed to the recuperating manatees.

Outside the sanctuary, visitors can swim with wild manatees in
the 72-degree waters.

Also try www.visitcitrus.com/diving.htm for places in which to
rent snorkeling or diving equipment and boats to take you to the
river. For lodging, guides, and information for both Crystal River
and Homosassa Springs, consult the Citrus County Tourist Development Council. Telephone 800-587-6667 or visit their website:
www.visitcitrus.com.

Blue Spring State Park

Blue Spring State Park 2100 West French Avenue, Orange City, Florida 32763. Tel: 386-775-3663; Website: www.funandsun.com/parks/bluespring/bluspring.htm.

A deep spring (120 feet, whose depths are open to cave divers only) attracts manatees to this park. Snorkelers can float over the manatee section, swim in another section.

Power Plants

If you're driving in Florida, watch for power plants, notably the Indian River and the Canaveral Power Plants: in the winter, the warm waters they discharge are a favorite gathering place for huge numbers of manatees.

Manatee Tour

Royal Palm Tours, Inc. P.O. Box 60079, Fort Myers, Florida 33096. Tel: 800-296-0249 (toll-free); 239-368-0760; E-mail: rptours@aol.com; Website: www.royalpalmtours.com.

This company offers a guided motorcoach tour of Florida's "marine stars": manatees (including both Crystal River and Homosassa Springs), dolphins, and sea turtles.

Rescue Centers

Three hundred years ago, manatees were so prevalent in Florida that English settlers named the whole state a manatee sanctuary. Three hundred years later, the Florida legislature actually passed an act making the state a "refuge and sanctuary for manatees," in order to protect the few that were left. Florida is now not only peppered with manatee rescue centers that provide medical help for injured manatees, it also boasts three world-class manatee critical care centers.

Veterinarians at **Sea World** (www.seaworld.org) in Orlando, which operates the world's largest manatee rescue center, were the first to put a cast on a manatee's broken flipper.

a, the **Lowry Park Zoo** (www.lowryparkzoo.org) has a
pital housed in an amphitheater reached by a boardwalk,
where visitors can witness critical care in action.

The third critical care hospital is in the **Miami Seaquarium**
(www.Miamiseaquarium.com).

Check out Miami Seaquarium's Overnight Adventures, Endangered Expedition, on which kids in grades one through eight can
learn about manatees, sea turtles, coral reefs, and more, and feed
and touch manatees under supervision. About $60 for each partici-
pant in a group of fifteen to thirty-two, which requires a deposit
(nonrefundable) of $250. Call 305-361-5705, ext. 520.

If you would like to adopt a manatee, visit www.sirenian.org, or
www.savethemanatee.com.

Manatees welcome
divers into their warm
shallow waters.
*James A. Powell,
U.S. Fish and Wildlife
Service, www.fws.gov*

19

AMERICAN ALLIGATORS

QUICK AND CLEVER

Trickier aquatic creatures do not exist. Hiding under blankets of algae, alligators are able to poke their little eyes up just enough to see an unsuspecting bird or beaver, and with lightning speed attack and acquire. Those who know them say alligators eat everything in sight, living or dead; their amazing stomach acid allows them to digest seashells, turtle shells, and bones. They wrestle prey underwater and drown it, eat a little, then store the rest underwater where it decays. But by the beginning of November, they begin a four-month fast.

Famously, they are not shy. Both male and female alligators roar during mating season. Family members are very articulate, grunting, gargling, hollering, and hissing when they are angry. Babies about to break out of their eggshells sound like video games.

Alligators are 220 million years old and resemble their ancient ancestors that walked on land and swam, limbs flat against their bodies, swinging their powerful tails for locomotion.

Along with crocodiles, alligators are very specialized. If you look closely at an alligator sleeping (safely behind a fence), you can see the thousands of tiny black bumps on their upper and lower jaws. Neuroscientist Daphne Soares at the University of Maryland recently studied these bumps and discovered that they are connected to sensory nerves able to detect the slightest ripple in the water. Coupled with alligator speed, these detectors mean prey don't have a chance.

In swamps, alligators pull their ancient reptile bodies out of the water to snooze and bring their cold blood up to speed. Their average length is about ten feet. If you meet an alligator on a canal or river bank, pass by quietly and cautiously and watch your back. Think twice before passing if the alligator has its head and tail lifted; this is a sign of aggression.

In the 1950s American alligators were all but written off as a species, mainly because they had been recklessly hunted for their skins. Federal and state legislation protected the alligator in the 1970s. For some Florida residents, alligators are now much too apparent; some are bred on farms for their meat and skins.

Should you ever encounter one in the water remember this story from Okefenokee Swamp about 1900. A hunter saw a large American black bear dive into the water and swim unperturbed next to a very curious alligator for a while. Then suddenly the bear stopped swimming, turned, reared up out of the water, and slammed the alligator on its snout. The bear safely resumed its swim to the bank and continued on its way.

Alligator Zoos

St. Augustine Alligator Farm   Route A1A South, St. Augustine, Florida 32084. Tel: 904-824-3337; Website: www.alligatorfarm.com.

Florida has some excellent alligator zoos. This is a historic site, home to hundreds of crocodiles and alligators, including two albino alligators that look as if they are made out of white chocolate.

Gatorland   Tel: 800-393-JAWS[5297]; Website: www.gatorland. com.

Located in Orlando, all things 'gators here, from wrestling shows to petting zoos. This is a captive breeding place for alligators; 'gator products are sold.

A white alligator glows in its shady pool at the St. Augustine Alligator Farm, Florida. This one is originally from Louisiana. *Roger Archibald*

Websites

For an update on alligator attacks, see the Florida Museum of Natural History attack file: www.flmnh.ufl.edu. Click Sharks, click Attacks, click Alligators.

You can identify a crocodile by its fourth tooth: it sticks up and out of the mouth. See The Crocodile Specialist Group website, an international conservation coalition of everyone, from biologists to fashion designers, who has anything to do with wild alligators, crocodiles, caimans, and gharials. Log on to www.flmnh.ufl.edu/natsci/ herpetology/crocs.htm.

Also, www.nationalgeographic.com stays in touch with crocodiles.

20

SWAMPS

Swamps are terrific places to experience life; every inch above and below water is occupied by some creature—insects, lizards, frogs, spiders, birds, bears, foxes, wolves, deer, reptiles, as well as exotic flowers, trees, and plants. A kind of heavy-duty wetland, it never dries out and is home to water-loving trees that grow to great heights, like cypress. Swamps can be dark even in midday, which is why they were the legendary preferred real estate of pirates and escaped prisoners.

OKEFENOKEE SWAMP

Georgia

The first ocean reptiles millions of years ago probably crawled onto land in coastal swamps: look any alligator or crocodile in the eye and you know you're looking at a dinosaur.

Okefenokee Swamp is unique. More than 250,000 years ago, it was a shallow lagoon protected from the deep ocean by a forty-mile-long sandbar.

Time passed, the ocean receded, and the lagoon and the sandbar became separated from the coast. Soon the saltwater in the lagoon dried up and it became a receptacle for rainwater. Because it supported a robust growth of tropical trees and plants that decayed over time into peat moss, the lagoon filled up. Today fifteen feet of peat resting on the bottom of the swamp have created what resident American Indians called "Trembling Earth" (*Okefenokee*): jump on the ground next to a pine tree on an island in the swamp, and it will tremble along with the ground under your feet.

Unlike other wetlands that depend on rivers, the collected rainwater in the Okefenokee feeds the Suwanee River, which empties into the Gulf of Mexico, and the St. Mary's River, which empties into the Atlantic. Okefenokee has no water problems; it's disappearing for another reason: the peat is piling up, one day making it a peat bog.

But today, about seventy-five miles from the Georgia coast and 120 feet above sea level, the narrow channels of dark tannin-laced water weaving through the mangroves and cypress hung with Spanish moss—with hefty alligators resting on tiny clumps of land—create a swamp experience that is as good as it gets.

Officially a National Wildlife Refuge and National Wilderness Area, the 25-by-38-mile area is loaded with animals and birds and world renowned for its resident amphibians. Black bears come out to fatten up for winter from October to December; rangers believe there are about 1,500 and chances of seeing them are good. Beginning in April for about six weeks, you can hear alligators bellowing out their mating calls and some twenty species of frogs happily singing along. Deer drift like ghosts through the prairies, and otters poke up from the white water lilies. A sharp eye sees turtles, lizards, snakes, bats, shrews, foxes, wolves, and maybe a Florida panther. Birds are too numerous to mention, from migrating birds to overwintering birds to endangered birds like the red-cockaded woodpecker.

Expect lots of mosquitoes, even though giant insect-eating pitcher plants proliferate here.

How to Relate

Three official entrances offer an abundance of information and opportunities to travel through the swamp. You can canoe by the day without a permit, but permits are required for two- to five-day canoe trips in the swamp. Apply two months in advance at 912-496-3331.

The East Entrance   Route 2, Box 3330, Folkston, Georgia 31637. Tel: 912-496-7836; E-mail: okefenokee@fws.gov; Website: www.okefenokee.fws.gov.

This is the official National Fish and Wildlife Service entrance and Visitors' Center. Guides take passengers through the swamp in covered power boats, or you can rent a canoe with or without a guide.

The North Entrance   U.S. 1, eight miles south of Waycross, Georgia 31501. Tel: 912-283-0583; E-mail: osp@okeswamp.com; Website: www.okeswamp.com.

This private concession leased by the National Fish and Wildlife Service is staffed by volunteers and offers boat rides, canoe rentals, a train ride, a replicated pioneer farm, boardwalk, and museum.

The West Entrance   Stephen Foster State Park, seventeen miles east of Fargo, Georgia 31631. Tel: 912-637-5274.

A state park leased by the National Fish and Wildlife Service also offers boat tours, furnished cabins, and a museum, plus if you apply for a permit, you can canoe on some of the 120 miles of canoe trails and stay overnight.

Bayou Country, Louisiana

The longest alligator on record—nineteen plus feet—grew up in Louisiana in the bayou south of New Orleans. These cypress swamps are below sea level, so low they are second only to Death Valley. They are also so dark and unpleasant that the pirate Jean Lafitte hid some of his treasure here, knowing it was as good as in a safe deposit box. For at least three centuries, sightings of Big Foot have been reported, most recently from a commercial fisherman who described a creature that was 300 pounds, seven feet tall with wide staring eyes, and covered with long orange hair.

Louisiana swamps have as many local legends as resident species, but the species you actually see are pretty interesting.

Honey Island Swamp Tours Tel: 985-641-1769; Website: www. honeyislandtours.com.

Dr. Paul Wagner is a wetlands ecologist who lives next to the swamp; he has been conducting eco tours through Honey Swamp for two decades. Small boat tours allow you to see eagles, alligators, herons, feral hogs, owls, and lots more, including Wookie, the local name of Big Foot. About $20.

Website

For complete data on frogs around the world, as well as some important museum amphibian and reptile collections, see: amphibiaweb.org.

21

BEARS

BROWN OR GRIZZLY BEARS

The grizzly is named after the color of its coat, light tips on brown hairs, called grizzled. But the word *grizzly* has become synonymous with the *Horribilis* part of its official Latin name, *Ursus Arctos Horribilis*, for two reasons: it is huge—up to ten feet tall on its hind legs, and it has been known to attack humans.

Tales from the Wilderness

Although the ratio of human attacks on grizzlies far exceeds grizzly attacks on human beings, for whatever reason, grizzly stimulates adrenaline. From way back, hunters seek out the biggest and baddest and recount legends about bear hunts, always involving a lone hunter in the wilderness at dusk who rounds a craggy corner and encounters a grizzly that rears up and is 12 or 15 or 20 or 50 feet tall. Park rangers who work with grizzlies say, on the other hand, that the bears rear up only when they are trying to look around, or to give a mock display of aggression, usually accompanied by snorts and growls. Grizzlies are as afraid and uncertain of people as people are of grizzlies. In any case, the hunter's story usually ends with a shot and a trophy.

If You Meet Alone in the Wilderness . . .

Rangers say that a grizzly will probably run if it hears hikers' bells or loud talk before it sees them in the wilderness. Additionally, bears

BEARS 179

generally do not eat human beings, they do not even like human meat, and the only thing to fear is surprising a mother with her cubs (expect no mercy) or meeting a hungry grizzly that has come to associate the smell of people with food. (See: mountain-prairie. fws.gov.) Then, if it lowers its nose, gets you in its sights, and begins to charge (at up to 50 miles per hour), you have a couple of options:

- Drop to the ground, freeze, and play dead, wrapping yourself up into a tiny ball, face down, preferably with a big backpack on your back.

- Wait until the bear is a few feet away and hit it with bear spray, a form of specially formulated pepper spray used by park rangers.

- Don't turn your back and run. Bears are much faster than human beings. Tiptoe backward slowly, saying soothing things to the bear.

- Don't climb a tree unless you have a head start and are a superb tree climber.

- If you are attacked in your tent, rangers say, *fight back*. Hit it with anything you can find and make a lot of noise.

The Numbers

Hunted for millennia, bears now are vulnerable to poachers who sell bear gall bladders and gall bile to China for use in medicine. Habitat reduction, from people muscling grizzlies out of their ranges, is a big problem in the United States. Officially in the United States grizzlies are listed as a threatened species.

Of about 1,100 in the lower forty-eight states, Yellowstone National Park (www.nps.gov/yell) has the healthiest population of grizzlies, about 500 to 600. Glacier National Park in Montana (www.nps.gov/glac) lists about 400 to 600, but the Cabinet-Yaak region of the Kootenai National Forest in Montana and the Selkirk Mountains in Idaho each have about 30 grizzlies left. Forty thousand live in Canada and Alaska, where logging threatens to clog the streams that salmon use; and about 100,000 inhabit Kamchatka and Russia and the Carpathians, where poaching is a peril.

The Menu, Please

Grizzlies are omnivorous and eat everything from huckleberries to dead musk ox. Fortunately, we are way down on their preferred diet list and can never hold a candle to a salmon freshly leaping out of an upstream path. Where salmon are, grizzlies are. Some catch the salmon mid-air in their mouths; others fish them out of the stream with their hugely long claws. Then, with the precision of a brain surgeon, grizzlies use their claws to fillet the fish, discarding the skin, bones, heads, and tails before eating the salmon meat. Grizzlies stock up on salmon, including the huge king salmon, in the weeks before they begin their winter sleep. Biologists say it is not really hibernation (low pulse and core temperature), but simply a six-

Grizzlies catch a rest on the shore in Kamchatka, Russia.
www.KamchatkaPeninsula.com

month sleepy fasting period, during which mothers give birth to as many as three cubs and nurse them through the winter.

Teddy bears, Paddington Bear, and Smokey Bear were created to make people love the wilderness they represent. Not as cute, grizzlies have several look-alikes: the brown coastal, or huge Kodiak bear, which weighs about 400 pounds more, and smaller brown bears across northern Europe. Many researchers believe they are the same species on different diets.

Alaska

Densely forested coastal mountains with salmon-running rivers is grizzly country, found along Alaska's southwest peninsula. Access to many of these sites is restricted to floatplanes or boats, which can make it pricey. Also, include what Alaskan tourism officials call buffer days in your plans, because weather is wildly unpredictable, and you might stay longer than you thought.

Katmai National Park

Katmai National Park has lots of grizzlies, lots of salmon, and lots of photographers at Brooks Falls. Bears bring their new cubs to teach them how to catch fish in the summer, and come to eat a lot before going into their annual slumber in the fall. In July, visitors are allowed in on one-hour passes. But the two overlooks—wood decks above the small waterfall filled with leaping salmon, and, at the head of the falls, tens of hungry grizzlies catching fish—are great.

Katmai National Park   P.O. Box 7, King Salmon, Alaska 99613-0007. Tel: 907-246-3305; Website: www.nps.gov/katm; www.katmai. national-park.com.

Katmai is about 300 miles southwest of Anchorage, accessible only by air or boat. You can reserve a campsite there in an area surrounded by an electric fence.

Brooks Lodge   Tel: 800-544-0551 (toll-free); 907-243-5448
E-mail: info@bear-viewing.com. Website: www.katmailand.com.
  About $400 per four-person room.

Katmai Coastal Bear Tours   Homer, Alaska 99603. Tel: 800-
532-8338 (toll-free). E-mail: ast@xyz.net; Website: www.
katmaibears.com.

  Taking advantage of the twenty-six-foot tides on the coast in
Katmai that wipe away all trace of human activity, these tours provide a live-aboard boat with a skiff that carries no more than ten
passengers to the tidal flats for bear viewing. A photographer's
dream, the Katmai coast (also the site of the Exxon *Valdez* oil spill)
is full of non-aggressive, timid grizzlies going about their business.
Low tide, you can see them digging for clams with their long claws;
high tide, you can see them fishing in pools. Each trip is accompanied by a naturalist guide, including some famous ones such as bear
expert Lynn Rogers. The seventy-three-foot R/V *Waters* is reach-
able by seaplane from Homer. One-day, about $800; four days,
about $3,300. Season runs from June 1 to September 15.

Lake Clark Bear Lodge

Great Alaska Adventure Lodge   (*Summer*): 33881 Sterling
Highway, Sterling, Alaska 99672. (*Winter*): Box 2670, Poulsbo,
Washington 98370. Tel: 800-544-2261 (toll-free); 907-262-4515;
E-mail: greatalaska@greatalaska.com; Website: www.greatalaska.
com.

  Located in southwest Alaska overlooking the Kenai Mountains,
you can go to fish for king salmon, or you can take a bush plane
over the roadless and remote backcountry in Lake Clark National
Park to the Bear Lodge. Bears gather unselfconsciously in this
remote Cook Inlet fishing area, and you can watch them from one
of twelve high-tech "weather ports"—safe, heated luxury tents, with
gourmet meals flown in daily. Two-day Bear Lodge stay, including
air from Anchorage, about $1,000. A seven-day wilderness safari
includes Chugach National Forest and Kenai Fjords National Park,

with kayaking, white-water rafting, bear viewing, fishing—you name it, about $2,800. *Outside Magazine* voted this Best Bush Camp.

McNeil River Falls

Alaska Department of Fish and Game   Wildlife Conservation, 333 Raspberry Road, Anchorage, Alaska 99518-1599. Attention: McNeil River State Game Sanctuary. Tel: 907-267-2182; Website: www.adfg.state.ak.us/mcneil.

Of about 150 resident grizzlies in this 200-square-mile state park, chances are good you will see as many as 70 at one time gathered at McNeil Falls waiting for salmon. The grizzly density makes this place high on the list of photographers and grizzly lovers. It doesn't come easy, however. For the protection of the animals and of the people who view them, the park is closely managed. Visitors and photographers must join a lottery to obtain permits to view and camp for four days.

The number of people allowed at viewing locations at any one time in the park between June 7 and August 25 is ten. Apply at least a year in advance: March 1 is the deadline with a flat fee of $25 per person. You will be notified in April if you have won. Guided viewing permits cost $350 for non-residents, $150 for Alaskans. Camp Standby viewing permit is $175 for non-residents, $75 for Alaskans.

Located about 250 air miles from Anchorage and 100 air miles west of Homer, McNeil River State Game Sanctuary is accessible by floatplane, which you must reserve in advance. Once you are there, sign a liability waiver, set up your tent, put on your hip boots (*required*), and join an armed ranger to see the bears.

To watch the McNeil bears from your computer, check out the National Geographic "Wildcam": www.nationalgeographic.com/bearcam.

Denali National Park

Denali National Park   Supervisor: P.O. Box 9, Denali Park, Alaska 99755. Tel: 907-683-2294; E-mail: denali_info@nps.gov; Website: www.nps.gov/dena.

Walking the World   P.O. Box 1186, Fort Collins, Colorado 80522. Tel: 800-340-9255 (toll-free); E-mail: info@walkingthe world.com; Website: www.walkingtheworld.com.

Combine walks through Denali National Park, considered one of the wildest and most beautiful of American parks, with stays in comfortable lodges inside the park. Walks are constructed to take you near grizzlies on the riverbanks.

Arctic National Wildlife Refuge

Arctic National Wildlife Refuge   Contact: Richard Voss, Refuge Manager, 101 12th Avenue, Room 236, Box 20, Fairbanks, Alaska 99701. Tel: 800-362-4546 (toll-free); 907-456-0250; E-mail: arctic_refuge@fws.gov; Website: http://arctic.fws.gov.

On the brink of nowhere and in the middle of a hot political debate, ANWAR is grizzly country at its American wildest. This roadless breathtakingly beautiful wilderness is home to not only grizzlies, but also polar bears, migrating caribou, wolverines, wolves, dall sheep, and musk ox. However, their range is so vast, you might or might not see them. In any case, if you want pristine, this is the place. You can go alone, but why not try the following companies:

Arctic Wild   P.O. Box 80562, Fairbanks, Alaska 99708. Tel: 888-577-8203; E-mail: trips@arcticwild.com; Website: www.arcticwild.com.

Using local guides, small groups, low-impact camping, and the best gear, this company offers a number of guided (and flexible) trips that hike or paddle through the wilderness. Coastal Backpack, for example, is an easy twenty-mile hike from the Kongakut River to the Arctic Ocean along the coastal tundra where grizzlies gather. Seven days, about $2,400.

Mountain Travel Sobek   6420 Fairmount Avenue, El Cerrito, California 94530. Tel: 800-586-1911 (toll-free); 510-527-8100; E-mail: info@mysobek.com; Website: www.akdiscovery.com.

Fly in from Fairbanks and paddle raft rivers on a selection of summer trips. Ten days, about $3,500.

Gates of the Arctic National Park

Gates of the Arctic National Park Contact: Bettles Ranger Station (Field Ops), P.O. Box 26030, Bettles, Alaska 99726 or National Park Service, 201 First Avenue, Fairbanks, Alaska 99701. Tel: 907-692-5494 (visitor information); E-mail: GAAR_Visitor_Information@nps.gov; Website: http://nps.gov/gaar.

This slightly smaller Arctic park in the Brooks Range, a Biosphere reserve, is also a roadless wilderness inhabited by grizzlies, black bears, caribou, Dall's sheep, and wolves. No facilities in the park.

Mountain Travel Sobek 6420 Fairmount Avenue, El Cerrito, California 94530. Tel: 800-586-1911 (toll-free); 510-527-8100; E-mail: info@mysobek.com; Website: www.akdiscovery.com.

Spend ten days canoe paddling and camping along the Noatak River to the Arctic Ocean. About $3,500, includes bush plane from Fairbanks.

British Columbia

Khutzeymateen Valley

The Khutzeymateen Valley, about twenty-five miles north of Prince Rupert, is home to about fifty grizzlies, in Canada's Grizzly Bear Sanctuary, managed jointly by British Columbia and the Tsimshian Nation since its inception in 1994. It consists of about 113,000 acres of temperate rain forest, ocean fjord, and rivermouth estuary, ideal for grizzlies. The best access is by boat.

Sun Chaser Charters Dan Wakeman, Box 1096, Prince Rupert, British Columbia, V8J4H6, Canada. Tel: 250-624-5472; E-mail: sunchase@citytel.net; Website: www.citytel.net/sunchaser.

Using the forty-foot motor sailing ketch *Sun Chaser* as base, visitors to the Khutzeymateen Grizzly Bear Sanctuary can take a Zodiac to shore to explore on foot or simply cruise the coast to see grizzlies, as well as moose and wolves. Trips run May to September. Four days, about CD$1,600; six days, about CD$2,400; ten days, about CD$4,000.

Ocean Light Adventures   No. 363-1917 West 4th Avenue, Vancouver, British Columbia V6J 1M7, Canada. Tel: 604-328-5339; E-mail: tour@oceanlight2.bc.ca; Website: www.litherland. ca/oceanlight.

Using the seventy-one-foot *Ocean Light II* as home base, visitors take Zodiacs ashore to explore, view, and photograph. Four-day trips May to June, about CD$1,500, plus CD$90 park fee.

Knight Inlet

Knight Inlet Grizzly Bear AdventureTours   Knight Inlet Lodge, 8841 Driftwood Road, Black Creek, British Columbia V9J 1A8 Canada. Tel: 250-337-1953; E-mail: grizzly@island.net; Website: www.grizzlytours.com.

Glendale Cove on Knight Inlet on the midcoastal region of British Columbia is a popular gathering spot for both grizzly and black bears. In the fall when the salmon run up the Glendale River, as many as forty cluster together. These tours run in the spring from boats, to see bears fishing for mussels; in the summer on logging roads; and in the fall (August) on five viewing platforms over the river when the salmon run. Two days, from about $750 to $900; eight days, from about $3,050 to $3,500.

Grizzly Bear Sanctuary

Grouse Mountain Refuge for Endangered Wildlife   Grouse Mountain Resorts, Ltd., 6400 Nancy Greene Way, North Vancouver, British Columbia V7R 4K9, Canada. Tel: 604-984-0661; Fax: 604-984-7234; E-mail: info@grousemountain.com; Website: www.grousemountain.com.

At this mountain resort in Vancouver, orphaned baby grizzlies can spend some growing-up time on their five acres, providing lots of information to biologists as well as to interested people and their children. You can take part in any of three interactive daily talks; volunteer; or click on to the Grizzly Cam and watch the current baby bears, Grinder and Coola, play or, in the winter, sleep in their den.

Kicking Horse Mountain Grizzly Bear Refuge   Kicking Horse Mountain Resort, Golden, British Columbia. E-mail: grizzlyrefuge@kickinghorseresort.com; Website: www.kicking horseresort.com.

When the orphaned bears outgrow their stay at Grouse Mountain, they move onto the twenty-two-acre enclosed grizzly bear refuge at Kicking Horse. "There is no protocol for the rehabilitation of orphaned bears in BC," says Gord Vizzuti of the resort. "The only alternative to captivity has been destruction." Here the bears will be rehabilitated, as researchers develop a protocol. The mother of the two current orphaned cubs, Cari and Boo, was shot illegally. Her cubs had to be rescued from a fifty-foot tree where they had sought refuge.

Russia

Kamchatka Peninsula

The wildest of bear-viewing places, Kamchatka is an amazing collection of twenty-seven active volcanoes, numerous still-smoking or inactive volcanoes, magnificent mountains, rushing rivers plowing through deep valleys, and literally hundreds of hot springs—110-degree-Fahrenheit water bubbling into natural hot tubs. If you want to experience grizzly life, this is the place.

The vast peninsula that pokes from the Arctic into the Pacific is home to no one knows how many brown bears, blue whales, hundreds of thousands of seals, as well as Steller's huge sea lions and Steller's huge sea eagle, reported to be able to pluck and carry away a forty-pound seal. German naturalist George Steller was among the first explorers who, along with Danish scientist Vitus Bering (whence the Bering Sea, Strait, and Island, where he died), joined the Russian-financed Great Northern Expedition sponsored by Peter the Great in the 1740s, sent to Kamchatka to find out what was there.

Poachers Beware.   With a human population of about one person per kilometer, the only danger to bears is poachers, and they are out in full force, killing bears, extracting their gall bladders, and selling them to Chinese medicine chop shops. To counter the profitable business, a few people are sponsoring ecotourism projects. Two Canadian bear researchers, Charlie Russell and Maureen Enns, spent eight years establishing a protected area for Kamchatka grizzlies to prove they and people can live harmoniously. In 2003 all of their bears were slaughtered by poachers. They nevertheless are continuing their study efforts, which in the past have included volunteers. (See www.cloudline.org.)

Because Kamchatka is huge and raw, it's better to go with an informed guide and a group for company. You can reach Kamchatka by direct flight from Anchorage, Alaska. You will need a visa.

Lost World Tours   5 Stoneway, Lynnfield, Massachusetts 01940. Tel: 202-746-0661; E-mail: info@kamchatkapeninsula.com; Website: www.kamchatkapeninsula.com.

A professional alpinist and his wife have been running tours to Kamchatka since 1993, reaching into some of the most remote areas on Earth. The spectacularly beautiful Kronotsky National Park—one of the places they visit—is the site of a lake, a caldera, nine active volcanoes, and the Valley of Geysers. With few human predators, the wildlife is abundant: grizzlies fishing in the river and gathering berries, lots of wild deer, and hundreds of swans. Lodging is in an old ranger's cabin, lodges, or camp surrounded by an electric fence. Travel is by boat and helicopter. At least one stop in a hot springs. Nine days, about $2,000, August/September.

Joint Stock Company VAO Intourist   150, Mira pr., Moscow 129366, Russia. Tel: 011 7-095-956-4206; E-mail: ecotours@ t.ru; Website: www.ecotours-intourist.ru.

This Moscow-based company, with links in Great Britain (www.intourist.co.uk) and Europe, takes you to the Kurilskoye Lake in the Yujrio-Kamchatsky Reserve for brown bear viewing as they feast on red salmon. Led by a Canadian biologist/bear expert, the tour begins with a helicopter flight to the lake. From the base of your lakeside campsite surrounded by an electric fence, you spend the days on easy to moderate hikes through the wilderness and to a bear-viewing platform overlooking a salmon-leaping river. An armed park ranger accompanies the hikes. Expect to see lots of bears, Arctic fox, Steller sea eagles, birds, and sockeye salmon. Traditional Kamchatka food and vodka for dinner in this spectacular place. Seven days, about $2,100.

WOLVES, BEARS, AND LYNX IN TRANSYLVANIA

Romania

Carpathian Large Carnivore Project   Str. Dr. Ioan Senchea, No. 162, 2223 Zarnesti, Romania. E-mail: iafo@clcp.ro; Website: www.clcp.ro.

Under an ecotourism project designed to census large carnivores in the Carpathian mountains in Romania (5,000 brown bears, 3,000 wolves, and 2,000 lynx), and to develop conservation areas to protect them, the CLCP has inaugurated "Wolves, Bears, and Lynx in Transylvania," to invite tourists to appreciate the area's abundant wildlife. Tourists fill the niche otherwise filled by poachers, and foreign dollars and the involvement of local folk in wildlife tourism increase the value of wildlife *alive*.

Staying with local Zarnesti families and in guest houses, visitors can take guided hikes through the interesting mountains and ancient-growth forests; observe brown bears, wolves, lynx, and boars, as well as visit habituated bear and wolf habitats; and meet shepherds and farmers. A roasted lamb over a campfire celebrates the tour. One to two weeks, leave by minibus from the airport or hotel in Bucharest. Contact for cost.

BLACK BEARS

Just Call Me Chubby

There are so many black bears (*Ursus americanus*) in the suburbs in the United States they should have voting privileges. As our urban sprawl reached into *their* natural habitat, they reached into *ours*, helping themselves to our garbage and seeking out the Golden Arches. Beekeepers expect them, during those moments when, like Pooh, they have a hankering for a certain something. A recent study found that not only are black bears gaining weight, but also they are bunking behind the shed, rather than returning to their leafy wilderness caves. So much for Smokey Bear.

The American black bear still inhabits the wild, especially around the Appalachian Mountain Range in eastern United States (an estimated 5,000 live in upstate New York); in a swath from New Mexico to Alaska; from northern California to northern New York; and in Newfoundland. The largest are about six feet tall and weigh about 400 pounds, and eat in a range about seventy square miles. Black bears can be aggressive if food is between you and them and have been known to open unlocked car doors and eat the picnic. They will also fight you for food in your tent if you break the cardinal camping rule against sleeping with your food.

Black bears have several colorful subspecies: the spirit bear, the rare blue bear, the cinnamon bear, the Eastern black, and the Newfoundland black.

Minnesota

The American Bear Association   P.O. Box 77, Orr, Minnesota 55771; E-mail: bears@rangenet.com; Website: www.americanbear.org.

In northern Minnesota on the shores of Pelican Lake sits the Vince Shute Wildlife Sanctuary. Here from an observation deck, you can view wild black bears in their natural habitat as they spend the summer evenings playing, eating, and climbing. May to September, 5 P.M. to dusk. Trained naturalists fill you in on their facts. Donations accepted. For lodging in the area, call 800-357-9255.

North Carolina/Tennessee

Great Smoky Mountains National Park 107 Park Headquarters Road, Gatlinburg, Tennessee 37738. Tel: 865-436-1200;
E-mail: grsm_smokies_information@nps.gov; Website: www.nps.
gov/grsm.

The largest national park in the East, Great Smoky is a World
Heritage Site (because of its wildlife diversity) and an international
biosphere reserve. It is also home to lots of wild black bears. Park
rangers warn visitors to keep their distance from the bears, keep food
locked up, back away if any bear appears aggressive, and aggressively
fight back if you are attacked. Make a lot of noise and hit the bear
with whatever you have handy to let it know you are not prey.

The park is open year-round, has 800 miles of hiking trails, and
costs between $10 and $20 a night for camp fee.

British Columbia

Tide Rip Grizzly Tours 1660 Robb Avenue, Comox, British
Columbia V9M 2W7 Canada. Tel: 888-643-9319 (toll-free);
250-928-3090; E-mail: tiderip@island.net; Website: www.tiderip.com.

A day tour from Telegraph Cove by boat will take you to the
thousand islands of the Broughton Archipelago off the British
Columbia coast. On the new and full moons, when the tides are
extremely low (and high), you can see black bears scooping up mussels and crabs and eating seaweed. May to October.

SPIRIT BEARS

Spirit bears, or kermode bears, are really black bears, with an astonishing white coat. Not albino, one in ten cubs of these clusters of
related families is white. In what's called the Great Bear Rainforest
of the north central coast of British Columbia, on small islands
between the coast and Queen Charlotte Islands, several bears live.
They stand out like ghosts, which is why the local Kitasoo/X
call them spirit bears.

Sea Kayak Adventures   1036 Pine Avenue, Coeur d'Alene, Idaho 83814. Tel: 800-616-1943 (toll-free); 208-765-3116; E-mail: info@seakayakadventures.com; Website: www.seakayak adventures.com.

This company runs four itineraries around the temperate rain forest of Princess Royal Island. Based in coastal huts, Spirit Bear Quest takes you by motorboat to access the remote areas where spirit bears seek out salmon. Five days, August and September, about $1,000. A five-day lodge-based tour explores the homeland of the resident Kitasoo/Xaixais and how the spirit bear fits into their culture, about $1,000. Or spend seven days kayaking Laredo Sound, camping, about $1,000—includes all gear.

Natural Habitat Adventures   2945 Center Green Court, Suite H, Boulder, Colorado 80301-9539. Tel: 800-543-8917; Website: www.nathab.com.

In the Great Bear Rainforest on Princess Royal Island, this trip allows you to search for the spirit bear by boat and helicopter. Seven days, lodges, about $5,000.

Ocean Light Adventures   No. 363-1917 West 4th Avenue, Vancouver, British Columbia V6J 1M7, Canada. Tel: 604-328-5339; E-mail: tom@oceanlight2.bc.ca; Website: www.litherland.ca/ oceanlight.

The seventy-one-foot *Ocean Light II* sailboat takes you to beautiful and remote places along British Columbia's midcoast region to appreciate the wide diversity of birds, fish, and animals that call it home. Their spirit bear tour allows you to sail to the coast, then take a zodiac ashore for closer viewing and photos. Four-day trips in May and June, about CD$1,450 (U.S.$1,150); plus CD$90 (U.S.$70) park fee.

POLAR BEARS

Polar bears are the largest carnivore on land, but their Latin name, *Ursus maritimus*, describes the land: ice on the Arctic Ocean. White to match their environment, polar bears are different from grizzlies:

their long necks precede them as they lope across the ice, and the fur on their legs resembles mucklucks. Good swimmers, they travel from ice floe to ice floe, living on a diet of seals, occasionally carcasses of walrus or whales, and they travel as much as forty-five miles a day, usually alone. In winter, females find a den in which to go dormant and give birth; males keep moving, but more slowly, occasionally falling into sudden naps.

When the ice breaks up in summer, polar bears move south into sub-Arctic land to eat and to mate in April and May. Their diet consists of everything from eggs to lichens to musk ox or caribou carcass. A polar bear even tried to munch on a submarine rudder that surfaced through the ice.

Manitoba

In October hundreds inhabit the tundra outside of Churchill, Manitoba, where they gather to watch the tourists. In November, when the ice congeals, they move back north.

Polar bears are not listed as threatened, but are a bit of a mystery. Thought to be delicately tied into their ecosystem, nevertheless, in 2002, six polar bears were found living with a traveling circus in the Caribbean. Kept as performers since they were cubs, the seven-foot-long, 1,000-pound creatures with heavy white coats were rescued from a five-by-eight-foot air conditioned trailer by agents from the American Zoo and Aquarium Association. One died in transit, but the other five were distributed to zoos throughout the country that had habitats more in keeping with their own. (See: www.aza.org.)

Several tour companies run trips to Churchill, Manitoba, in October. Most travel across the tundra in tundra buggies, with lots of stops when polar bears are in view, especially when they are play-fighting, which is a behavioral habit unique to Churchill.

Check out the following selections:

Travel Wild Expeditions P.O. Box 1637, Vashon Island, Washington 98070. Tel: 800-368-0077 (toll-free); 206-463-5362; E-mail: info@travelwild.com; Website: www.travelwild.com.

This tour leaves Winnipeg and guarantees three days of tundra buggy viewing, plus includes hotels in Churchill and Winnipeg, naturalist guides, and all meals. Six days, about $2,500.

Arctic Odysseys   3409 E. Madison Street, Seattle, Washington 98112. Tel: 206-325-1977; E-mail: arctic4u@aol.com; Website: www.arcticodysseys.com.

This naturalist-guided tour operates out of a naturalist lodge on the shore of Hudson Bay in the mouth of the Seal River. Here polar bears wander, too, as do lots of other wildlife: Beluga whales, Arctic fox, Arctic wolves, and lots of sea birds, getting ready for their winter migrations. Take a tour by boat, helicopter, or floatplane to better to see polar bears; walking tours are best to examine the flora and fauna of the coast. You can take an ocean kayak or canoe for a paddle trip, swim with the Belugas, or go fishing. In a six-wheel ATV, explore the tidal environment of the Seal River Estuary. Eight days, about $5,000.

International Expeditions, Inc.   One Environs Park, Helena, Alabama 35080-7200. Tel: 800-633-4734 (toll-free); E-mail: nature@ietravel.com; Website: www.internationalexpeditions.com.

With expert guides, and a unique twenty-four-hour tundra buggy viewing marathon on days 4 and 5, this trip incorporates other wildlife areas in Manitoba and introduces visitors to Inuits. Eight days, about $4,200.

Join a Scientific Project

Earthwatch   3 Clock Tower Place, Suite 100, Box 75, Maynard, Massachusetts 01754-0075. Tel: 800-776-0188 (toll-free); 978-461-0081; Fax: 978-461-2332; E-mail: info@earthwatch.org; Website: www.earthwatch.org.

Why do male polar bears play-fight so much when they are in Churchill? In the wild, males have encounters only during mating. The second question this project asks is, How much do tourists influence their behavior? With global climate change melting the extent of their sea ice home, will polar bears adapt to living more on

the mainland? Join two university animal behaviorists traveling in
tundra buggies across the ice in Churchill and take digital photos of
the play-fights. Seven days, lodging at the Churchill Northern Studies Center, about $3,300.

Norway

Lindblad Expeditions   720 Fifth Avenue, New York, New York
10019. Tel: 800-397-3348 (toll-free); 212-765-7740; E-mail:
explore@expeditions.com; Website: www.expeditions.com.
    Polar bears also migrate south to places other than Manitoba.
On this trip to the archipelago of Svalbaad by cruise ship *Endeavor*,
with Zodiac trips to the mainland, you will see polar bears, reindeer, walrus, seals, and Arctic foxes enjoying the summer fields
among the fjords. Leaves from Oslo. Eleven days, from $4,700 to
$6,200, depending on berth.

Websites

For many facts and fancies about bears, log on to www.bearden.org.
    The website of the Fish and Wildlife Service contains brochures
of all national wildlife refuges (fws.gov).

In the Canadian Arctic, a handsome polar bear surfaces to take a
look at the people a few feet away in a boat. *Susan Voorhees,
Arctic Odysseys, www.arcticodysseys.com*

22

WOLVES AND ELK

WOLVES

Of all the carnivores on Earth, wolves win the literary inspiration award, hands down. As long ago as ancient Greece, parents told bedtime stories to their kids about wolves that ate children if they went into the woods alone. In Europe, when writers wanted to create a man's most savage alter-ego, did they think of writing stories about Bear Man? No, Wolf Man stole center stage, the consequence of the effects of an unknown substance on a perfectly normal human being who grew lots of body hair, howled in the full moon, and became a carnivore.

So Blame It on Little Red Riding Hood

When settlers arrived in this country 300 years ago, they were saturated with ideas that wolves were big and bad. Unfortunately for the great gray wolf that roamed coast to coast, American settlers shot them on sight. When settlers moved into the Far West, the government put a bounty on wolves' heads.

By 1930, the overkill was so complete there were only one or two wolves anywhere in the United States. For Native Americans, who had grown up hearing stories about wise and good wolves and who look on the wolf as a spiritual brother, the "extirpation" of the wolf, as it was officially known, was just another symptom of the earth's illness.

The Reintroduction

In North America, only Canada teemed with gray wolves, mostly because the tundra was unpopulated with people. Packs of wolves roamed here and there, and one day crossed the boundary into the United States, slipping quietly into the Boundary Waters area in Minnesota, as well as into Idaho and Montana.

By the 1980s, wildlife biologists began to realize that wolves are good: they control elk herds, attacking the sick and keeping the elk population in check, and just might be an important part of the wild ecosystem. The reintroduction of the gray wolf into the American wild began in 1995 and 1996, when eight packs of Canadian gray wolves were captured and relocated in Yellowstone National Park, Wyoming. The object was ten breeding pairs, which form the center of the pack, in Montana, Idaho, and Yellowstone.

Today wolves number close to 100 in each of Montana, Idaho, and Yellowstone, with even more in Michigan and Wisconsin. Minnesota (see below) has a couple of thousand. There are about 8,000 gray wolves in Alaska and 50,000 in Canada.

Still the Big Bad Wolf

The story of the gray wolf now is that not everyone is happy about its reintroduction. Some ranchers oppose it, claiming they can't afford to lose livestock to wolves; hunters don't welcome the competition for elk and deer. Organizations like the National Park Service realize that the story of the wolf these days is a little like the Middle East: How do you manage a peace plan? Park managers are creating safe buffer zones in which mapless wolves can safely wander, private organizations such as Defenders of Wildlife are compensating ranchers for the loss of any wolf-killed livestock, and schools are teaching children that wolves are interesting and can be beneficial. Tourism companies hope to bring in people who are open to understanding where the gray wolf fits in American society today.

A pensive little wolf at the International Wolf Organization charms kids, schoolgroups, and adults. *Lynn and Donna Rogers, www.bearstudy.org*

Who Are Gray Wolves?

Statistics indicate that wolves don't attack human beings. There are so few substantiated facts of wolf/human attacks that wildlife biologists believe the stories of wolf attacks were created in Europe, when wolves were observed feeding on people killed in wars. Wolves will grab sheep or cattle, but only when there is nothing else to eat. According to the National Wildlife Federation, wolves attacked a total of only 76 cattle and 192 sheep—spread over the past ten years. Generally, wolves stick to themselves, serenading remote communities with their beautiful voices.

Like lions of the Serengeti Plain, wolves hunt in packs, which is how they are able to bring down a moose or an elk that is at least twice their size. Wolves are big proponents of family values and mate for life, share a den, and let the young stick around if they want when they are adolescents.

Wolves spray urine to mark their territories, and stay in touch by howling. They also bark, whine, and growl, just like domestic dogs, whose ancestors they are.

The best way to experience wolves is to go into the ~~ with knowledgeable guides.

Wyoming

Yellowstone National Park: North American Safari Country
Supervisor, P.O. Box 168, Yellowstone National Park, Wyoming
82190-0168. Tel: 307-344-7381; E-mail: yell_visitor_services@
nps.gov; Website: nps.gov/yell.

Often called the Serengeti of North America, Yellowstone National Park, which occupies Wyoming and Montana, is an amazing geological wonder. It is an International Biosphere Reserve and a World Heritage Site. Although geologists hold their breath for its imminent explosion, Yellowstone keeps bubbling away, sitting on an ancient caldera that sends out geysers (Old Faithful) and huge jets of steam, and bubbles up in brilliantly colored hot springs. The park has valleys, rivers that shoot through canyons, mountains, and stretches of plateaus or savannah-type grasslands. Here grazers and browsers, like elk and bison, spend their days.

Unique to North America are moose, the largest of deer species, with huge antlers and characteristic throat bag; they live also in Maine and Minnesota. Pronghorn antelope, also unique to North America, have recently been discovered to be faster than cheetahs, running 55 miles an hour for four miles. Unlike cheetahs, these graceful antelopes graze in small herds, marking their territory with some twenty scent glands from various parts of their bodies. They race to elude the Yellowstone predators, including grizzlies, black bears, coyotes, and wolves.

You can also see bison herds, big horn sheep, mule deer, white-tailed deer, foxes, bald eagles, golden eagles, and trumpeter swans.

See www.yellowstone-natl-park.com for sightings, news, and a wolf map of the park.

You can stay in the park in lodging that ranges from "rustic cabins to luxury suites." Campsites, numerous small lodges and hotels are located outside the park.

Pronghorns, native to North America, can outdistance cheetahs in fast sustained runs. *Dave Menke, U.S. Fish and Wildlife Service; www.fsw.gov*

Yellowstone Association Institute   Tel: 307-344-2294; Website: www.YellowstoneAssociation.org.

The Educational division of the Yellowstone Association in partnership with the National Park Service, the institute offers several courses on the Yellowstone wolves, from one-day introductory courses to four-day field intensives given by wildlife biologists. The field intensives are held at the Park's Lamar Buffalo Ranch, where you will be able to stay in log cabins for about $22 a night.

Winter Wolf Discovery   Tel: 307-344-7311.

A "lodging and learning" program is based at Mammoth Hot Springs Hotel in the park. After lectures, you go into the field with a wildlife biologist who will show you how to use high-powered wildlife spotting scopes. Two days, about $250; three days, about $375, depending on room.

Wildlife Ed-Ventures   Tel: 307-344-2294.
A one-day field trip with a wolf expert, about $55.

Several companies offer tours centered around the wolf:

Fischer Outdoor Discoveries   Hank and Carol Fischer; E-mail:
info@fischeroutdoor.com; Website: www.fischeroutdoor.com.
Hank and Carol, authors of the *Montana Wildlife Viewing Guide*,
know the area well. "The Great Yellowstone Wolf and Bear Quest"
takes you on a weeklong tour through the park in early June when
thousands of elk calves are being born. In a ritual similar to that of
lions and wildebeest in the Serengeti, wolves stalk, pounce, and
attack elk calves, competing only with grizzlies. A typical trip, they
say, will spot ten to fifteen grizzlies and the same number of wolves.
You will also witness at least one kill, and the Fischers will help you
understand the predator/prey relationship that keeps things in balance. Eight days, hotel and lodges, about $2,500.

Travel Wild Expeditions   P.O. Box 1637, Vashon Island,
Washington 98070. Tel: 800-368-0077 (toll-free); 206-463-5362;
E-mail: info@travelwild.com; Website: www.travelwild.com.
Augmented by evening slide shows and lectures about wolves and
their reintroduction, this five-day winter wolf tour through Yellowstone concentrates on the Lamar Valley, where the wolves live. Five
days, about $2,000, includes everything while you are there.

Off the Beaten Path   7 E. Beall Street, Bozeman, Montana
59715-9943. Tel: 800-445-2995 (toll-free); E-mail: travel@
offthebeatenpath.com; Website: www.offthebeatenpath.com.
In a small group, celebrate the new year in snow-covered Yellowstone, the best time to spot wolves (the grizzlies are dormant). This
trip also includes a New Year's Eve ranch stay in Montana, with a
horse-drawn sleigh ride and ice skating. Seven days, about $3,000.

Natural Habitat Adventures   2945 Center Green Court, Suite
H, Boulder, Colorado 80301-9539. Tel: 800-543-8917; Website:
www.nathab.com.

Wolves and Wildlife of Yellowstone begins in Grand Teton National Park, then visits the National Elk Refuge, where herds of close to 7,000 elk live. Where elk are, wolves are never far behind. Crossing the upper northwest corner of Yellowstone, you will stop at Lamar Valley—wolf country. Because wolves hunt in the daylight here, you might see a pack in search of prey. Search for tracks and signs. Seven days, stay in historic lodges close to wildlife, about $2,900.

Minnesota

Superior National Forest   Forest Supervisor, 8901 Grand Avenue Place, Duluth, Minnesota 55808. Tel: 219-626-4300; E-mail: r9_superior_nf@fs.fed.us; Website: www.snf.org.

The Boundary Waters Canoe Area Wilderness in Superior National Forest has been a healthy home to several packs of gray wolves. Because their territories are small (about six to twelve miles), they have become big vocalizers to protect their territories and to stay in touch with members of their own packs.

International Wolf Center   Teaching the World About Wolves, 1396 Highway 169, Ely, Minnesota 55731. Tel: 218-365-4695; Website: www.wolf.org.

This educational center seeks to "advance the survival of the wolf" and offers Adventure Programs in Minnesota, Canada, and Yellowstone. Wildlife biologists at the center radio-collar and track wild wolves to understand their habitat; and several "ambassador wolves," habituated wolves, are available at the center for further education (see their Wolf Watch Cam).

The Wolf Center's Adventure Programs offer weekend and weeklong programs for kids and adults. One, for example, takes you dogsledding in the Boundary Waters Canoe Area Wilderness, while you radio-track some collared wolves. Four days, about $600, including meals and lodging.

Participants in an adventure program at the International Wolf Center learn how to howl to attract wolves. *International Wolf Center; www.wolf.org*

Michigan

Join a Scientific Project

Earthwatch   3 Clock Tower Place, Suite 100, Box 75, Maynard, Massachusetts 01754-0075. Tel: 800-776-0188 (toll-free); 978-461-0081; Fax: 978-461-2332; E-mail: info@earthwatch.org; Website: www.earthwatch.org.

Moose and Wolves in Michigan studies the relationship between predator and prey, wolf and moose. In the Isle Royale National Park, join thirty-year investigator Rolf Peterson with aerial photos, topo maps, and compasses, as you hike about ten miles a day off trail in the backwoods of upper Michigan. It's rigorous—experienced hikers will be happier here. But it's great if you love the lure of a mystery, in this case, finding moose bones from old wolf kills in the middle of the wilderness. Eight days, backpacking, about $800, food included, but you cook over a single-burner stove.

Idaho

Several packs of reintroduced wolves live in the Nez Perce Tribal Lands in northern Idaho, where Nez Perce help manage them in conjunction with the U.S. Fish and Wildlife Service.

Wapiti River Guides   Box 1125, 128 Main, Riggins, Idaho 83549. Tel: 800-488-9872 (toll-free); E-mail: wapitirg@spro.net; Website: www.wapitiriverguides.com.

This interesting company combines wolves, Native Americans, and river rafting in some of the most beautiful country in the United States. Experienced river guides Barbara Gaskell and Gary Lane, a wildlife biologist, invite a Nez Perce wolf specialist on their trips to introduce visitors to Native Americans who look upon the reintroduction of wolves as the beginning of healing of the earth.

A typical trip on the Salmon River begins with a visit to the Nez Perce Wolf Education Research Center in Winchester, Idaho (see: www.wolfcenter.org) to visit wolves raised in captivity but kept for educational purposes on twenty wild and fenced acres. Here you learn that "wolves are not a renewable resource. They are a nation of beings who share the planet with us." Then you put in to the river in a wooden dory for five days of rafting and camping, in four canyons, through class I to class IV rapids, depending on the season. (Midsummer is easiest and warmest.) You have lots of time to look for wolves and to talk about where predator and prey fit together in the wilderness. "When the Nez Perce tribal member speaks," says Gary Lane, "it comes from the heart." Five days, about $1,500, includes all camping gear and food.

Canada

Great Canadian Ecoventures   P.O. Box 2481, Yellowknife, Northwest Territories X1A 2PB, Canada. Tel: 800-667-9453 (toll-free); 867-920-7110; E-mail: tundra@thelon.com; Website: www.thelon.com.

Dance with the Wolves will take you to the remote parts of Canada to see (unobtrusively) some of the many wolf dens that have grown up in response to a population boom among musk ox. Fly in, camp, and be immersed in wolf country. Great for photographers. Seven days, about $3,500, June and July only.

Slovakia

Biosphere Expeditions   Sprat's Water near Carlton Colville, The Broads National Park, Suffolk NR33 8BP UK. Tel: 011 44 1502 583085; E-mail: info@biosphere-expeditions.org; Website: www.biosphere-expeditions.org.

In the other part of the Czech Republic, join a local scientist and a mountain guide in the Nizke Tatry Mountains, monitoring the health of chamois, the goat that is the chief prey of brown bears and gray wolves. The overall purpose is to find out how many chamois and wolves exist here, to get an idea if the predator/prey balance is working. Twelve days, about $1,700.

Mongolia

Biosphere Expeditions   Sprat's Water near Carlton Colville, The Broads National Park, Suffolk NR33 8BP UK. Tel: 011 44 1502 583085; E-mail: info@biosphere-expeditions.org; Website: www.biosphere-expeditions.org.

In Mongolia's Hustai National Park, where Prezwalski's horses are being reintroduced to the wild, you can join wolf expert Dr. Tungalagtuya, who is studying the gray wolf in Mongolia. Gray wolves are remarkable for their ability to live in forests, mountains, and deserts, and on this trip, you seek out wolves in all those terrains. Twenty days, lodging in tents, gers, and hotel in Ulaanbaatar, about $3,500. Includes food and tent equipment.

Wolves help keep elk populations manageable. A herd of elk graze in Yellowstone National Park. *Glen Smart, U.S. Fish and Wildlife Service, www.fws.gov*

ELK, OR WAPITI

Wyoming

National Elk Refuge Jackson, Wyoming; Website: nationalelkrefuge.fws.gov.

About 7,500 elk migrate here every fall, seeking the higher elevation from Grand Teton National Park and southern Yellowstone National Park. From October to May Jackson is home. Listen for elk bugling in September and October; it's the mating call. It's also the time in which elk shed their antlers, which Jackson Boy Scouts collect to put into the Annual Jackson Boy Scouts Antler Auction. (About 80 percent of the proceeds go back to the refuge.)

Kentucky

Elk, an antlered member of the deer family, once roamed the mountains and forests of the Appalachian Range, as did wolves. Human habitation and hunting "extirpated" the elk, until 1997, when the Kentucky Department of Fish and Wildlife Resources decided to reintroduce the elk. By 2001, the herd had reached close to 1,500, proving that the area of about 475,000 acres reclaimed from surface coal mining could support close to 7,500 elk. Plans are underway to reintroduce the wolf to Kentucky, as well.

Kentucky Dept. of Fish and Wildlife Resources   1 Game Farm Road, Frankfort, Kentucky 40601. Tel: 800-858-1549; Website: www.kdwr.state.ky.us

The Department of Fish and Wildlife provides information on visiting the Cumberland Plateau and new elk population.

Rocky Mountain Elk Foundation   Website: www.rmef.org/index/htm.

This foundation offers additional facts on the elk population in the United States.

23

HORSES

WILD HORSES

Przewalski's horse, the only truly wild horse in the world, was hunted until the species was reduced to fewer than a hundred. Most of these were sent off to private zoos in Europe. In the wild, the last recorded sighting of a Przewalski's horse was in 1969.

When it became clear they were close to extinction, a foundation was formed in 1977 for the horse's preservation (see: www.treemail.nl/takh). Now the horses are part of captive breeding-and-reintroduction programs that are returning them to the Hustain Nuruu Reserve in Mongolia, about sixty miles west of Ulan Baatar. Named after a Russian count, the horses, a favorite of prehistoric cave painters and the ancestors of domestic horses, are called Takhi in Mongolia.

In Ohio

To see a herd of Przewalskis racing over the green hills of Ohio, visit:

The Wilds   14000 International Road, Cumberland, Ohio 43732. Tel: 740-638-5030; Website: www.thewilds.org.

On ten thousand acres of reclaimed surface-mined land given by the American Electric Power Company, several hundred animals from Asia, Africa, and North America roam. In a one-hour tour, you can see American bison and African black rhinos grazing, along with the Przewalski wild horses and lots of other species. Many are part of conservation study programs of animal and land management. Others, such as the Przewalskis, are being bred to reintroduce healthy and stable populations to the wild. The wild horses are part of the Species Survival Plan of the AZA in conjunction with the National Zoo.

This place offers many study opportunities for kids and students, from camp to internships, and it's a great place to learn about problems that animals experience around the world. To visit, you can do a Sunset Safari, eat a buffet dinner, talk with the management staff, and take a tour of the residents. Three hours, about $50; reserve in advance by contacting btreadway@thewilds.org. Tel: 740-638-2286. June to September.

A herd of Przelwalski horses, the only true wild horse species in the world, are bred in captivity at the Wilds in Ohio as part of the Asian Wild Horse Species Survival Program. Small populations will be reintroduced to their former home range in Mongolia. For more information, visit the Wilds at their website, www.thewilds.org.

Join a Scientific Project

Volunteer to follow, count, monitor, and help Przewalski horses return to the wild:

Samar Magic Tours Co., Ltd.   Cristo Camilo Gavilla Gomez. Tel: 011 976-11-311051; Fax: 976-11-327503; E-mail: ecovolunteers@samarmagictours.com; Website: www.samarmagic tours.com. In the United States: Voice mail or Fax: 206-888-4286.

If you are at least eighteen years old, speak English, can ride horseback (Mongolian steeds are small and pesky), and don't mind camping or staying in a Mongolian ger, you can sign on to the project to participate in activities that might include tracking down a Przewalski harem (stallion, females, and foals). Three weeks: summer (June to September), about $1,800; winter (October to May), about $1,850.

Wild Wings   First Floor, 577/579 Fishponds Road, Bristol, BS16 3AF, UK. Tel: 011 79 65 8333; E-mail: wildinfo@wildwings. co.uk; Website: www.ecovolunteer.org.

Some of the horses are kept in a semi-wild area before they are released into the wild. Volunteer to help monitor their movements with a GPS, noting their behavior; when they form a harem with a protecting stallion, they are released into the wild. You must be eighteen or older, able to speak English, and ride horses. Three weeks, camping or gers, about £750 ($1,200) in summer, £850 ($1,350) in winter.

Horse Adoptions

Feral Horses, United States

Przewalskis are the only wild horse in the world, but feral horses, whose ancestors were once tamed, roam many parts of the earth, from Namibia to Australia to the American West. Herds roamed the grasslands around the Rockies, undisturbed until the 1970s, when the U.S. Bureau of Land Management, in an effort to control their healthy breeding populations, began capturing them and offering them for adoption.

The offering price is $125, which at auction might go up a bit. Buyers must be at least eighteen years old, not have any convictions of animal abuse, can prove they are able to shelter and keep a horse, as well as feed and water it. About 6,000 to 8,000 horses and 500 to 1,000 burros are offered a year at places across the country. See: www.wildhorseandburro.blm.gov, or www.adoptahorse.blm.gov for time and place of auctions.

Crosswinds Equine Rescue, Inc. 1476 North County Route 1350E, Tuscola, Illinois 61953. Tel: 217-832-2010; E-mail: cross windseqresq@aol.com; Website: www.crosswindsrescue.com.

Sometimes people buy horses at auction with an intent to sell them to slaughterhouses. This organization buys horses at auction to keep them from slaughter. It also works to bring an end to horse slaughter, rescues horses, including racehorses that have been abused, and educates horse owners in the arts of gentle training. (See AnnMarie Cross's online gentling course.) After six months of rehab, most horses are offered for adoption; some become "permanent guests."

ReRun P.O. Box 96, Carlisle, Kentucky 40311. Tel: 859-289-7786; E-mail: rerunhorse@kih.net; Website: www.rerun.org.

This nonprofit has chapters in eight states across the country, each with horses up for adoption.

Adopt a Former Racehorse

Racehorses are bred for one thing: racing. Whether they win or lose, they have a short career, and the choices, if they don't have a sympathetic caretaker, are few. Many wind up in slaughterhouses.

To give them a chance to come down from the fast life and to find new loving homes, a few places offer these beautiful animals for adoption. The initial fee is not very much, but you must have a place to keep your horse and be able to afford the hay.

Thoroughbred Retirement Foundation   PMB 351, 450 Shrewsbury Plaza, Shrewsbury, New Jersey 07702-4332. E-mail: trfinc@msn.com; Website: www.trfinc.org.

At farms in upstate New York and in Vermont, TRF rehabilitates and retrains former race horses, helped by prisoners as part of their rehabilitation. Then TRF tries to place the horses with the right adoptive owners, matching them in "temperament, appearance, soundness, and age." Once adopted, TRF monitors the horse to make sure the new owner and the horse are as happy as they were when they first met.

Many of the formerly feral and race horses are kept in prison grounds as part of the rehabilitation of prisoners; others are used in cities with former teen gang members to help youths care for something that is both wild and dependent.

For information on all horse organizations, including racehorse sanctuaries: www.kingdomkeepers.net See also: www.savehorses.com and horsewelfare.8k.com.

RANCH VACATIONS

If you want something more than a dude ranch, try signing on with a working ranch vacation. You'll ride horses and spend time finding out how modern-day ranchers deal with wild animals living very close to their livestock. It's a Rubik's Cube of a problem, making sure that the grass you plant and where you plant it is enough for your livestock as well as a few migrating creatures.

The following two unusual ranch vacations offer a chance to understand the problems, do a little ranch work, eat some ranch food, and have fun.

Wyoming

Elk Mountain Ranch   Box 74, Elk Mountain, Wyoming 82324.
Tel: 307-348-7440; E-mail: recreation@elkmountain.com;
Website: www.elkmountain.com.

This unusual bison ranch, founded in 1866, is an example of Nature
Conservancy's Wild Spaces, Working Places. The fifty-square-mile
ranch monitors its water sources, rotates its pastures, leaves forage for
wildlife that migrates through the ranch, while it controls and nur-
tures its healthy bison herd. Bison are bred, and some are sent to
market for buffalo meat. Bison, since they have no predators except
man, are kept in check in guided big game hunts in the fall.

The ranch also opens its doors to corporate and family vacations
and it's a great place to understand the workings of a ranch. Elk
Mountain offers:

- Interactive, educational tours of the bison herd. Learn something about how to keep a range herd healthy.
- Mountain ecology. Ranch hands will take you up the mountain (about 11,000 feet) where you see elk, deer, antelope,
  black bears, and lots of birds as well as learn about wildlife
  corridors.
- Fishing, hiking (Butch Cassidy lived nearby, and some U.S.
  Cavalry soldiers were stationed here), biking, shooting instruction, working on the ranch, and star gazing.

Guests stay in the lodge, located at 7,300 feet, and eat in the
ranch cookhouse. The guesthouse accommodates ten people. Four
nights for four people, starts at $3,000; six nights, four people, starts
at $4,750.

California and Wyoming

Environmental Restoration Adventures, LLC   550 Hamilton
Avenue, No. 240, Dept. W, Palo Alto, California 94301.
Website: www.eradv.com.

Choose from among four working ranches, two in Wyoming, two in California, and jump in to learn what the problems are in ranching. These are no dude ranches: the work you do contributes to a better understanding of how a working ranch can incorporate wildlife by improving the health of streams, planting seedlings, or building a trough.

At the Big Bluff Ranch, in Red Bluff, California, a 4,000-acre environmentally sensitive cattle ranch, for example, you can help collect data to assess health of the animals or landscape and participate in a restoration project. Three days, about $900, includes lodging and food.

HORSE WHISPERING

Ever since the film by Robert Redford (*The Horse Whisperer*, 1998), horse whispering has gained momentum as the best way to train not only an unbroken or difficult horse, but to resolve any management problems you might be having at the office.

Also called *horse gentling* and *natural horsemanship*, horse whispering is a complex of techniques designed to bring a horse to full cooperation in a matter of minutes, by using nonverbal body movements that mimic wild herd behavior and by trying to see things from the horse's point of view. These minimize a horse's fear, which is the source of much of its resistance. Horses are also supersensitive to visual stimuli, to the point of not recognizing an owner who has a new limp.

To learn horse whispering, you can attend seminars, buy videos, or take an inexpensive online course.

As for the office, that's a training that involves singling out one problem that compromises your ability to be a good leader; for example, not being able to delegate. Originally, training for leadership was done in the ring with horses, which have an uncanny ability to size up the take-charge abilities of a rider and can dump an uncertain one. Now the course is more metaphorical. But those who teach techniques of horse whispering for horses emphasize that owners personally benefit as well. Following are a small sampling.

Australia

Horse Whispering Lodge   Hunter Valley, 72 Sandy Creek Road, Quorrobolong, New South Wales 2325, Australia.
Tel: 02 4998 6086; E-mail: clove@kooee.com.au; Website: www.horsewhisperinglodge.com.au.

This lodge, about sixty miles from Sydney, teaches natural horsemanship privately or in groups or workshops. Bring your own horse, or use a loaner. A three-night package in Harmony Cottage includes ten hours' horse training and accommodation, about $1,000. Instructor Diamond Porter emphasizes understanding horse "survival, comfort, and play" by reading their body language, understanding their games, and joining them in their games.

Illinois

DownUnder Horsemanship   Clinton Anderson, 24232 Lincoln Road, Sterling, Illinois 61081. Tel: 888-287-7432 (toll-free); E-mail: outback@cin.net; Website: www.clintonanderson.net.

An Aussie transplanted to Illinois, Clinton Anderson gives a weekly horse gentling training course on satellite television. Check out his videos. A three-day clinic is about $750; two weeks is about $3,000.

California

Dennis Reis   411 Highland Avenue, Penngrove, California 94951. Tel: 800-732-8220 (toll-free); 707-792-0629; E-mail: dreis@reisranch.com; Website: www.reisranch.com.

Using his own system, Reis gives demonstrations in techniques that bring you and your horse closer together in a deeper relationship. He gives two-day seminars, and five-day and one-month clinics. $200 a day.

Online Course

Gentling/Training the Young Horse is a four-week online course in trust and alpha leadership offered by AnnMarie Cross, of Crosswinds Equine Rescue (see above); www.suite101.com.

For people horse-whispering techniques, see www.alphaleaders.com.

HORSE FESTIVALS

Mongolia

Historically, horse festivals were times in which young athletes or warriors-in-training could compete in horse races. Traders took advantage of the festivals to increase their herds or sell horses that were no longer useful.

Naadam Games

This celebration held on a national holiday in early June pits wrestler against wrestler and archer against archer. The big event is composed of horse races run by six- to ten-year-olds. Most of the horses are broken, but some are two-year-olds. Depending on the age of the horse, the boys race bareback or with saddles, over courses that range from 5 to 30 km (about 3 to 18 miles). For a young warrior in training, wrestling, archery, and above all horsemanship are the skills he needs to master.

The following companies run tours to the Naadam Games.

Boojum Expeditions   Tel: 800-287-0125; Website: www.boojum.com.

Ride out from your basecamp lodge in Khovsgol on a horse trek to the games. About 17 days, about $3,500.

Nomadic Expeditions   1095 Cranbury-South River Road, Suite 20A, Monroe Township, New Jersey 08831. Tel: 800-998-6634 (toll-free); 609-860-9008; E-mail: info@nomadicexpeditions.com; Website: www.nomadicexpeditions.com.

Visit historic sites and monasteries heading to the Gobi Desert and the games. Twelve days, about $2,600.

Tibet/China

Litang Horse Festival

The Litang Festival of the Khampa Warriors in Tibet (called Kham, West Sichuan, by the Chinese) is a gathering of about 2,000 competing horsemen who race and do acrobatics on horseback. Competitors and traders set up colorful camps under waving flags. This weeklong festival held every August 1 to 7 sponsors a series of competitions between horsemen, but also affords a chance for traders to trade everything from tools to yaks. Lots of singing and dancing under the stars.

Myths and Mountains   976 Tee Court, Incline Village, Nevada 89451. Tel: 800-670-MYTH[6984] (toll-free); 775-832-5454; E-mail: travel@mythsandmountains.com; Website: www.mythsandmountains.com.

This company will guide you to the Litang, introduce you to many of the locals, then take you to places in China. Twenty days, about $4,000.

HORSE VACATIONS

Several companies sponsor horse vacations, many for families, in countries around the world—from the American West to Wales to Mongolia. A couple of examples follow.

Equitours   P.O. Box 807, 10 Stainaker Street, Dubois, Wyoming 82513. Tel: 800-545-0019 (toll-free); 307-455-3363; Fax: 307-455-2354; E-mail: equitours@wyoming.com; Website: www.ridingtours.com.

Cross Country International   Equestrian Vacations, P.O. Box 1170, Millbrook, New York 12545. 800-828-8768 (toll-free); Fax: 845-635-3300; E-mail: info@xcintl.com; Website: www. equestrianvacations.com.

It's spring, and the stallions fight to lead their feral herd at the Pryor Mountain Wild Horse Range, Montana. *U.S. Bureau of Land Management, www.blm.gov*

24

TRACKING

DECODING THE PRINTS

Ever wonder whose prints preceded you on the trail? And when they were there? And how far away they are now?

Animals do this all the time: they either leave traces, such as urine marks or claw scratchings, or they look for them to find out who's in the neighborhood.

Animal tracking schools and courses teach you how to decode all of this, plus the thrill of the mystery. You start tracking by knowing only the footprints; as you get drawn in, you pick up other clues, "until," veteran tracker Tom Brown Jr. wrote in *The Tracker* (1978), "you know the maker of the track like a lifelong friend." You return to the real world as a keen observer, trusting your own senses.

If animal tracking appeals to you, you can try outdoor survival skills—backpacking without a backpack. Then move on to living with ancient technology (i.e., stone tools). Or you can get into the field of tracking down human fugitives, not always in the wild.

New Jersey, Florida, and California

Tom Brown's Tracker School   P.O. Box 173, Asbury, New Jersey 08802. Tel: 908-479-4681; E-mail: info@trackerschool.com; Website: www.trackerschool.com.

Tom Brown has been a tracker since childhood, and now, when he's not in demand as a consultant to the film industry or on a

Dinosaurs left tracks around the world, like this one frozen in time at the Red Gulch Dinosaur Tracksite, Wyoming. Jerry Sintz, *U.S. Bureau of Land Management; www.blm.gov*

television show, he gives one-week courses in tracking and nature observation. You will learn observation of nature and how to trust your five senses and not leap to conclusions. You will also learn stalking, camouflage, and track identification, as well as how to read pressure releases (different in running than walking), for example. Seven days, about $700 to $900. Read one of the many books Tom has written about tracking before you get hooked; then move on to his Advanced Tracking, Scout, Philosophy, and Advanced Awareness courses.

Wisconsin

Tracks and Trees Learning Center, LLC   N7597 County Y,
Watertown, Wisconsin 53094. Tel: 920-699-3217; E-mail: dugtracs
@execpc.com. Youth programs, Kari Chaussee. Tel: 262-903-5974;
E-mail: owltracker@aol.com; Website: www.tracksandtrees.com.

Spend a fall weekend tracking gray wolves in Black River Falls,
Wisconsin, where there are many. Hiking two to four miles a day,
you will locate and interpret footprints, scat, and any kills. You will
also make plaster casts of the prints. Bring your own camping gear;
they provide the food. Three days, about $250.

Washington

Wilderness Awareness School   P.O. Box 5000, PMB 137,
Duvall, Washington 98019. Tel: 425-788-1301; E-mail: wasnet@
wildernessawareness.org; Website: www.natureoutlet.com

On a Summer Wolf Tracking Expedition, you immerse yourself
in the landscape, following wolf tracks, always staying "one day
behind" so the wolves won't know they are being tailed. Believing
that tracking is "an interpretive art," this school will teach you how
nature "encourages us to open all of our senses to the subtle clues
hidden everywhere." They offer weeklong wolf-tracking expeditions
separately for adults and for teens. About $750 to $850, includes
food and camping gear. The school also gives courses in mentoring
and inner tracking; and a yearlong Wilderness Awareness Residen-
tial Program for adults (about $10,000).

New York

The Ndakinna Wilderness Project   23 Middle Grove Road,
Greenfield Center, New York 12833. Tel: 518-583-9980;
Fax: 518-583-9741; E-mail: asban@earthlink.net; Website: www.
ndakinna.com.

This education center offers a banquet of wilderness skills to
adults, teens, kids as young as six, and families. In keeping with

Native American tradition, many of the tracking and wilderness courses include storytelling. One- and two-day tracking courses are held in the Pocono Mountains in New York. A four-day wolf and grizzly tracking course is held in Yellowstone National Park. James Bruchac, director, and Ivan Erchak, head instructor, have appeared frequently on national television shows.

Website

For a list of wilderness schools, see: www.wildernessdrum.com.

25

DOGSLEDDING

DOGS IN CHARGE

Early fur traders found this was the only real way to get around the frozen wastes—a sled, or sledge, for portering people and goods, and a good team of six or eight strongly bred dogs. The leader, or musher (from the French, *marchez*), is responsible for the dogs' health and well-being; the dogs are responsible for carrying the sled to civilization. In the frozen wilderness, man and animal are one.

(Please note: You will need all of your waterproof winter clothes for dog-sledding: think ice and cold wind.)

Minnesota

A good place to take lessons, if you have never dogsledded, is in northern Minnesota, where lakes freeze early.

Gunflint Trail   P.O. Box 205, Grand Marais, Minnesota 55604. Tel: 800-338-6932 (toll-free); Website: www.gunflint-trail.com.

January is the Dogsled Moon, according to the Ojibway people, whose territory this is. Minnesota Lake country is filled with trails where man and wild animal overlap in the Superior National Forest and Boundary Waters Wilderness. Take lessons in dogsledding, and when you are good at it, take the dogs along trails across frozen lakes or through the woods.

Boundary Country Trekking   173 Little Ollie Road, Grand
Marais, Minnesota 55604. Tel: 800-322-8327 (toll-free);
E-mail: bct@boundarycountry.com; Website: www.boundary
country.com.

Two nights' lodging, one day mushing will teach you the basics.
Start with the dogs at the kennel, where you meet your team and
learn how to harness five or six huskies. About $370.

Two days includes seventy-five to eighty miles of mushing, with
you at the helm. Nights spent in a wilderness yurt. About $750.

White Wilderness   P.O. Box 727, Ely, Minnesota 55731.
Tel: 800-701-6238 (toll-free); 218-365-6363; E-mail: info@white
wilderness.com; Website: www.whitewilderness.com.

Dogsled from yurt to yurt through the Superior National Forest
and Boundary Waters Wilderness. (A yurt is a heated circular tent.)
This company arranges a variety of options, five nights from $1,100
to $1,500.

Alaska

Denali

Denali West Lodge   P.O. Box 40, Lake Minchumina, Alaska
99757. Tel: 888-607-5566 (toll-free); 907-674-3112; E-mail: info@
denaliwest.com; Website: www.denaliwest.com.

Get lessons on the trail from Tonya Schlentner, who taught
dogsledding in the Italian Alps for ten years. To become a musher,
choose six days based in a lodge with a hot sauna, with dogsledding
along an interesting historic trail, stopping for photos, and
tracking; or nine days mushing in the wilderness, staying in
heated tents, learning winter camping skills, and appreciating the
magic of Denali. Learn also how to make the dogs comfortable in
beds of straw after preparing them a hearty well-deserved meal.
Both these treks are in winter. Six days, about $3,500; nine days,
about $7,000.

Wasilla

Alaska's Trails and Tails   P.O. Box 874293, Wasilla, Alaska 99687. Tel: 800-300-MUSH[6874] (toll-free); 907-373-1408; E-mail: info@dogsledtours.com; Website: www.dogsledtours.com. Located in the same town as the headquarters of the Iditarod Sled Dog Race, this company will put you up in their bed-and-breakfast and let you get to know the dogs in their kennel. One-half day Rookie Run includes instruction and a chance to try out your skills, about $250. Two days, with one spent in instruction, the other on the Iditarod Trail, about $600. Lots of other options, as well.

Canada

Baffin Island

Arctic Odysseys   3409 E. Madison Street, Seattle, Washington 98112. Tel: 206-325-1977; E-mail: arctic4u@aol.com; Website: www.arcticodysseys.com.

Weather fosters flexibility, and this Arctic Dog Sled Odyssey will introduce you to not only Inuit-style dogsledding, but also the inner strength that's required to live on the east coast of central Baffin Island, where fogs, blizzards, and melting or forming sea ice are factors in everyday life. Start in Ottawa, and get outfitted with an Arctic parka, pants, boots, and sleeping bag. Then fly to Iqaluit and harness your dogs. If all goes well, you can spend as many as six days exploring the icy outback on dogsled, spending downtime fishing for Arctic char, or photographing Arctic birds in spring/summer. Eight days, about $4,400; five days, about $3,800.

British Columbia

Alaskan Husky Adventures   Dunn Lake Road, Box 236, Clearwater, British Columbia V0E 1N0 Canada. Tel: 866-587-0037 (toll-free); 250-587-0037 (outside North America); E-mail: info@ dogsleddingadventures.com; Website: www.dogsleddingadventures.com

Through beautiful snow-covered Wells Gray Park, drive or ride with a team of highly trained Alaskan Racing Dogs with professional guides. Go overnight on a twenty-four-hour trip, where you cook over an open fire, and camp on the trail, like the mushers in the annual Iditarod Trail Sled Dog Race in Alaska in March. One person riding, about $420; driving the team, about $560. Or stay in a lodge (with a pool and hot tub) for five nights, mushing each day, about $800. This company welcomes families; ask about special kids' rates.

Russia

Lost World Tours   5 Stoneway, Lynnfield, Massachusetts 01940. Tel: 202-746-0661; E-mail: info@kamchatkapeninsula.com; Website: www.kamchatkapeninsula.com.

Spend nine days mushing your way across the Nalycheva Valley in Kamchatka, after instructions and preparations at a hotel in Petropavlovsk. Then head out across the snow, with overnight stops in cabins and lodges and daily dips in geothermal springs, before returning to civilization. Nine days, includes city tour and museums, as well as the sleds and dogs and guide, about $1,600.

Greenland

Dogsledding in Greenland is the only means of transport of seal hunters and fishermen who bag their quarry, then carry it home on dog sledge. Along the line of their routes are seal huts, which are places to overnight.

You can dogsled for one day, from your hotel, or for several weeks, if you have a hankering for the tundra and mountains of Greenland. On long treks, you stay in seal huts or pull a tent over your sled and nestle into furs.

The best time to dogsled is from March to May, when the ice is still firm, but the sun rises and the day is light.

To connect with a hotel package, contact Greenland.com at www.greenland.com or e-mail: info@greenland.com.

Wildlife here is sea-oriented, with beluga, humpback, narwhal, minke whales, and seals. In the northeast in the largest national park in the world, you will find polar bears, musk ox, wolves, walrus, foxes, ermine, lemmings, and reindeer, or caribou.

Websites

For information on the Iditarod Race, held in March, starting in Anchorage, Alaska: www.iditarod.com. During the race, keep up to date with the web cam.

General site on everything pertaining to dogsledding: www. sleddogcentral.com.

International Sled Dog Racing Association: www.isdra.org.

Skijoring is a sport that attaches a skier to one or two dogs, which can be the family pooch. Skijoring information: www.skijorama.com.

For places to skijor with your own dog: www.xcski.org.

Adopt a retired sled dog: www.norsled.org. This is the site of the Northern California Sled Dog Rescue, with links to many other adoption sites.

26

DINOSAURS AND MAMMOTHS

UNCOVERING THE DRAGONS

The former major tenants of the planet were reptiles. Dinosaurs ruled the roost for about 150 million years, from the earliest, bipedal meat eaters—the size of a large dog—to the latest, feathered, horned, armor-plated omnivores—the size of a small cruise ship.

Mammals struggled into existence about the same time in the Late Triassic period, some 200 million years ago, but they were about two inches long and lived in trees and couldn't really compete with dinosaurs who made their way around all of Pangea, the original single continent of Earth. Fifty million years later, during the Jurassic period, Pangea split into two, Gondwana in the south—modern-day South America, Australia, Africa, and Antarctica; and Laurasia in the north—North America, Europe, and Asia. Dinosaurs, never short on adaptation, moved right along and multiplied like, well, rabbits.

As a result of this, dinosaur traces are everywhere, from big bones in front of the pyramids to footprints in Connecticut. Sometimes the same species poke out of Mongolian cliffs and dry Montana riverbeds. Tragedies such as getting caught in floods in ancient rivers, fires in ancient forests, or bitter internecine fights have left

228

dinosaur fossils—bones, coprolites, eggs, and tracks—on every continent, with the oldest so far in Madagascar and Argentina.

Dinosaurs range from one the "size of a large paperclip" (recently found in China) to thirty-foot-long multi-tonned meat eaters with horns. By the Cretaceous period, 150 million years ago, dinosaurs were big, really big. Many of them ran in herds across the Arctic and the American West, where hundreds of triceratops pounded across Texas, New Mexico, Colorado, Wyoming, Montana, North Dakota, and Alberta. Long-necked sauropods ate plants and trees, whereas therapods, T Rex among them, with long nails and teeth like steak knives, ate meat. Food-getting was serious: paleontologist Paul Serena found a nasty marine dinosaur, fondly referred to as Super Croc, buried in the desert in Niger. Once the terror of the swampy banks of a long-gone Saharan river, it was about forty feet long with a six-foot skull and jaws that could crack steel.

Over their 150 million years, dinosaurs adapted to a panoply of environmental changes, from developing continents, droughts, and changing vegetation, to volcanoes, freezes, and floods. Theories of why they died off (with some exceptions) about 65 million years ago are flashpoints for paleontologists: Did an asteroid create havoc on Earth for a decade or more? Did dinosaurs simply eat everything in sight? Or was it a combination of volcanoes, rising ocean levels, drought, diseases, *and* an asteroid hit? Whatever happened, about 65 million years ago, close to 70 percent of species went extinct.

Paleontologists today are looking less for the behemoths that fill museums and more for the small creatures that lived during that time—early mammals, lizards, insects, and turtles—that might give greater insight into exactly how complex the smaller creatures were, and why some species like dinosaurs took center stage for so long and refused to leave.

Into the Field

If you enjoy working usually in hot or cold and dry areas all day, either trekking over unmapped hills looking for fossils or chipping away at rock sediment, often thinking you have found something which turns out to crumble in your hands, and if you are engulfed by the romance of the earth when oversized species dominated, and so far there seem to be zillions of them, then a dinosaur fossil dig is for you. You will learn how to spot dinosaur traces in dry riverbeds and remote deserts, how to dig with toothbrushes as you uncover something that could be the size of the Statue of Liberty, and how to make plaster casts and get the plaster off you before it hardens. Most of all, you will understand why paleontologists always have enough energy to shout and dance when they find something, even after slaving away all day in breathless heat.

NORTH AMERICA

The Judith River Formation

Late Cretaceous floods (about 75 million years ago) and later glacial melts (about 10,000 years ago) from northern Montana to Alberta, Canada, sent thousands of dinosaur carcasses into an area that in 1955 became Dinosaur Provincial Park, a World Heritage Site. More than thirty-six dinosaur species have been uncovered here, with more to come.

Canada

Royal Tyrrell Museum of Paleontology   Box 7500, Drumheller, Alberta T0J 0Y0. Tel: 888-440-4240 (toll-free); E-mail: fieldexp@ tyrrellmuseum. com; Website: www.tyrrellmuseum.com.

Located in the middle of Dinosaur Provincial Park, the museum serves as a center point for field research. This is tyrannosaurus country; come prepared for the big stuff. Day Digs for families, adults, teens, and seniors are very popular; reserve in advance. Also popular are the one-week digs in Dinosaur Provincial Park (about $1,200). A 73-million-year-old hadrosaur, or duckbilled dinosaur, will take about three years to extract from a rock ledge. Kids five to thirteen can take part in a Camp-In, join an in-house "dig, " cast a dinosaur part, and examine live reptiles before bedding down for Friday or Saturday night among the dinosaurs in the museum hall (under $50).

UNITED STATES

Montana

The Judith River Dinosaur Institute   Box 429, Malta, Montana 59538. Tel: 406-654-2323; E-mail: nmurphy@ttc.cmc.net.

This is a good place to get an overview of the Judith River Formation and to join the many researchers who flock here in the summer months to work some of the many sites. "Expedition— the 75-Million Year Journey" is the name of the program open to amateurs in conjunction with the Phillips County Museum for a five-day instruction and field dig that currently centers around an armor-plated stegosaurus. July and August, about $850. Lodging is extra, in Malta.

Egg Mountain, Montana

Museum of the Rockies   Montana State University, 600 West Kagy Boulevard, Bozeman, Montana 59717-2730.
Tel: 406-994-DINO[3466] (information); 406-994-6618; E-mail: wwwmor@montana.edu; Website: www.museumoftherockies.org.

In 1979 paleontologist John Horner found the first dinosaur nesting colony, with babies and eggs, near a rise north of Helena, Montana, that he dubbed Egg Mountain. Horner's babies were young hadrosaurs; in the museum, a model of a hadrosaur mother, named Maiasaura, resembles a large camel. Gentle plant eaters, several thousand of them died from the outpouring of an ancient volcano in the Rocky Mountains. They fell over an area about a mile long, giving amateur dinosaur lovers today a chance to delve into life during the Late Cretaceous, about 73 million years ago. The museum is a fulcrum for Horner's excellent dinosaur imagination. (For a good detective hunt for bones, see John Horner, *Dinosaur Lives*, 1997.) Montana State University crews dig in the summer.

Old Trail Museum   823 North Main Street, Choteau, Montana 59422. Tel: 406-466-5332. E-mail: otm@3rivers.net.

In 1978, at Egg Mountain, John Horner found the eggs of Troodon, a ferocious many-toothed meat eater with a large brain that lived about the same time as the gentle hadrosaurs. The Old Trail Museum has a small exhibit (a more extensive exhibit is in the Museum of the Rockies, *above*), and runs tours of Egg Mountain. It also offers two-day field courses for amateur diggers at the site in the summer. Lodging (extra) is in Choteau. Instruction in field techniques, tools, transportation to the site, and lunch, about $200 a person. Adults, families, and kids fifteen and older are welcome.

North Dakota

Marmarth Research Foundation   P. O. Box 5, Marmarth, North Dakota 58643. Tel: 701-279-6601; Website: www. marmarthresearchfoundation.org.

Whether you are a student, teacher, or interested person on the street, you can learn it all here in the summer at established sites with hadrosaurs, triceratops, as well as turtles and crocodiles from the ancient sea. Field techniques as well as fossil preparation and preservation are topics covered in the field. One day, about $75; one week (includes lodging and food), single person, about $700; family (two adults, two children), about $1,100.

The Morrison Formation

A serious flood or several floods rushed over a Jurassic plain with such force that huge species like brachiosaurus, some almost ninety feet long, were swept to their deaths. Stretching north to south across the western United States, the Morrison Formation was an ancient ocean shoreline that captured lots of footprints. Several sites with a jumble of dinosaur fossils document the many environmental events that shaped the dinosaurs' lives, from flash floods to droughts during which thousands of creatures died in crowded waterholes. Some paleontologists believe this is the most diverse collection of Jurassic dinosaurs in the world.

Colorado

Dinosaur National Monument   Dinosaur, Colorado 81610. Tel: 435-789-2115.

Recognizing the number of years it would take to extract the mismatched bones from a wall of the Morrison Formation, paleontologists built a visitors' center over and around the wall. The area of the dinosaur remains stretches from Colorado into Utah and includes the Carnegie Quarry with several hundred tons of bones. A good overview.

Dry Mesa Quarry   U. S. Forest Service, 2505 South Townsend, Montrose, Colorado 81401. Tel: 970-240-5400.

This quarry in the Uncompahgre National Forest was once a waterhole. It tells a sad story of what happens when drought overtakes an area and waterholes gradually shrink: everything from fish to mammals to some of the largest dinosaurs yet found on Earth have made this their cemetery. A mostly intact skeleton of a dinosaur 120 feet long (its shoulder blade is 8 feet), named Supersaurus, was found here. Nearby were the bones of a 35-foot-tall carnivore, Torvosaurus, that might have been competition for T Rex.

The quarry is uncovered from Memorial Day to Labor Day when paleontologists continue the dig. You can join the dig for free with the following conditions: bring your own lunch, snacks, and water, and you must drive a high-clearance vehicle to clear the rocks and ruts of the dirt road (which is dangerously slick in the rain). Digs are weather-dependent: call 970-874-6638 for weather cancellations, or to schedule a guided quarry tour, given Fridays and Saturdays at 10 A.M.

Museum of Western Colorado   233 South Fifth Street, Grand Junction, Colorado 81502. Tel: 888-488-DINO[3466] (toll-free); 970-241-9210; E-mail: mmenard@westcomuseum.org; Website: www.dinosaurjourney.org.

The first brachiosaurus (or apatosaurus, now in the Chicago Field Museum) was found near Grand Junction in 1900, an astounding seventy feet long from its waving neck to its waving tail. Check out the museum's animatronic dinosaurs. In Grand Valley, a few miles west of Grand Junction, join summer day digs on Mondays and Tuesdays (about $100, reserve early); and three-day field digs, about $700 for a family.

National Geographic Expeditions   P. O. Box 65265, Washington, DC 20035-5265. Tel: 888-966-8687 (toll-free); Website: www.nationalgeographic.com/ngexpeditions.

Spend seven days in the rugged and fascinating dinosaur country around the Museum of Western Colorado. This trip for all ages includes hikes to spot the differences between rocks and bones, a horseback trip to the Uncompahgre Plateau, and a day spent digging at the Mygatt-Moore Quarry. About $3,000.

Wyoming

Wyoming Dinosaur International Society   Box 50768, Casper, Wyoming 82605-8768. Tel: 877-996-3466 (toll-free); E-mail: info@wyodino.com; Website: www.wyodino.com.

Another Morrison Formation cache was found near Thermopolis, Wyoming. With paleontologist Robert Bakker, you can join digs in the middle of the giant plant eaters like camarosaurus and diplodocus. Dig for one day, with lunch, about $100 for one; $250 for a family of two adults, two children.

Wyoming Dinosaur Center   Box 868 Thermopolis, Wyoming 82443. Tel: 800-455-3466 (toll-free); 307-864-2997; Website: www.wyodino.com.

To have land on which to salvage some of these huge dinosaurs, researchers bought Warm Springs Ranch and built the Dinosaur Center to contain what they found.

SOUTH AMERICA

Argentina

Earthwatch   3 Clock Tower Place, Suite 100, Box 75, Maynard, Massachusetts 01754-0075. Tel: 800-776-0188 (toll-free); 978-461-0081; Fax: 978-461-2332; E-mail: info@earthwatch.org; Website: www.earthwatch.org.

Once part of Pangea, the northwest corner of Argentina, a rugged area so torn by volcanoes it is called the Valley of the Moon, might hold evidence of the oldest dinosaurs on Earth. The Ischigualasto Formation, located in Provincial Park, a World Heritage Site, has an undisturbed sequence of triassic (the earliest) dinosaurs that had begun to develop into different species. One of the first finds of early dinosaurs, eoraptor, a six-foot bipedal meat eater, was made here.

If you like camping out in a really remote desert area that is alternately hot and cold and often windy, where water is rationed for bathing, and your private bathroom is "a shovel, a roll of toilet paper, and a great view, " then this dinosaur hunt is for you. With three Argentinian paleontologists, you will excavate, map, wrap in plaster, catalog, and spend evenings immersed in dinosaur talk. Twelve days, including food, wine, and campsite, about $1,900.

ASIA

Mongolia

In 1927 Roy Chapman Andrews took a team from the American Museum of Natural History to the Flaming Cliffs in Mongolia to find ancient human bones. Instead, he uncovered the first dinosaur egg nest, a discovery that led to hundreds of dinosaur bones that more closely resemble birds than reptiles.

Paleontologists who dig the cliffs play with the idea that these fossils were the basis of the myth of griffins among ancient Greeks. The lion-bodied, bird-headed creatures with a sharp, hooked claw were often sculpted in marble to defend royal palaces and were believed to have been ferocious creatures that guarded caves of gold in the north. To modern paleontologists who found the bones of what looked like bird-headed, lion-bodied dinosaurs with a sharp, hooked claw at the entrance to caves in the Flaming Cliffs in Mongolia, griffins have become more than a fable. (See Michael Novacek, *Dinosaurs of the Flaming Cliffs*, 1996.)

Nomadic Expeditions, Inc.   1095 Cranbury-South River Road, Suite 20A, Jamesburg, New Jersey 08831. Tel: 800-998-6634 (toll-free); 609-860-9008; E-mail: info@nomadicexpeditions.com; Website: www.nomadicexpeditions.com.

Join Canadian paleontologist Phillip Currie from the Royal Tyrrell Museum in Alberta and Mongolian paleontologist Dr. Baramgarav from the Mongolian Academy of Sciences to dig the Flaming Cliffs, described by Roy Chapman as looking like a medieval city with "castles and turrets with spires." Spend the days prospecting and excavating and the nights in traditional Mongolian ger camps or tent camps. Seventeen days from Ulan Bataar, about $3,800. The climate has preserved fossils well, and you can expect to find Cretaceous dinosaurs. Previous digs have uncovered huge eggs and fragments of velociraptor and protoceratops, a chunky dinosaur with a kind of rhino horn.

Selena Travel Co., Ltd.   *In the U. S.:* Sokol Tours, 357 W. Fourth Street, No. 1, Boston, Massachusetts 02127. Tel: 617-269-2659; E-mail: sokol@sokoltours.com. *In Mongolia:* P. O. Box 320, Ulanbataar, 26 Mongolia. E-mail: selena@magicnet.mn; Website: www.selenatravel.com.

To get to know the area around the Flaming Cliffs and many

other dinosaur sites in the Gobi Desert, Selena Travel will take you to sites where you can camp, and to Vulture Gorge to see rare argali (wild sheep), ibex, and Asiatic wild ass. Eight days, all meals, no international airfare, about $1,100 double occupancy, $1,400 single.

Websites

For a basic list of dinosaurs with lots of information on sites and species: www.dinodata.net.

Also see www.bbc.co.uk/dinosaurs.

DINOSAURS TODAY

Plesiosaurs in Lakes: The Loch Ness Mystery

Do dinosaurs still exist? Birds, sea turtles, alligators, crocodiles, several species of insects, and amphibians such as the Komodo dragon and marine iguana have direct lineages to the Cretaceous. But tantalizing tales of plesiosaurs—large, long-necked, marine creatures that took to the oceans when other dinosaurs became land-dwelling plant eaters—persist throughout the world and throughout history.

If a plesiosaur got stuck in a lake that no one lived near, it might never make the news. No one knows how many large ancient dragons are trapped in deep lakes around the world with no one to notice; their presence is in direct proportion to the presence of interested researchers and tourists. A "sea serpent" terrorized the New England coast in the late 1800s—visits enthusiastically documented by natural historians and local newspapers advertising trips to see it. Lake Champlain in Vermont (and Canada) harbors "Champ," a plesiosaur-type creature that plays regular cat-and-mouse games with shore residents and tourists.

Arguably, the lake with the greatest number of sightings of a very long reptile-like, small-headed, long-necked resident is Loch Ness in northern Scotland, near Inverness. Long draped in legend—a monk from the island of Iona was said to have been attacked by a lake monster and rescued by a fellow monk who later became St. Colomba—the 800-foot deep, long and narrow lake (twenty-five miles long by one mile wide), seems to host an obscure large "something" that ruffles the water and troubles researchers. The murky waters have been charted with side-scan sonar and photographed with submarine strobes; its underwater sounds have been recorded and analyzed at all frequencies; its bottom has even been trekked by a marathoner in a diving suit. But Nessie the unknown resident still refuses to produce proof. Is it a dinosaur? A giant sturgeon? Electromagnetic waves from a sunken UFO? Theories fly.

In the 1930s when highway engineers blasted the area on one side of the lake for what became the A82, the number of creature sightings soared, leading some to speculate that the sound of the blasting irritated Nessie and brought it out of its nest.

More recently, researchers have begun to correlate sightings with the seismic activity under the lake. Loch Ness sits on a fault line that produces about three earthquakes a century—mostly north of the lake where the majority of sightings occur. Are the waves on the surface of the lake seismic activity? Or a leftover Jurassic reptile coming up for air and its close-up?

Lots of sites keep you up to the minute: www.lochness.co.uk (has a web cam); www.simegen.com; www.loch-ness.org. Loch Ness is flush with little hotels and boaters ready to take passengers for a spin on the lake. Summer is the season to see Nessie, although local tour operators are stretching the season into winter.

Iain and Kellie Mackay   Highland Voyages, c/o Distillery Cottages, Brackla, Nairn IV12 5QY, Scotland. Tel/Fax: 011 44 01667 40 44 41; E-mail: highvoyages@freeuk.com; Website: www. highlandvoyages.co.uk.

You can sail on a "retired herring drifter," a completely refitted sixty-foot wooden sailing vessel that was a fishing boat. Named *Eala Bhan*, which means "white swan" in Gaelic, the boat, which has heated cabins for twelve guests, carries an echo sounder whose results you can watch simultaneously on a screen. Weekend trip, from about £100 to £150 (about $150 to $225).

Early Mammals: The Big Pig Dig

Badlands National Park   P. O. Box 6, Interior, South Dakota
57750. Tel: 605-433-5240.

Between dinosaurs (65,000 years ago) and mammoths (12,000
years ago), mammals took the stage and developed into creatures
like archeotherium, or the big pig that resembled a rhinoceros but
was equally at home in the water. In 1993, tourists in the Badlands
National Park in South Dakota were the first to spot its backbone
sticking out of the shale. Since then, paleontologists have found
8,000 bones of mammals of the Oligocene period: three-toed
horses, saber-toothed tigers, a foot-tall deer, and the giant pig.

Located among 244, 000 acres of unusual rock spires and sharp
hills, the Big Pig Dig takes place from June to August. Students and
pros do the work, but visitors are welcome to watch and listen to
paleontologists tell the story of the mammals and their adaptations,
as well as how paleontologists work.

Mammoths: The Ice Age

Woolly mammoths and mastodons populated Earth during the Ice
Age, or Pleistocene epoch, from about 25,000 to 10,000 years ago.
Some mammoths fell into pits or were caught in glaciers and locked
in blocks of ice. Jarkov, the famous Siberian mammoth, excavated in
1997 after 20,000 frozen years, was slowly warmed to be analyzed
scientifically. Other mammoths ran out of vegetation or suffered
from disease, stopped reproducing, and ultimately became extinct.
Elephants, however, count mammoths as their ancestors.

Mammoths were the largest thing of the Pleistocene era, or Ice
Age, but they had some colorful companions: saber-toothed tigers,
lions, giant ground sloths, camels, dire wolves, and short-faced
bears.

George C. Page Museum of La Brea Discoveries   5801
Wilshire Boulevard, Los Angeles 90036. Tel: 323-857-6311.

To get a terrific overview of this period, you can visit not only a museum with reconstructed creatures, but the Tar (or asphalt) Pit into which they fell and from which they were retrieved several thousand years later. Still bubbling, black, and unappealing, the La Brea Tar Pits, or Pit 91, nearby, are still yielding evidence of this period. And all this in the middle of downtown LA.

The Page Museum offers the opportunity to volunteers to join a Pit 91 dig for two months during the summer, but with the following conditions: you must be at least sixteen and, before you join the dig, be willing to work one day a week for three months in the paleontology lab, helping to sort microfossils and to learn how to clean and polish and catalog fossils. Apply at the museum by filling out an application and having an interview.

The Mammoth Site   Box 692, 1800 Highway 18, Truck Route, Hot Springs, South Dakota 57747. Tel: 605-745-6017; E-mail: mammoth@mammothsite.com; Website: www.mammothsite.com.

About 25,000 years ago near Hot Springs, South Dakota, a giant sinkhole masqueraded as a waterhole that trapped a huge variety of Pleistocene creatures. It was not discovered until 1974. So far, geologist and anthropologist Larry Agenbroad (who helped excavate Jarkov, the Siberian mammoth) has dug up the remains of several species of mammoths, short-faced bears, and, recently, lion. Large lions (bigger than present-day African lions) hunted from Canada to the tip of South America until 10,500 years ago.

For two months in the summer, you can join Agenbroad at the Mammoth Site as part of an Earthwatch team on an ongoing, long-term excavation.

Earthwatch   3 Clock Tower Place, Suite 100, Box 75, Maynard, Massachusetts 01754-0075. Tel: 800-776-0188 (toll-free); 978-461-0081; Fax: 978-461-2332; E-mail: info@earthwatch.org; Website: www.earthwatch.org.

Fifteen days, shared rooms, ranch food, about $1,800.

27

PANDA BEARS

If giant pandas did not exist, they would probably be invented by an enterprising toy company. The ultimate cuddly creature, with a perpetual smile, improbable black eyes, and a roly-poly physique, the giant panda bears that don't live in toy stores live in heavily forested mountain ranges in Sichuan Province, southwestern China. It is an ever-dwindling habitat, however, due to increasing human population. Solitary, shy, and almost exclusively bamboo eaters, the giant panda survives in isolated mountain pockets, guarding its young from predator cats and poachers.

They are not easy to track or see in the wild, but both Chinese and Western conservationists believe there are about 1,000 giant pandas in the wild, in need of help if their species is to survive. That's why they are the logo for the World Wildlife Foundation, whose website is www.panda.org. They have become the poster herbivore for endangered species, chosen because pandas make such a good celebrity "flagship species" for conservation, more appealing than the equally endangered fruit bat.

ANCESTORS

Cousins of raccoons, other bears, and the much smaller fox- or cat-like red panda, black-and-white giant pandas are unique. They have six toes, don't stand on their hind legs as other bears do, and vocalize only in the presence of the opposite sex during their brief mating season, which lasts for a couple of months in the spring.

Apparently pandas have always lived in China; pandas' grinding molars have been excavated from a Chinese cave dated to a few hundred thousand years ago, during the early Pleistocene.

About six feet from tip to toe, they weigh about 280 pounds and spend most if not all of their waking hours eating bamboo—shoots in the spring, leaves in the summer, and stems in the winter—although their molars allow them to crush bone, which they have been known to do on rare occasions when they eat meat.

In the 1920s they were the last exotic trophy to be bagged as exhibits for museums. The chic found them amusing and adorable; in a poem titled "That Reminds Me," poet Ogden Nash wrote of a young man courting a young woman in the most ideal circumstances. Standing together in the moonlight, he asks her softly what she is thinking, and she replies, "I was wondering how many bamboo shoots a day it takes to feed a baby giant panda."

In the 1930s, a few giant pandas wound up in zoos. It wasn't until the early 1970s that diplomatic relations between the United States and China warmed enough for President Nixon to trade a pair of Alaskan musk ox for a pair of giant pandas. No one knows how many Chinese fell in love with our musk ox, but the pandas in the National Zoo began to convince whole generations of children that conservation is important, and the endangered giant panda is at the top of the list.

Enter: The Market

In the 1990s the giant panda became a rainmaker for China, and the days of giving giant pandas as gifts were over. The international demand for pandas prompted the Chinese government to allow certain zoos to keep pandas temporarily, at a yearly fee of more than $1 million. After a ban on pandas (because they were endangered) in this country was lifted, pandas were allowed to spend a year, with renewable option, at the San Diego Zoo (Shi Shi and Bai Yum arrived in 1998, and now have a baby); Zoo Atlanta (Lun Lun and Yang Yang came in 1999); the National Zoo in Washington (Mei

Xiang and Tian Tian in 2000 replaced the late Hsing Hsing and Liang Liang); and the Memphis Zoo (Le Le and Ya Ya, 2003, the latest to arrive in the United States).

Part of the American Zoo and Aquarium (AZA) Species Survival Plan, the rented giant panda bears come with certain conditions: if they can be bred in zoos successfully, China owns the babies as well, and equal funds will be given to helping pandas survive in the Sichuan wild, what Wildlife Conservation Society zoologist George Schaller has called "a moral obligation to maintain species in the wild." This involves money to develop more reserves in China and train specialists to care for pandas as well as educate the public on their meaning.

So far, zoo breeding hasn't been a great success. Most of the tiny 2½-ounce cubs that have been born have not lived beyond six months. Not big breeders in the wild—although some Chinese scientists maintain they are doing okay—giant pandas are not interested in sex until they are between five and six; they tend to have single births separated by two to three years. Currently researchers are trying to identify why artificial insemination seems to be the only reliable way to reproduce pandas in zoos—observers speculate that maybe the pheromones are wrong, or maybe familiarity breeds disinterest. (See Susan Lumpkin and John Seidensticker, *Smithsonian Book of Giant Pandas*, 2002; and George Schaller and Lu Zhi, *Giant Pandas in the Wild*, 2002.)

Giant pandas are a national treasure in China. They are a lot of zoo-goers' private treasures, as well. Somehow, when giant pandas roll around, climb and tumble, or lie on their backs and chew bamboo, they personify a kind of innocence that we need to protect.

Zoos

San Diego Zoo   Balboa Park, 2090 Zoo Drive, San Diego, California 92101. Tel: 619-234-3153; Website: www.sandiegozoo.org.

Check out the panda cam, which also tracks the baby cub.

Giant panda bears do well in captivity and charm everyone who sees them, like this one that plays with its dish at the National Zoo, Washington, *D.C. Gary Stolz, U.S. Fish and Wildlife Service; www.fws.gov*

Zoo Atlanta   Grant Park, Atlanta, Georgia 30303. Tel: 888-945-5432 (toll-free); 404-624-5600; Website: www.zooatlanta.org.

The United Parcel Service donated one of their Boeing 767s to transport the giant pandas to Atlanta. UPS also donated a $625,000 five-year grant for the pandas. Their panda cam is operative Tuesday through Friday, 10 A.M. to 5 P.M.

National Zoo   3001 Connecticut Avenue, NW, Washington, D.C. 20008. Tel: 202-673-4800 (info); Website: www.natzoo.si.edu.

The National Zoo's pandas are the center of a lot of educational projects. Check out the panda cam.

Memphis Zoo   2000 Galloway, Memphis, Tennessee 38104. Tel: 901-276-WILD[9453]; Website: www.memphiszoo.org.

The Panda Exhibit is so popular, the tickets are timed. You can watch the pandas on the panda cam, or take advantage of the Zoo's Panda Hotel Package trips.

China

The Chinese government has set aside more than thirty areas in Sichuan for giant panda reserves and national parks. The main center for conservation studies is the **Chengdu Giant Panda Research Base**, and, seventy-five miles northwest, the **Wolong Giant Panda Protection Research Center**, where giant pandas are bred (often with artificial insemination and in vitro fertilization), and allowed to grow up in a semi-natural area, called Giant Panda Park, where they are not allowed to forget their wild roots to be adept at living in the wild when they are reintroduced.

Pandas injured in the wild are also treated here and released when they have recovered; and long-term panda conservation research is ongoing. The center is in the process of developing tourism facilities on more than 400 acres.

Both Chengdu and Wolong are open to the public for tours, or you can offer to spend the day as a volunteer, tending to food preparation, cleaning, and so forth.

In-Country Tour Companies

If you are in Beijing, these companies can arrange trips to some of the Sichuan Panda Reserves, as well as the Chengdu Research Station.

Log on to www.chinagiantpanda.com to arrange everything from a half-day (about $20) to seventeen-day ($1,500) giant panda–oriented trip.

See also: www.4panda.com; and www.chinaonlinetravel.com.; and www.wildgiantpanda.com, which also has some interesting photos and news of giant pandas in the wild.

United States

World Wildlife Fund   Membership Travel Program, 1250 24th Street, NW, Washington, D.C. 20037-1182. Tel: 888-993-8687 (toll-free); 202-778-9683; Website: www.worldwildlife.org/travel.

Visit Chengdu and Wolong Panda Preserve and meet with Chinese experts to hear the latest on panda research, plus see as many as forty at one time at Wolong. Fourteen days, about $7,000, includes airfare from San Francisco.

Posh Journeys   530 E. Patriot Blvd. No. 172, Reno, Nevada 89511. Tel:/Fax: 775-852-5105; E-mail: contact@poshjourneys.com; Website: www.poshjourneys.com.

Posh Journeys has designed an interesting tour that includes everything from a visit to the Summer Palace, the Terra Cotta Warriors, a silk factory, and two days as a volunteer at the Wolong Giant Panda Bear Reserve. After a briefing, you will help clean, take bamboo to the hillside bins, and hand-feed the pandas. You actually are able to cuddle a young panda on the final day. Fourteen days, about $3,700.

Geographic Expeditions   2627 Lombard Street, San Francisco, California 94123. Tel: 800-777-8183 (toll-free); Fax: 415-346-5535; E-mail: info@geoex.com; Website: www.geoex.com.

The Wild and the Sacred takes you by car through the Sichuan Province to the Wanglang Panda Reserve, plus a stop at Chengdu, before heading off to other nature reserves and monasteries in the area. Sixteen days, about $5,000.

Natural Habitat Adventures   2945 Center Green Court, Suite H, Boulder, Colorado 80301-9539. Tel: 800-543-8917 (toll-free); Website www.nathab.com.

Visit at the Chengdu Research Base and see the pandas inside and out in the vast enclosures. Then travel to Wolong Panda Reserve and spend two days among pandas with Chinese panda experts. Twelve days, about $6,000.

28

SNOW LEOPARDS

DISAPPEARING CATS

Masters of illusion, snow leopards have a way of vanishing before your eyes if you are lucky enough to see one. Besides being beautifully camouflaged to fit into the gray craggy ledges and white snow patches of their habitat, they are, like the Yeti, few and far between. Hard facts on their numbers are hard to come by—estimates range from the hundreds to the low thousands; but researchers do know that for decades they have been hunted by poachers for their pelts for fur clothes, and bones and body parts for Oriental medicines. Farmers on Soviet collective farms used to trap them for a few extra dollars; current farmers kill them because they eat their livestock. Today snow leopards are listed as critically endangered.

Snow leopards like high altitudes, from about 6,000 to 20,000 feet, which is also the habitat of their chief prey: ibex, Markhor goats (which have spiral horns, 5 feet long), endangered Argali sheep (also with 5-foot horns), blue sheep (really brown, with a bluish tint to their white underbelly), musk deer, marmots, and hares. They can tolerate temperatures as low as minus 21 degrees Fahrenheit and range across political boundaries from the Himalayas in India north to the Altai Mountains in Central Asia.

Unlike their tiger-lion-leopard-jaguar cousins, snow leopards do not roar. Slightly smaller, they also have a round head and a thick, long tail that allows them to fairly fly through the air as they leap from crag to crag or on top of prey. No incidents of any attacks on human beings have been reported, and they are fairly docile when they are caught. They are breathtakingly beautiful; Peter Mathiessen wrote a whole book searching the Himalayas for the snow leopard (1978) and concluded that just to know that the snow leopard exists, "that its frosty eyes watch us from the mountains—that is enough."

The International Snow Leopard Trust is working with other conservation groups in snow leopard enterprises to compensate villagers from Mongolia to the Kyrgz Republic for *not* killing snow leopards by giving them a bonus for crafts goods they sell. (Goods range from finger puppets of animals and cashmere mittens to an entire authentic twenty-foot Mongolian ger, or tent; see: www.snowleopard.org; www.artfortheanimals.org.)

In Hemis National Park in the Ladakh Range in northern India, the Snow Leopard Trust is helping to train local nature guides to spot the urine spray markings, claw prints, pieces of fur left on rocks, and spoor of snow leopards, to be able to lead tour groups. The trust is also helping to build predator-proof corrals for farmers' livestock.

Since practically nothing is known for certain about snow leopards, you can join any of several field research groups engaged pri-

Secure at a sanctuary, a young snow leopard plays. *www.BigCatRescue.org*

marily in doing snow leopard census counts, trying to gauge their natural range (forty to sixty square miles, maybe), and what small mammals they rely on for food when their usual diet is interrupted by local overhunting. Work ranges in high altitudes and can be challenging; no company guarantees ever actually seeing a snow leopard.

But you might.

Southern Mongolia

With a Conservation Group

International Snow Leopard Trust   4649 Sunnyside Avenue N., Seattle, Washington 98103. Tel: 206-632-2421; E-mail: info@ snowleopard.org; Website: www.snowleopard.org.

In the southern end of the Gobi Desert at Mount Noen in Mongolia, the International Snow Leopard Trust, a conservation group devoted to saving the snow leopard from extinction, runs a Mission to Mongolia, a trip designed to introduce visitors to the environment in which snow leopards thrive. Hoping each day that one will show itself, you look for snow leopard scrapes, pawprints, scent sprays, and scat. You also do snow leopard transects and interviews with local villagers to find out what problems they have with snow leopards. The Snow Leopard Trust has built predator-proof corrals to protect farmers' livestock, routinely killed by hungry snow leopards. Overhunting of wild sheep and goats has left snow leopards without prey.

Sponsored by Karakorum Expeditions in Mongolia, the trip is fifteen days: lodging in gers, three square meals a day, travel by 4-WD; about $2,800. Fly in from Ulaan Bataar.

Kyrgyzstan

Join a Scientific Project

WildWings   First Floor, 577/579 Fishponds Road, Bristol, BS16 3AF UK. Tel: 0117-965 8333; E-mail: wildinfo@wildwings.co.uk; Website: www.ecovolunteer.org.uk.

Part of the International Ecovolunteer Network, WildWings sponsors a field research expedition to Issyk-Kul Biosphere Reserve in eastern Kyrgyzstan, Russia, to participate in a snow leopard census. Located within the 26,000-square-mile reserve at about 7,800 feet altitude, the research camp is near Lake Issyk-Kul, the second largest high-altitude lake in the world. Data you will help collect are geographic information system (GIS) positions from transects; signs of snow leopard activity, from kills to claw marks; and counts and locations of snow leopards' prey, especially marmots. A translator will help, working with local zoologists. Travel to research stations will be on horseback and on foot. You need to consider yourself fit enough to work at high altitudes and to deal with radical weather changes from 40 degrees Celsius (>100 degrees Fahrenheit) to snowsqualls. Stay in all-male and all-female comfortable yurts, which serve as bedroom and living room, and expect to eat well. The meeting point is Bishkek Airport. You must commit to two weeks; you can stay longer if you wish; about £850 (about $1,300.). May to October teams.

Central Asia: Altai Republic

Biosphere Expeditions   Sprat's Water near Carlton Colville, The Broads National Park, Suffolk NR33 8BP UK. Tel: 011 44 1502 583085; E-mail: info@biosphere-expeditions.org; Website: www. biosphere-expeditions.org.

In the Altai Mountains in Central Asia, where China, Russia, Mongolia, and Kazakhstan come together, join a field team that will track snow leopards and their prey. Their prey are equally interesting, because rarely seen: the Altai ibex, a hefty goat with horns shaped like a scimitar, and the endangered and aggressive Argali sheep with huge horns that curve outward. Base camp is 6,500 feet. From here you travel in Land Rovers and on foot upward to 7,500 feet to track snow leopards by their signs. You will spend one night in an observation hut to use video traps and field scopes in the hope of seeing snow leopards. You will find areas where the sheep and ibex tend to congregate, and identify such small mammals as marmots, which inhabit the region and might serve as alternative prey for the snow leopards.

Trips take place in the summer, but weather is very variable. The locale is breathtakingly beautiful, remote, with a huge biodiversity, and largely untraveled. And virtually nothing is known about snow leopards in this corridor between Mongolia and Russia.

Meet at the airport in Novosibirsk, then spend two days traveling on good roads in a comfortable Land Rover 300 miles each day past steep gorges and waterfalls, stretches of tundra, and through astonishing mountain passes to the remote field station in the foothills of the Altai Mountains. Lodging about 6,000 feet is in one- and two-person dome tents, with showers, toilets, and good food. You must have a moderate to high fitness level; expect to walk up to ten miles a day on uneven terrain. Every team member will be rotated on tasks and have rest days. Two weeks, about $1,900.

Tour Snow Leopards' Range

Hemis National Park, Ladakh, India

Discovery Initiatives   The Travel House, 51 Castle Street, Cirencester, Gloucestershire, GL7 1QD, UK. Tel: 011 44 01285 643333; E-mail: Enquiry@discoveryinitiatives.com; Website: www. discoveryinitiatives.com.

"The predator is tied to the prey," and on this trip you concentrate on the prey, which just might lead you to the snow leopard itself. From Delhi you travel to the Hemi National Park in historic Ladakh, slowly getting acclimated. Then you hike to the village of Zinchen at 10,000 feet, camp, then up to Rumbak at 13,000 feet, camp, then up to the base of Chortenchen at 13,500 feet. Overnight in Stok Kangri at 15,000 feet before you begin your descent. You finish the trip visiting monasteries in Ladakh before returning to Delhi.

You *will* be among Bharal (blue) sheep, ibex, wild ass, marmots, Tibetan hares, wolves, and foxes. You will see golden eagles and vultures. You have as good a chance as any for seeing snow leopard, and you will certainly understand its territory and the people who share that territory. Clearly this trip is not for everyone because of the demands of hiking on uneven terrain in extreme altitudes. Trips in March and October, fourteen days; about $1,900, from Delhi to Delhi.

Altai Mountains, Mongolia

Mountain Travel Sobek   6420 Fairmount Avenue, El Cerrito, California 95430-9962. Tel: 800-687-6235 (toll-free); 510-527-8100; Fax: 510-525-7710; E-mail: info@mtsobek.com; Website: www.mtsobek.com.

From Ulaan Baatar, spend seven days hiking up to 10,000 feet in snow leopard country, the Altai Mountains in Mongolia among the Kazakh nomads. With horses carrying the gear, spend three days hiking to a mountain campsite beside a glacier among snow leopard prey, Argali sheep and ibex. Also spend a day in the Altai Tavan Bogd National Park, and hike to the site of petroglyphs on Tsagaan Ereg Mountain. Fitness is a requirement: moderate to strenuous hiking on uneven terrain. Nine nights in tents, three in hotels, all meals, good guides, about $4,600.

Websites

For more information on snow leopards, see: www.snow.leopards.com (or www.lazycat.org).

For the Cat Specialist Group, see: lynx.uio.no/catfolk.

To watch snow leopards, live, on a web cam at the Bronx Zoo: www.earthcam.com/usa/newyork/snowleopards.

To adopt a snow leopard: www.snowleopard.org; or call 206-832-2421.

www.tigerhaven.org.

Various zoos have snow leopards, which can be adopted. Examples are:

St. Louis Zoo: www.stlzoo.org.

National Zoo: www.natzoo.si.org.

New England: www.zoonewengland.org.

29

TIGERS

INVISIBLE CATS

In the 1960s the U.S. Navy hired popular Italian fashion designer Emilio Pucci to design a pattern for a battleship that would make it invisible on the high seas. Using exactly the same swirling curves in lavender, hot pinks, and greens that he used in his dress designs to paint the vast walls of the battleship, Pucci miraculously made the ship disappear.

Somehow, light breaking across the irregular black-and-orange stripes of a tiger give it that same ability to blend in to tree trunks, waving grass, even rocks in a stream. Tigers become invisible; many people might have seen one and not known it. That's why there is no guarantee that you will see tigers on a trip through an Indian national park.

Weighing about 500 pounds, nine feet long, and powerfully muscular, tigers are the largest cat on Earth. Some of the tigers that were killed by British hunters a century ago measured close to twelve feet. Hidden most of the time in the tall grass, they nevertheless are good swimmers, their big heads incongruously moving across a wide stream. Not as fast as lions, they use a stealth attack, waiting until their prey is about six feet away, then leap. Tigers are also the only cat documented to be man eaters—deliberately seeking out human beings to devour.

Where Have All the Tigers Gone?

Despite the fact they are ferocious, greatly feared, and very good at not being seen, tigers are literally disappearing as a species. Of the original eight species of tiger covering most of Asia from Siberia to Indonesia, only five species are left, and some of them are counted in the hundreds. A 1998 census of all Asian tigers found there are between 5,000 and 7,000, most of them Bengal tigers in India. Researchers believe there are only between 300 and 400 Siberian tigers, the largest tiger in the world, and between 20 and 30 in South China.

Tiger Cure-All

Squeezed off their range like many other large cats, tigers are trying to manage a need for meat and the space in which to hunt it, and they keep abutting small farms or new villages with police with guns. Poachers, outlawed and illegal, stalk tigers more for their bones than for their skins. Hunted all over Asia, tiger body parts are sold for use in Oriental and folk medicines: whiskers curb toothache; claws are a sedative; bones alleviate rheumatism. In a market in a small Chinese town, a tiger jawbone sells for $15; rib bone for $4.50 an inch. Because they can be tracked in the snow in winter, Siberian tigers are especially at risk of poachers.

Researchers found they had to start from scratch to piece together tigers' private lives. To figure out its hunting range, they start with a census, counting individuals by noting idiosyncrasies in whiskers and stripes. Because tigers are completely elusive, darting and radio-collaring give insights.

Socially, tigers are happy alone. Males visit females only to mate; otherwise the social group is mother-and-cubs. Tigers fiercely guard their territories marked with urine spray and claw marks, and males have access to all the females within a particular territory. In Royal Chitwan National Park, Nepal, a radio-tracking study found that females had a home range of about eight miles; males, between twenty-three and forty miles.

Tiger Ancestors

In 1998, researchers from the American Museum of Natural History did a mitochondrial DNA study of the Sumatran tiger and discovered that it was a completely different species from other tigers, and therefore, unable to breed with other tigers. Physically it is the smallest, about seven to eight feet long. What researchers realized was that some of the 500 or so Sumatran tigers that exist need to be in captive breeding programs, or risk extinction.

Not descended from saber-toothed tigers that went extinct, modern tigers began as tiny tree mammals about 250 million years ago. The first real evidence of a tiger comes from skulls dating from the middle Ice Age in China. By the late Ice Age, tigers moved into Siberia and India and were much bigger than they are today. Extremely adaptable, they live in arid lands, wet marshlands, snowy mountains, hot humid tropics, and forests. They eat fish, birds, mammals; in India they prefer chital, deer that travel in herds of a hundred, and sambar, an eight-foot tall deer with four-foot horns. Given the chance, they also eat moose (in Siberia), rhinos, water buffalo, and elephant babies.

Why Eat Human Beings?

Why they eat people is not understood. In studies done in Nepal's Royal Chitwan Park, Fiona Sunquist and Mel Sunquist (see *Tiger Moon*, 1997) found that lone males defeated by other males and ejected from their territory were most likely to become man eaters. Others believe that it happens only in extreme situations, when a tiger is wounded and in pain, or surprised in a nest with cubs. A British bird-watcher who stumbled upon a tiger den in the high grass in the 1980s in India was immediately attacked and eaten. Some speculate that a mother could teach her cubs to add an occasional human being to the diet.

Always a symbol of power and beauty, tigers confound Indians. In fact, some Indian villagers believe tigers have the ability to shape-shift back and forth into human form. Villagers' ambivalent feelings about tigers extend to the death of a man eater: when it is killed, villagers scatter flowers over the dead tiger's body.

One story is told of a Brahmin who came upon a tiger that had fallen into a well. The tiger begged him to help; the Brahmin refused, saying he didn't want to be eaten. But the tiger called him back and promised it would not eat the man once it was freed. So the trusting Brahmin saved the tiger. The end of the story is that the tiger bestowed upon the Brahmin gold, happiness, and prosperity. Conservationists are hoping to convince villagers of the same thing.

Trips to See Tigers

India has about twenty-seven wildlife reserves and national parks. The best for possibly seeing tigers are Bandhavgarh National Park in central India, and Corbett National Park in the north. Ranthambore National Park is popular, and the resident tigers tolerate being watched. In Nepal, the Royal Chitwan Park has been in the vanguard of tiger preservation since 1984 when they set aside more than 300 square miles for tigers in the Parsa Wildlife Reserve, east of Royal Chitwan.

Monsoon season, from about June to September, is not a good time to travel to India. Some of the parks are closed.

Betchart Expeditions, Inc.   17050 Montebello Road, Cupertino, California 95014-5435. Tel: 800-252-4910 (toll-free); 408-252-4910; E-mail: karen@betchartexpeditions.com; Website: www.betchartexpeditions.com.

Betchart runs an annual trip to Ranthambore and Bandhavgarh national parks, as well as Bharatpur bird sanctuary with expert naturalist guide James Jiler. Fourteen days, about $3,500, plus international airfare from Paris to Delhi.

Mountain Travel Sobek   6420 Fairmount Avenue, El Cerrito, California 95430-9962. Tel: 800-687-6235 (toll-free); 510-527-8100; Fax: 510-525-7710; E-mail: info@mtsobek.com; Website: www.mtsobek.com.

With profits donated to the conservation group Fund for the Tiger, this Save the Tiger trip explores some of the measures being taken by conservation groups against poachers. Traveling on foot, by Land Rover, and elephant back, you visit Bandhavgarh National Park to see tigers and meet those in charge of a new conservation project; see what antipoaching patrols are doing in Corbett National Park; and meet with Belinda Wright of the Wildlife Protection Society of India and producer of the National Geographic special on tigers. Then you go to Royal Chitwan National Park in Nepal on the trail of poachers with conservationist Charles McDougal, author of *The Face of the Tiger*. In Nepal, you stay at Tiger Tops Jungle Lodge in the Royal Chitwan Park. Expect to see tigers, greater one-horned rhino, and the ungainly sloth bear, as well as marsh muggers (Indian crocs), and gharial crocodiles (the big ones with a long narrow snout and lots of super sharp teeth). Fourteen days, about $3,800, plus $550 internal airfare. International airfare extra.

International Snow Leopard Trust 4649 Sunnyside Avenue N., Seattle, Washington 98103. Tel: 206-632-2421; E-mail: info@snowleopard.org; Website: www.snowleopard.org.

Somehow the stripes become a disguise in the reeds and grass.
www.BigCatRescue.org

This seventeen-day trip takes you to Ranthambhoi   azi-
ranga National parks (as well as Delhi and the Taj Ma   et
with the Snow Leopard Trust's India program director (t
Mishra who will take you to the Darjeeling Zoo and discus
An optional trip is offered to the Sasan Gir Forest to see the
lions. Seventeen days, about $6,200, includes round-trip a.
from Seattle (or another U.S. gateway) to Delhi.

Discovery Initiatives   The Travel House, 51 Castle Street,
Cirencester, Gloucestershire, GL7 1QD, UK. Tel: 011 01285
643333; E-mail: Enquiry@discoveryinitiatives.com; Website:
www.discoveryinitiatives.com.

This company runs four tiger trips to India with various
emphases. One in-depth tiger tour examines the problems of tigers
in Kanha, Bandhavgarh, and the new Panna national parks. The trip
will donate $1,000 to tiger conservation and is especially recom-
mended for photographers. Fourteen days, about $4,500.

The following companies offer general wildlife trips:

Bestway Tours and Safaris   Suite 206, 8678 Greenall Avenue,
Burnaby V5J 3M6, British Columbia, Canada. Tel: 800-663-0844
(toll-free); 604-264-7378; E-mail: bestway@bestway.com; Website:
www.bestway.com.

Exotic India and Nepal visits Nepal and northern India and
includes a visit to the Sariska National Park near Delhi, originally
formed to protect tigers. Fourteen days, about U.S.$2,300.

International Expeditions, Inc.   One Environs Park, Helena,
Alabama 35080-7200. Tel: 800-633-4734 (toll-free); E-mail:
nature@ietravel.com; Website: www.internationalexpeditions.com.

Visit the parks and palaces in India to help understand the place
of the tiger in Indian society. Fourteen days, about $3,000.

In Nepal:

ɔyal **Chitwan National Park**   Website: www.welcomenepal.com.

Tiger Mountain   E-mail: info@tigermountain.com; Website: www.tigermountain.com/ttops/tigertops.htm.

Stay at Tiger Tops, a lodge, or a tented camp (on stilts) in the park. Take solar-heated showers, read by kerosene lamps, take an elephant safari.

Websites

For updates and information on tigers, see the tiger information site: www.5tigers.org.

To see tigers happy in a zoo, visit the six Siberian tigers installed at Tiger Mountain in the Bronx Zoo. Website: www.wcs.org.

Project Tiger, the Indian conservation site: envfor.nic.in.

Save the Tiger Fund is a project of the U.S. Fish and Wildlife Foundation in conjunction with Exxon Mobil Corporation. See www.nfwf.org.; www.savethetigerfund.org.

See also: www.tigeraid.org.

www.wildaid.org is the WildAid website, an activist wild animal protection organization that targets and arrests poachers.

Adopt a Tiger Sites

Hornocker Wildlife Research Institute   University of Idaho, P.O. Box 3246, Moscow, Idaho 83845. Tel: 888-844-3744; E-mail: hwi@uidaho.edu.

Maurice Hornocker, tiger researcher and senior conservationist of the Wildlife Conservation Society, will help you adopt a tiger.

[See *Tigers in the Snow* (2000) by Peter Mathiessen, with photos by Maurice Hornocker, about Siberian tigers in the wild.]

World Wildlife Fund, www.panda.org.

www.friendsoftheforest.org.

Wildlife Conservation Society, www.wcs.org.

www.forevertigers.com.

30

CAMEL FESTIVALS

THE MEANING OF CAMELS

For most Western tourists, camels are the creatures you ride a few feet for a photo op. But for the people who live where camels are the chief bus, train, and truck, and source of milk, meat, fuel, and hair for warmth, camels signify worth: how many you have, or your bride-to-be is willing to put up, indicates your standing among other camel owners. More are definitely better, decorated to the nines, if possible, on the day of exchange. No cattle corrals here.

Evolving over the years, a camel fair is not only a place in which to sell or trade camels, it is also a time of great celebration, sometimes involving marriages, always with dances, music, plays, lots of good food, and drink. For a tourist, a camel fair is a great event in which to understand not only how people relate to animals, but how animals are completely written into the culture.

Although dromedaries (single hump) can go for several months without a drink of water, they depend on human beings to give them water of which they can consume thirty gallons in a matter of minutes. Camels browse and graze, eat grass and thorn trees, and store fat in their hump. For a tribe of desert traders, camels are the ultimate low-maintenance domesticated animal.

Few truly wild camels exist, because they have been domesticated for so long. Pockets of feral camels, left over from old armies, roam parts of the Sahara and Australia. The South American version of the wild camel—the guanaco and the smaller and endangered vicuna—still inhabit the high grasslands of the Andes, but llamas and alpacas, which date from the Incas who bred them, have always been domesticated.

India

Pushkar Camel Fair, Rajasthan

Pushkar means "lotus"; and the lotus-shaped lake where Hindus come to "dip" and pay homage to Lord Brahma is there because that's where Brahma dropped a lotus flower. In this sacred town in the northern province of Rajasthan each November when the moon is in the right phase, tens of thousands of camel traders pull and ride their decorated mounts into town, where several hundred thousand people gather to trade camels, donkeys, or cattle, buy and sell crafts, get tattooed, or simply to watch the spectacular events of the fair. Pilgrims visit the monasteries and take a holy dip in the sacred lake; visitors marvel at the former Raj palaces here and in nearby towns.

Dates for the Pushkar Fair: *2005:* November 12–15; *2006:* November 2–5; *2007:* November 21–24; *2008:* November 10–13; *2009:* October 30–November 2; *2010:* November 18–21.

Pushkar India Festival Tours   16 Timber Ridge Road, North Brunswick, New Jersey 08902. E-mail: us@pushkarfestivals.com; Website: www.pushkarfestivals.com.

Choose from a wide variety of package tours with this Pushkar- and Delhi-based company.

Myths and Mountains   976 Tee Court, Incline Village, Nevada 89451. Tel: 800-670-MYTH[6984] (toll-free); 775-832-5454; E-mail: travel@mythsandmountains.com; Website: www. mythsandmountains.com.

Not your average tour, this trip takes you to the Pushkar where you watch the camel activities with camel herders and their families. After the fair, take a camel safari into the desert; visit Jaisalmer, a magical city, once heavily fortified, in the middle of the desert;

explore the hills on a narrow-gauge train; and have tea with a noble Raj family. Nineteen days, about $4,700.

Geographic Expeditions   2627 Lombard Street, San Francisco, California 94123. Tel: 800-777-8183 (toll-free); Fax: 415-346-5535; E-mail: info@geoex.com; Website: www.geoex.com.

At the Pushkar Festival, stay in a private tented camp, and immerse yourself in camels and the goods they bring to the market: crafts, jewelry, many interesting things. Eighteen days, about $4,600.

American Museum of Natural History   Discovery Tours, Central Park West at 79th Street, New York, New York 10024-5192. Tel: 800-462-8687 (toll-free); 212-769-5700; Website: www.discoverytours.org.

This trip begins with a visit to the Bateshwar Animal Fair, where a day is set aside to honor the Hindu deity Lord Shiva with the trading of animals and other goods on the banks of the Yamuna River. Then visit a bird sanctuary in Jaipur before going to the Pushkar Camel Fair, where you stay in the Royal Tented Camp. Ride the Palace on Wheels, a vintage luxury train, across the desert to where the ninety-nine sandstone bastions of the fort of Jaisalmer rise out of the desert. Here, you can explore the palaces and take a camel safari into the desert. Spend a day at Ranthambore National Park, with the tigers. Sixteen days, about $7,700.

Mongolia

Thousand Camel Festival

In the land of Ghengis Khan you would expect excellent archers and a tradition of the warrior, and that's what is there—plus nomads with yaks, horses, and camels. Mongolia has only recently recognized its tourism potential, and now fills the niche of being one of the last little-explored places on Earth. It is also one of the least populated, and the last wild place of the Bactrian (two humps, long

A young man rests next to his Bactrian camel in Mongolia. *Stephan Salladin, www.Selenatravel.com*

fur) camel. The fewer than 2,000 truly wild camels that exist in the world exist in Mongolia and western China.

In fact, in a land of traditions dating at least to Ghengis Khan and maybe to the Bronze Age, their Thousand Camel Festival dates from only a couple of years ago. Begun by a non-governmental group whose aim is conservation of the few remaining Bactrian camels in the wild, this festival is unique: (domesticated) Bactrian camels are raced—fifteen kilometers for the mature camels, ten kilometers for the two-year-olds—and awarded bronze, silver, and gold medals for the winners in each age category.

The tradition of the race is old, but the import is brand new: conservation of the wild Bactrian. That is also the topic of a workshop discussion, a photo exhibit by camel trek guide Do Byamba, and a drawing contest of "The Camel, My Friend," in the local schools, open to the public. Don't miss the camel polo game at the end of the day of the Thousand Camel Festival.

Nomadic Expeditions   1095 Cranbury-South River Road, Suite 20A, Monroe Township, New Jersey 08831. Tel: 800-998-6634 (toll-free); 609-860-9008; E-mail: info@nomadicexpeditions.com; Website: www.nomadicexpeditions.com.

Staying at the eco-efficient Three Camel Lodge (www.three camellodge.com), in the Gobi Desert, participants in the Thousand Camel Festival tour will celebrate the Mongolian Lunar New Year, Tsagaan Sar, in the Gobi with the camel festivities and perform- ances by colorful dancers and musicians. Check out the Flaming Cliffs and some dinosaurs. This trip is preceded by four days in Ulan Bataar, visiting with Mongolian families for a shot of vodka and steaming dumplings and watching the traditional New Year wrestling matches. Ten days, from about $1,650 to $2,300, depend- ing on the number of travelers.

Niger

Cure Salée

At the end of the rainy season in September, Tuareg traders gather en masse at a salt deposit near InGall in Niger in the Sahel, the border of the Sahara Desert, for their dromedary camels to rest and eat and to take the salt cure after a season of traveling. This end-of- the-season get-together is also the time for the men of the Wodaabe tribe of the Fulani pastoralists to dress up and put on a talent show for the girls, an event called the Gerewol. Attractive and stylish, the Fulani costume is a combination of body paint, beads, and colorful weavings draped on their lithe bodies. They parade and make faces at the women they hope to engage, who are too young to be any- thing but modestly shy.

Between the two Sahara nomadic peoples, the Fulani and the Tuareg, you will see ancient camel and cattle cultures in full array in ways that are barely documented; their Gerewol ceremonies will seem a normal expression of people whose lives revolve solely around the health of their animals.

Mountain Travel Sobek   6420 Fairmount Avenue, El Cerrito, California 95430-9962. Tel: 800-687-6235 (toll-free); 510-527-8100; Fax: 510-525-7710; E-mail: info@mtsobek.com; Website: www.mtsobek.com.

Ultimate Sahara is a trek that Mountain Travel has been doing for twenty-five or so years. After the Cure Salée and the Gerewol, visit the terminus of many camel caravans, the desert city of Agadez and the nearby salt mines, source of many a caravan across a brutal route. Farther into the desert are ghost encampments from old wars. Twenty-five days, about $5,000.

Wilderness Travel   1102 Ninth Street, Berkeley, California 94710. Tel: 800-368-2794 (toll-free); 510-558-2488; E-mail: info@wildernesstravel.com; Website: www.wildernesstravel.com.

From Niamey, Niger, travel from oasis to oasis across the Air Mountains through the Grand Erg du Bilma, and an ancient salt works. Travel by 4-WD, except for the final two days when you trek through the Ténéré Desert on camels, sleeping under the stars. This trip runs three times a year; for the Cure Salée, leave in September. Twenty-two days, about $5,200.

Dreamweaver Travel Company   1185 River Drive, River Falls, Wisconsin 54022. Tel: 715-425-1037; E-mail: dudley@dreamweavertravel.net; Website: www.dreamweavertravel.net.

Dreamweaver donates a portion of each trip to community projects within Niger, a country always struggling with the encroachment of the desert and droughts. Their fifteen-day trip includes a family homestay, a three-day camel trek either in the Air Mountains or the Ténéré Desert, and a chance to get to know both the Berber-descended Tuareg and the Fulani—and their camels and cattle. Enjoy the Cure Salée and the Gerewol, as well. Fifteen days, itinerary can be customized, about $3,000.

31

PETS

PET TRAVEL

Pets are in. If you and your pet get along fabulously, take to the road together; it can be an amazing experience for your pet and an enlightening one for you. Your cat might raise an eyebrow at the thought of traveling, but your dog, if he is like Jack London's in *The Call of the Wild*, will trust your judgment and give you "credit for a wisdom that outreaches his own."

The New Eloise

Once reserved for the very rich and their arm-candy dogs, five-star hotels now routinely open their doors to the family pooch or cat, with a few conditions of tidiness. Call ahead, and your pet's name is already imprinted on its feeding bowl and the chef has noted its special dietary requests. Expect the doorman or the concierge to provide its daily airings.

At the Ritz-Carlton Bachelor Gulch on Beaver Creek Mountain, Colorado (970-748-6200), a resident golden lab welcomes people and pets alike. Named Bachelor, he's on hand for kids who need an instant buddy and for hikers who don't like to hike alone.

It's not only five-star hotels that welcome pets these days; many hotels will accommodate you and your pet—unless you travel with a pair of mastiffs.

Pray Together

In Vermont at the foot of Dog Mountain is a chapel designed for people and their dogs (near St. Johnsbury). Built like a small village church, it sports a weathervane in the shape of a Labrador retriever with wings (www.dogchapel.com).

Adventure Together

For people who take their dogs very seriously, a few companies have designed special places and trips for them and you—if your dog decides to take you along.

Summer Camp, Vermont

Camp Gone to the Dogs   Website: camp-gone-tothe-dogs.com.
    Starting in June in Marlboro, Vermont, Camp Gone to the Dogs offers educational and fun activities for your dog, and you, if you choose. Your dog can learn everything from agility to flyball to freestyle dancing. You can go to lectures that range from Tick Management to the Tellington Touch. Together, you can do arts and crafts and enjoy the Doggie Costume Party.
    All of this takes place at two campuses in Marlboro (a 250-acre spread) and Stowe (at the Mountaineer Inn), Vermont. Elect to stay on campus or off, in pet-friendly places that give discounts. Seven day camps: onsite, $950 to $1,100; offsite, about $900.

Take to the Lake, Ontario, Canada

Dog Paddling Adventures   177 Idema Road, Markham, Ontario, Canada L3R 1A9. Tel: 416-992-2216; E-mail: jessie@dogpaddlingadventures.com; Website: www.dogpaddlingadventures.com.
    Paddle wilderness rivers in the summer, go skijoring in the winter, hiking in the back woods in spring and fall with your best

canine buddy. Skijoring is cross-country skiing with your dog in a harness attached to you (it has a snap release if your dog suddenly chooses another route). About $99 Can. ($75 U.S.) a day.

Dogs take to canoes like Lewis and Clark, sitting up front as if they are the scouts. Dog Paddling Adventures offers a number of options on various waterways at about $100 Can. ($75 U.S.) a day, which includes lunch and all safety gear for you and your pet.

If your dog is a true adventurer, try some white-water paddling on the Madawaska River. Your dog wears everything but the hard hat. Three-, four-, or five-day "Ruff Water" trips, from about $375 to $550 Can. per person-and-dog. Dogs love it.

Beach Dogs

Not all beaches welcome dogs, but some beach-loving owners have put together a list: see www.dogfriendly.com. If you're in Key West, Florida, with-dog, you have not only a variety of places to stay, but a beach—not very big—that's all yours: Dog Beach at Vernon and Waddell avenues.

Dog Triathalon, California

California dogs are expected to work out, and the Triathalon at Long Beach, California, starts with a 40-yard swim (20 out, 20 back); hurdle-jump on the beach; then a 100-yard dash. Winners gain a certain panache when they run leash-free on the beach, which they can do once a month, spring and summer, when 300 to 450 dogs whoop it up at the shore. For this and a lot more, check out www.hautedogs.org. (That's pronounced "hot dogs.")

Communicate

Something called the Bow-Lingual, an electronic device that fits on your dog's collar, will translate what your pet is really saying. A database will collect and store your pet's "home alone" barks, so you can analyze how your dog handles an empty house; keep an archive of barks for historical comparison; do a medical check; and read your pet's body language, so you won't miss the nuance of a tail twitch. This costs about $100, but Americans spend close to $31 billion a year on pets, according to the pet industry.

To read to your pet or write a poem or story inspired by your pet, pick up a copy of *Bark* (www.thebark.com), a literary magazine devoted to guess who.

Websites

For lists of pet-friendly hotels, B&Bs, resorts, campgrounds, and beaches worldwide, see: www.petswelcome.com.

See also: www.travelpets.com; www.petsonthego.com (good pet blog); www.takeyourpet.com (some of these are membership organizations).

For travel information, see: www.interpetexlorer.com.

For hikes in national parks: www.hikewithyourdog.com. This is a British Columbia site but has links to American national and state parks.

For the Tellington Touch, a holistic dog-training technique: tteam-ttouch.com.

To adopt a former racing greyhound: www.greyhounds.org or call 800-446-8637. See also: www.grey2kusa.org.

Dogs outraced their owners getting geared up for the paddle. *Kathryn Howell, www.dogpaddlingadventures.com*

32

SANCTUARIES

OUT OF THE STORM

Sanctuaries tell you why the exotic pet trade and people do not go together. "You can train a wild animal, but you can never tame it," says animal trainer Jack Hanna.

Easy to buy, baby carnivores—lions, tigers, bears—amuse their owners until the animals grow up, become overwhelmingly expensive to feed, and attack their owners for reasons that are not always clear. Owners then come face-to-face with the fact that their pet is wild, and wild genes die hard.

The illegal trade in exotic pets was dealt a blow in 2003 when Congress passed a law making it illegal to transport exotic pets across state lines (for legislative updates, see the site of the Doris Day Animal League at www.ddal.org). Advocates like actress Tippi Hedren from Shambala Preserve in southern California (see below) argue that the trade has to stop completely to save animals from further abuse. "You can't know what a wild animal is thinking," she says, recalling a completely surprise attack from a "tame" cat while she was making a film.

Enter Sanctuaries

In the United States alone, hundreds of sanctuaries exist as safe havens to meet the increasing demand of rescued abused animals

270

that are neither wild nor tame. Zeus, an African lion used to a range of hundreds of miles, was starving in an unheated Colorado garage until he was discovered and rescued by the Rocky Mountain Wildlife Sanctuary. Shaquille, a black leopard used in a nightclub act, was found so severely beaten his eye sockets had been broken. He now lives peacefully at Big Cat Rescue in Tampa.

Equally tragic are circus animals no longer able to perform—elephants get arthritis, tigers get tired; laboratory animals no longer needed for experiments; animals born in zoos that boost the population beyond what the cages can contain; or native wild animals that are found orphaned or wounded in the wilds or on highways. A sanctuary near the Grand Canyon harbors discarded domestic and feral pets; a sanctuary in Texas shelters some of the wild horses that the Bureau of Land Management decided were too many.

How to Relate

Most of these sanctuaries operate as nonprofits, which means they depend on donations, adopt-an-animal programs, and volunteers. On average a lion costs about $9,000 a year to feed; an elephant, $15,000. Some sanctuaries open their doors to visitors and school groups for a small fee for guided educational tours. Others are closed to visitors because the animals have been too traumatized to be around people.

Rescue and Rehab Sanctuaries

(For a complete list of sanctuaries approved by the Association of Sanctuaries, see: www.taosanctuaries.org; or call 830-336-3000.)

Black Beauty Ranch   The Fund for Animals, Murchison, Texas 75778. Tel: 903-469-3811; E-mail: blackbeautyranch@aol.com; Website: www.blackbeautyranch.org.

Longtime animal advocate Cleveland Amory established Black Beauty Ranch on 1,300 acres in the 1970s. Since then, the ranch has been home to abused and retired elephants, "extra" wild horses and burros whose herds were thinned on federal lands, and chimpanzees from laboratories, among them the famous Nim Chimpsky, the first chimp to learn American sign language. He was released from study at the age of nine and sent to the ranch where he died at the age of twenty-six. The ranch is open to visitors on Saturdays, except in August. Chimps, however, do not welcome visitors and can be viewed only from a distance.

The Fund for Animals operates three other sanctuaries around the country: in southern California, for injured wild and urban animals, and in South Carolina, for rabbits who have become "throwaway pets." In New York City, the fund operates a free clinic to spay and neuter pets of low-income families.

Big Cat Rescue   12802 Easy Street, Tampa, Florida 33625. Tel: 813-885-4469; Fax: 813-885-4457; E-mail: SAFEinthewild@ aol.com; Website: www.bigcatrescue.org/visitus.htm.

Some of the cats in this sanctuary were rescued starving and abused from the backs of U-Hauls, from pet shows where the owner died, or from farms that raised certain cats only for the fur on their

This tiger cub was rescued before it was no longer wanted.
www.BigCatRescue.org

stomachs (the cats were electrocuted, their stomach fur sold to the clothing trade). Kinder owners leave their wild pets at the doorstep: an unwanted palm civet was a recent gift. The sanctuary also rescues animals in trouble—a sheep that was lost on a highway was given a place to stay.

Formerly known as Wildlife on Easy Street, Big Cat Rescue offers guided day tours and night tours, tours for kids, photo safaris, and Expedition Easy Street: A Big Cat Adventure. On this, start with a morning tour, help make toys and food puzzles for the cats' intellectual enrichment, then help feed tigers, cougars, lynx, caracals, and servals. Spend the night in a bed-and-breakfast cabin located within the park, where you can hear the roars of the night hunters. Minimum age eighteen, about $100. Ask about opportunities to intern for six months to a year, volunteer; or adopt an animal.

Shambala Preserve   6867 Soledad Canyon, Acton, California 93510. Tel: 661-268-0380; Fax: 661-268-8809; E-mail: info@ shambala.org; Website: www.shambala.org

Actress Tippi Hedren (Alfred Hitchcock's *The Birds* is one of her films) opened the doors of Shambala as a sanctuary to lions, tigers, leopards, servals, cheetah, snow leopards, mountain lions, a Florida panther, and one elephant, all of which had been discarded by owners who had bought them as pets or to use in the entertainment industry. The founder of the Roar Foundation, Hedren is an active proponent of animal rights and was a big supporter of the Big Cat Protection Act, passed into U.S. law in 2003, which bans interstate commerce in the exotic pet trade.

You can visit Shambala one weekend in each month on a three-hour safari tour for guests over eighteen ($35 donation payable one month in advance to the Roar Foundation, P.O. Box 189, Acton, California 93510). Wear shoes, no shorts. Between May and October, spend an overnight at the Malaika Marquee, an African safari tent (with feather bed), with catered gourmet dinner, midnight walk-about the sanctuary, and breakfast. About $2,500 for two, donation (a portion is tax deductible). Apply well in advance.

The Performing Animal Welfare Society   P.O. Box 849, Galt, California 95632. Tel: 209-745-2606; Fax: 209-745-1809; E-mail: info@pawsweb.org; Website: www.pawsweb.org.

Begun by former Hollywood animal trainers Pat Derby and Ed Stewart, PAWS rescues, shelters, works to strengthen laws to protect animals, and educates the public at three sites in Galt, Herald, and San Andreas, California. On ample acres, big cats, elephants, bears, primates, and a wolf hybrid are able to live out their lives in peace. In Ark 2000, a 2,300-acre site in Calaveras County, California, live two happy African elephants—Mara and 71—retired from their lives as performers in the film industry. Take advantage of the PAWS' three-day getaway, which includes a chance to help prepare food, feed the elephants, and take a tour of the site with elephant experts. You stay at a bed-and-breakfast there. Lodging and meals; about $750, donation. To make reservations, contact Kim Gardner at info@pawsweb.org, or call 916-488-3991.

Carnivore Preservation Trust   1940 Hanks Chapel Road, Pittsboro, North Carolina 27312. Tel: 919-542-4684; E-mail: info@cptigers.org; Website: www.cptigers.org.

Both big cats (tigers, leopards, and jaguars), and small cats (such as civet-like Binturong), live on fifty-five acres of this privately funded reserve. More than 130 carnivores from eleven species, all rescued either from dire circumstances or discontinued breeding programs of rare species, call this home. Twice a day on weekends, you can take a two-hour educational tour (about $10). Volunteers more than twelve years old are invited to help. Please wear shoes and long pants and no perfume. To take photos, sign a release form and pay $3.

International Exotic Feline Sanctuary   P.O. Box 637, Boyd, Texas 76023. Tel: 940-433-5091; Fax: 940-433-5092; E-mail: richard@bigcat.org; Website: www.bigcat.org.

More than sixty exotic cats have been rescued from abhorrent situations by the IEFS, which is the only rescue sanctuary that is a member of the AZA (American Zoo and Aquarium Association). The sanctuary recently acquired three very rare leopards, a clouded leopard and two amur (Russian) leopards. You can take a guided tour and hear each heartbreaking story while you gaze into the animal's eyes; fill out an online request or call in advance. Donation, about $20 adults, $10 children above the age of seven. Ask about their one-day photography class (lecture and shoot). Volunteers are welcome. Check out their live web cam and library of sounds.

Tiger Haven, Inc.   237 Harvey Road, Kingston, Tennessee 37763. Tel: 865-376-4100; Fax: 865-376-0284; E-mail: tigerfriends@tigerhaven.org; Website: www.tigerhaven.org.

Lions, tigers, and smaller cats find sanctuary here for life. Tours are aimed at educating the public in the ways of big cats, as well as illustrating why they need our care. Adopt a big cat, volunteer, take a tour, or just enjoy their website.

Rocky Mountain Wildlife Conservation Center   1946 WCR 53, Keenesburg, Colorado 80643. Tel: 303-536-0118; E-mail: information@wildlife-sanctuary.org; Website: www.wildlife-sanctuary.org.

Zeus, the starving lion rescued from a cold Denver garage, has been here for almost fourteen years, healthy, happy, and in charge of all the other residents—from bears to people. In business as a rescue organization for almost twenty-five years, the RMWCC lets in visitors only on a limited basis, to respect the animals. They are especially open to people anxious to learn more and to school-age children. Call and arrange a time. Volunteers are always welcome, if they can make a commitment. It costs close to $9,000 a year to feed Zeus, and he is just one of about seventy-five large animals. Donations are always accepted.

Primate Sanctuaries

Animal Protection Institute's Primate Sanctuary P.O. Box 22505, Sacramento, California 95822. Tel: 916-447-3085; Fax: 916-447-3070; E-mail: info@api4primates.org; Website: www.snowmonkey.org.

Formerly the Texas Snow Monkey Sanctuary, this primate home is located in Dilley, Texas, on 186 acres. Approximately 400 primates, including baboons, have been rescued from road zoos, medical labs, and people who changed their minds about their primate pet. Serious students can apply for a four- to six-month internship, which includes $250 a month and housing. Volunteers willing to work with the care and feeding of the primates or in the office are also welcome.

Jungle Friends Primate Sanctuary and Rehabilitation, 13925 North State Road 121, Gainesville, Florida 32653. Tel: 386-462-7779; E-mail: kari@junglefriends.org; Website: www.junglefriends.org.

Home to otherwise homeless and unwanted monkeys, Jungle Friends provides medical and loving care to more than thirty primates. Check out their original watercolors ($150 framed, $75 unframed). Volunteers always welcome. Contact LTW@jf.org, or fax your request to 386-462-7780.

Game Farms: Photography

Lassie lived on a game farm, and Hollywood can be credited with being the first to create a space for "tame" wild animals used in the film industry. Amateur photographers looking to polish their wildlife portrait abilities and professional photographers looking for magazine and calendar covers turn to game farms. Some farms began with rescued wild animals; more often the animals were born in captivity. The fees help support the animals.

Triple D Game Farm P.O. Box 5072, Kalispell, Montana Tel: 406-755-9653; Fax: 406-755-9021; Website: www.mefarm.com.

Located a few miles south of Glacier National Park, Triple D was the first game farm to operate in the United States. Twenty-four species from Siberian tigers to minks are available for close-ups and snapshots in the wild. The big ones, so-called primary species (tigers, grizzlies, snow leopards) cost about $400 per session per day; secondary species (minks, raccoons, etc.) cost about $100 per session per day. A session lasts from one to two and a half hours. An onsite log cabin accommodates visitors.

Wild Eyes Animal and Photo Adventures   894 Lake Drive, Columbia Falls, Montana 59912. Tel: 406-387-5391; Fax: 406-387-5863; Website: www.wildeyes-usa.com.

Wild Eyes has a collection of handsome carnivores from around the world, and you don't have to have a camera to visit. Guided by a handler, spend the day with the animals and the night in an on-site cabin (about $90), or let them design a tour package for you. For photographers, three-day package, six sessions with animals, about $1,300; five-day package with ten sessions; about $2,400; seven-day package with fourteen sessions, about $3,400. Price includes lodging in cabins and meals. Wild Eyes also offers single sessions from about $100 (secondary species) to $750 (two Siberian tigers).

Turpentine Creek Wildlife Refuge and Foundation   239 Turpentine Creek Lane, Eureka Springs, Arkansas 72632. Tel: 479-253-5841; Fax: 479-253-5059; E-mail: tigers@turpentinecreek.org; Website: www.turpentinecreek.org.

Located in the heart of the Ozarks, Turpentine Creek has about 150 lions, tigers, cougars, leopards, as well as bears, monkeys, deer, and birds. Long a refuge for neglected, abused, or unwanted big cats, this refuge offers two PhotoWild options for photographers. The open sessions, with big cats without fences (carefully monitored) cost $125 an hour, two-hour minimum; and closed sessions, cats behind fences that are easily disguised, cost $100 an hour. Contact Scott Smith at scott@turpentinecreek.org. You can also stay in a treehouse overlooking the reserve, about $100 a night for two.

Lakota Wolf Preserve   89 Mt. Pleasant Road, Columbia,
New Jersey 07832. Tel: 877-733-9653 (toll-free); 908-496-9244;
E-mail: Jim@lakotawolf.com; Website: www.lakotawolf.com.

Tundra, timber, and Arctic wolves, all born in captivity, live in
this preserve in the mountains of the Delaware Water Gap. Educational Wolf Watch programs are given twice a day throughout the
year, about $15 for adults, $7 for kids.

Serious photographers can reserve a place for a guided photography session with wildlife photographer Dan Bacon for unob-
structed picture opportunities. About $125 for one and a half hours,
$300 for a half day, $500 for a whole day. Contact Dan or Pam at
908-479-4369, or email: photography@lakotawolf.com.

No-Visitors-Allowed Sanctuaries

Save the Chimps, The Center for Captive Chimpanzee Care
P.O. Box 12220, Fort Pierce, Florida 34979; *second address:*
1300 LaVelle Road, Alamogordo, New Mexico 88310. E-mail:
info@savethechimps.org; Website: www.savethechimps.org.

In an amazing story, Enos, a five-year-old chimp, was launched
into space in 1961 on a two-orbit voyage preparatory to the manned
flight made by astronaut John Glenn. Enos was well prepared, but
a technological snafu gave the chimp an electric shock for each cor-
rect maneuver he performed. Undeterred, Enos ignored the shocks
and with great cool performed the designated tasks.

That was the good news. The astronauts got all the glory, but
after their flights, the Air Force Space Chimps became guinea pigs
in harsh biomedical research experiments. Now given a sanctuary
where they can be themselves, the twenty-one "depressed and shell-
shocked" chimps, well beyond retirement age, are beginning to
experience a new-found joy. (Check out their portraits on the
website.)

Meanwhile, about 200 other chimps, rescued from the same
ental laboratory in New Mexico that was closed by the U.S.
ent of Agriculture in 2001, wait for housing to join the

Space Chimps on their 200 acres in Florida. Until that time, Save the Chimps is making life more tolerable for them in New Mexico.

It costs about $7,000 a month for fruit and vegetables to feed the chimps, and even more to move the remaining chimps into their new home. Donate or offer to volunteer in a number of ways, both on- and off-site. The main objective is to help chimps develop social skills, which they have never had the opportunity to do. No "hands-on contact" with the chimps, however: trauma leaves its mark.

Chimp Haven   710 Spring Street, Shreveport, Louisiana 71101. Tel: 888-982-4467 (toll-free); 318-425-0002; E-mail: ikoebner@ chimphaven.org; Website: www.chimphaven.org.

Both wild born and laboratory born, these aging chimps have given their lives to federally funded medical research and now deserve to relax in a cageless environment around caring people. The newest of retired-chimp facilities, Chimp Haven encourages education about our closest relatives on Earth and how we can communicate with them. Kids can check out lots of information at Gigi's Corner at their website. Volunteers are always welcome; email: smiller@chimphaven.org. Become a member; email: mwands@ chimphaven.org. Donations always accepted.

The Elephant Sanctuary   P.O. Box 393, Hohenwald, Tennessee 38462. Tel: 931-796-6500; E-mail: elephant@elephants.com; Website: www.elephants.com.

Home to seven endangered Asian elephants, who were "old, sick, or needy," each with a terrible story to tell, the Elephant Sanctuary is truly that: a place where a few elephants may live out their lives without being beaten, cramped, underfed, and otherwise abused. On this 800-acre spread, with a 3,000-acre buffer zone, the elephants are able to play in streams and pools, graze at their will, and enjoy treats like watermelons. All females, they have bonded as a group as they would naturally in the wild. Six-week "labor intensive" internships are available. Adults over eighteen (or over fifteen if accompanied by an adult) are invited to take part in occasional

Volunteer Days, on which they perform whatever tasks need to be done. Visit the website for some photos and bios, and take a look at the live web cam. Patron-level donors do get to visit.

Former-Pet Sanctuaries

Best Friends Animal Society   5001 Angel Canyon Road, Kanab, Utah 84741-5000. Tel: 435-644-2001; E-mail: info@ bestfriends.org; Website: www.bestfriends.org.

Located in Angel Canyon, a stone's throw from Grand Canyon, Zion National Park, Bryce Canyon, and a lot of other colorful places, Best Friends is a sanctuary for hundreds of unwanted dogs and cats, with some bunnies, birds, and burros thrown in. Visitors are more than welcome to meet and get to know the residents on sixty- to ninety-minute guided tours. Volunteers are especially welcome and encouraged to stay for a day, a week, or a month, if you can spare

Volunteers get the buckets of food ready to feed the 650 dogs at the Best Friends Animal Society Dogtown in Kanab, Utah. *Harry Munro, www.bestfriends.org*

the time. Walk the dogs, feed the animals, tidy up the cemetery, learn to use a pooper scooper. Or help dogs, cats, and feral animals in your community. Internships are available. Stay at the Angel Canyon guest cottages, about $125 for two people; members receive 15 percent discount. Reserve at visiting@bestfriends.org.

The Heart and Soul Animal Sanctuary   Natalie Owings, 369 Montezuma Avenue, No. 130, Santa Fe, New Mexico 87501. Tel: 505-757-6817; E-mail: info@animal-sanctuary.org; Website: www.animal-sanctuary.org.

Natalie Owings has dedicated her life to the care of abandoned and abused pets and farm animals, and lives with her twenty-five or thirty dogs in "the Giant Doghouse," a large room with one human bed and thirty dog beds. The sanctuary provides medical help to rescued animals and teaches school-age children "compassion and respect" for all animals. To schedule a visit for a weekend afternoon, call in advance.

Websites

Feral cats: www.alleycat.org.

Farm Sanctuaries

When farm animals retire, they are usually put out to pasture or killed. Some have spent their lives as breeders in tiny cages. A few places give pigs, donkeys, horses, goats, sheep, rabbits, cows, even turkeys a sort of retirement home.

PIGS, A Sanctuary 1112 Persimmon Lane, Shepherdstown, West Virginia 25443. Tel: 304-262-0080; E-mail: farmmanager@ pigs.org; Website: www.pigs.org.

Potbellied and farm pigs, rescued from factory farms and genetic engineering labs, come here "where a pig can be a pig." You can enter this safe haven by becoming a volunteer.

Farm Sanctuary   P.O. Box 150, Watkins Glen, New York 14891.
Tel: 607-583-2225; E-mail: info@farmsanctuary.org.; Website:
www.farmsanctuary.org. In California: Tel: 530-865-4617, ext. 10;
E-mail: cashelter@farmsanctuary.org.

Located on both coasts, the Farm Sanctuary provides shelter for
food animals that are abused in factory farms and slaughter houses
(details on the website). Visit cows, turkeys, goats, sheep, ducks,
pigs, and rabbits. In New York, stay in a B&B cabin on the farm,
about $65 for one person, includes a tour. In California, stay in a
country cabin and pitch in to help with farm chores, about $75 for
one person, includes a tour.

See also:

Black Beauty Ranch   Murchison, Texas;
  www.blackbeautyranch.org.

Animal Place   Vacaville, California; www.animalplace.org.

Dreamtime Sanctuary   Elgin, Texas;
  www.dreamtimesanctuary.org.

Websites

Humane Societies

Humane Society   www.hsus.org.

**American Society for the Prevention of Cruelty to
  Animals**   www.aspca.org. (The SPCA was begun in 1826 by
  English philospher Jeremy Bentham who could not bear to
  see horses whipped.)

International Fund for Animal Welfare   www.ifaw.org.

National Humane Society   www.nationalhumane.com (offers
  free spaying and neutering).

~~rban animals:
  ~~ww.wildneighbors.org.

www.fund.org/urbanwildlife. The **Fund for Animals** (Urban Wildlife) gives lots of facts on coexistence with everything from bats to coyotes, with references to helpful websites.

National hotline: 203-389-4111 (weekdays); 203-393-1050 (after hours).

Primates:

For interesting studies of twenty-five species of lemurs, see the **Duke University Primate Center** site: www.duke.edu/web/primate/projects.html.

Shop:

Shop online and support sanctuaries (a portion of the price goes to the animals): www.aidforanimalsinc.com.

33

Zoos

Small Zoos

The United States is peppered with hundreds of small zoos. Some of them began as rescue centers to house an injured or orphaned wild animal, or as exhibits of "exotic" animals like big snakes or captured wild cats. Some were the gifts of successful men to their community. Today they are tourist destinations whose contributions support the health of the animals. Florida has more than its share. Following are examples.

Florida

Babcock Ranch Wilderness Preserve   8000 State Road 31, Punta Gorda, Florida 33982. Tel: 800-500-5583 (toll-free to make reservations for tours); E-mail: adventure@babcockwilderness.com; Website: www.babcockwilderness.com.

On this 90,000-acre, family-owned, private working cattle ranch, you can take a tour by swamp buggy or mountain bike (they provide the bikes, helmets, trail mix, and water) on back roads through the Telegraph Swamp, a cypress swamp in old Florida. The wildlife comprises alligators, one of the last remaining herds (in the East) of ¹   black bears, turtles, endangered whooping cranes and wood-
       aybe a Florida panther, and Lulu, a resident three-horned
           an eye open for a crested caracara, an imposing two-foot-
            at lives in a crazy nest made of twigs.

Parrot Jungle Island   1111 Parrot Jungle Trail, Miami, Florida
33132. Tel: 305-2-JUNGLE [258-6453]; E-mail: info@
parrotjungle.com; Website: www.parrotjungle.com.

Located literally in the middle of Miami, between downtown and
South Beach, this oasis of lush rain forest opened its doors in 1936
and was completely refurbished in 2003. Its 18.6 acres supports
3,000 animals from an albino alligator in the "Everglades Habitat,"
to an orangutan, to more than 200 parrots and macaws chattering to
their hearts' content and enjoying a replicated clay lick from Manu,
Peru. In the Parrot Bowl, you can see parrots ride bikes. This, and
much more, including a petting zoo.

Monkey Jungle   14805 S.W. 216 Street, Miami, Florida 33170.
Tel: 305-235-1611; Fax: 305-235-4253; Website; www.monkey
jungle.com.

In 1933 Joseph DuMond introduced six java monkeys to his
South Florida property as part of a primate behavior study. Fifty
years and two generations later, the DuMond family oversees a
thirty-acre private primate reserve, with more than eighty members
of the original java monkey group. In addition, you will find thirty-
four other primate species, including King, a western lowland
gorilla, part of a memory study and the kernel of a projected science
center. He will live in the new habitat Cameroon Forest. Visitors
are welcome daily, 365 days a year, from 9:30 to 5:00.

Central Florida Zoological Park   3755 NW Highway 17-92 at
I-4, Exit 104, Sanford, Florida 32771. Tel: 407-323-4450; E-mail:
cenflzoo@totcon.com; Website: www.centralfloridazoo.org.

This zoo began in the 1920s when a traveling circus left some
animals behind. The Sanford Fire Department took care of them
until 1941, when the zoo opened on the shores of Lake Monroe.
Today the zoo has several hundred animals in natural habitats spread
over a 116-acre park, and participates in the AZA's Species Survival
Program by breeding the endangered clouded leopard, ruffed lemur,
mandrill, cotton-top tamarin, and several other species.

revard Zoo 8225 North Wickham Road, Melbourne, Florida
32940. Tel: 321-254-9453; Website: www.brevardzoo.org.

Less than a dozen years old, this zoo supports ten acres called
Expedition Africa, which replicates an African savannah. Visitors
can kayak the Nyami Nyami River, take the Cape to Cairo Express,
or watch from a nine-foot viewing platform some of the more than
sixty African animals, such as Masai and Reticulated giraffes, white
rhino, oryx, impala, ostrich, and an African hornbill. The park also
provides an in-depth behind-the-scenes tour, called Wildside Tours.

Lowry Park Zoo 1101 West Sligh Avenue, Tampa, Florida
33604-4756. Tel:813-935-8552; Website: www.lowryparkzoo.com.

This zoo began in the 1930s with a few raccoons, alligators, and
birds, and has grown into a major zoo with a manatee rehabilitation
hospital with viewing pools, an African safari, Primate World, Asian
Domain, a native wildlife section, and an Australian exhibit ("Wal-
laroo Station"). The zoo supports a vigorous education program for
school kids and tots as young as one-and-a-half, and offers the
opportunity to kids and adults to be "Zookeeper for a Day."

Caribbean Gardens The ZOO in Naples, 1590 Goodlette-
Frank Road, Naples, Florida 34102. Tel: 239-262-5409; E-mail:
info@caribbeangardens.com; Website: www.caribbeangardens.com.

To learn more about American panthers, visit the Naples ZOO's
Panther Glade, a habitat for living cousins of the Florida panther,
the western cougar. In league with the National Wildlife Refuge,
the zoo has an educational exhibit of the Florida panther.

Missouri

American National Fish and Wildlife Museum 500 West
Sunshine Street, Springfield, Missouri 65807. Tel: 877-245-9453
(toll-free); 417-890-9453; Website: www.wondersofwildlife.org.

This unusual combination museum-aquarium-zoo is a tribute to
American species, thanks to John L. Morris, who founded Bass Pro
Shops (flagship store is next door). Dedicated to conservation, the

museum illustrates where hunting fits in the big picture. The museum itself has lots of stuffed animals, but 260 live specimens swim in the aquarium (four sharks), or the lake (Ozark fish), or live on the shores (frogs, lizards, beavers) or in the woods (a pair of bobcats). Missouri song birds fly about in the open-air aviary, and wild turkeys roam free. Lots of interactive stuff for kids plus Teddy Roosevelt's replicated library. Adults, about $10; kids four to eleven, about $7.

Dickerson Park Zoo   3043 North Fort Street, Springfield, Missouri 65803. Tel: 417-864-1800 (info line); E-mail: info@ dickersonparkzoo.org; Website: www.dickersonparkzoo.org.

As part of the American Zoo and Aquarium Association's Species Survival Plan, this zoo participated in the captive breeding of the endangered Asiatic elephant. A $4 million makeover in 2004 opened up the Tropical-Asia collection of Asian elephants, tigers, and gibbons, as well as an expanded Missouri Habitat that contains native mountain lions and wolves.

Pennsylvania

Trexler Lehigh County Game Preserve   5150 Game Preserve Road, Schnecksville, Pennsylvania 18078. Tel: 610-799-4171; Fax: 610-799-4170; E-mail: info@gamepreserve.org; Website: www.gamepreserve.org.

Active since 1906 when a wealthy industrialist created a private habitat for the endangered bison (fewer than 1,000 were left), this game preserve offers an excellent educational visit. Today more than fifty species from around the world—zebras, kangaroos, Arctic wolves, elk—live together. Kids from four up are invited to spend four days at Zoo Camp, with activities for each age level (about $90 to $210). Explore and Snore includes a night nature hike, zoo tour, and animal presentations. Then sleep—safely indoors (about $15 to $30). Internship program is available; volunteers are always welcome. The preserve is open daily from 10 to 3. The animals are very much a part of the family.

WILD ANIMAL SAFARIS

Florida

Better than an IMax, wild animal safaris are a good way to experience an African safari in miniature: the animals are real and wild and dangerous, and a fast-food restaurant is never more than a mile or two away.

Lion Country Safari   2003 Lion Country Safari Road, Loxahatchee, Florida 33470-3977. Tel: 561-793-1084; E-mail: info@lioncountrysafari.com; Website: www.lioncountrysafari.com.

Located near West Palm Beach, this 500-acre site, begun by a South African and a Brit who wanted to bring Africa to the States in 1967, was the first "cageless zoo" in the country. Accredited by the American Zoo and Aquarium Association, Lion Country Safari takes part in international conservation programs for the endangered white rhino and the Jane Goodall ChimpanZoo Observer Program, which trains volunteers to study chimp behavior. Driving and walking tours are offered daily. For information on children's programs plus staying in the adjacent campgrounds call 561-793-9797 for information or 800-562-9115 for reservations. This, by the way, is the only place in the country where a male African elephant was born in captivity.

California

San Diego Zoo Wild Animal Park   15500 San Pasqual Valley Road, Escondido, California 92027-7017. Tel: 760-747-8702; Website: www.sandiegozoo.org.

Located on 1,800 acres thirty-two miles north of the San Diego Zoo, the Zoo's Wild Animal Park has 3,500 animals, many of them from Africa. Visitors can take the Wgasa Bush Line Railway or jump on an open caravan truck, which also gives special tours for photographers and for families. Walk on the Wild Side Tours are for curious people who want to know what's going on behind the scenes. Kids and their parents can camp out in safari tents.

Big Zoos

Some animals look on zoos as low-security prisons: they take their square meals, work out, and prepare for the day when they're paroled. Most zoos spend lots of raised, donated, and grant money making sure animals will never *want* to be paroled: architects create habitats deceptively designed to resemble animals' native homes, friends-of-the-zoo organizations train docents who explain the animals to visitors and sponsor sleepovers for kids and their parents, and zoo directors put much time and effort into maintaining the animals' physical and mental health. After Little Joe, a gorilla dealing with adolescent hormones, attempted to escape from Boston's Franklin Park Zoo and headed for the subway, zoo managers put him on a rigorous diet of mentally stimulating projects. They also tightened security.

The AZA

Most zoos do what they can to get accredited by the American Zoo and Aquarium Association, the governing agency of zoo management. But the AZA is much more. When Marjan, the male lion in the Kabul Zoo, came helplessly under fire during the overthrow of the Taliban in Afghanistan, members of the AZA, along with vets from the London Zoo, flew to Kabul and examined the aging lion to make sure he and others were in good health. When Marjan died shortly after (at an age guessed to be between twenty-three and twenty-eight years), Afghanis placed flowers on his grave.

With the International Foundation for Animals in the Wild (www.ifaw.org) and Wild Aid, an organization that saves animals from disaster, the AZA through the North Carolina Zoo is also involved in restoring the Baghdad Zoo and looking after the big cats—cheetahs and lions—from the private collections belonging to Saddam and his sons.

Species Survival Plan

The AZA's Species Survival Plan oversees captive breeding programs of endangered species and reintroduces them to the wild, if that seems like the best idea. The Przewalski Horse Project, for example, in conjunction with Washington's National Zoo (www.natzoo.si.org) and The Wilds in Ohio (see www.thewilds.org), realized the successful breeding of three foals. After a couple of years of living in the semi-wild, when they are mature, they will be shipped to their ancestral home in the Hustain Nuruu Reserve in Mongolia and join a few other reintroduced Przewalskis.

Kids Can Save the Animals

The AZA also trains zoo professionals and encourages education of the public, especially kids. A poll taken by the AZA in 2003 to gauge the level of interest of kids in animals found that an amazing 95 percent of the polled six- to eight-year-olds wanted to know how they could help animals. Eighty-seven percent were interested in volunteering to help animals.

Websites

See: www.aza.org for more information and for lists of accredited zoos and aquariums.

Wild Aid   See the scope of their work fighting poachers and statements by active supporters Ralph Fiennes and Jackie Chan: www.wildaid.org.

Electronic zoo has sites for kids and general information on species: www.netvet.wustl.edu/e-zoo.htm.

Also see: www.ananova.com, a general news site. Click on Quirkies, then on Animal Tales, for animal stories from around the world.

Give a giant panda a stalk of bamboo and he's one happy panda. *National Zoo, Washington. Gary N. Stolz, U.S. Fish and Wildlife Service, www.fws.gov*

Index

Mexico: butterflies, 156–57; sea turtles, 86;
    sharks, 71–72, 73–74; tide pools, 91
Miami Seaquariurn, 170
Miami zoos, 285
Michigan wolves, 203
Midway Atoll National Wildlife Refuge,
    78
Mikongo Primate Research Center, 35
Minchumina, Lake, 224
Mingan Island Cetacean Study, 97–99
Minke whales, 102–3, 105–6
Minnesota: bears, 190–91; dogsledding,
    223–24; wolves, 202
Missouri: zoos, 154–55, 286–87
Missouri Botanical Garden, 154–55
Molokini, 109
Monarch butterflies, 156–57
Mongolia: camel festivals, 262–64;
    dinosaurs, 235–37; horses, 210,
    216–17; snow leopards, 249, 250–51,
    252; wolves, 205
Monkey Jungle (Florida), 285
Monkeys. *See* Apes
Montana: dinosaurs, 231–32; game farm,
    276–77
Montana State University, 231–32
Montana Wildlife Viewing Guide, 201
Monterey Bay Aquarium, 84
Montreal Insectarium, 153
Moose, 149, 198, 199
Moremi Game Reserve, 19, 59, 61
Morrison Formation, 232–35
Moss, Cynthia, 8, 47, 48, 49, 51
Mote Marine Laboratory, 86–87
Mountain Gorilla Conservation Fund, 39
Mountain gorillas, 36–39
Mountain Travel Sobek: African safaris,
    14–15, 16–17, 22; Arctic bears,
    184–85; camels, 265; chimpanzees,
    33; Galapagos, 144; snow leopards,
    252; tigers, 256–57
Mount Kinabalu National Park, 42
Mount Noen, 249
Mud beetles, 152
Museum of the Rockies, 231–32
Museum of Western Colorado, 234
Mygatt-Moore Quarry, 234
Myths and Mountains, 217, 261–62

Naadam Games, 216–17
NACOBTA Booking and Information
    Office, 26

Nalycheva Valley, 226
Namib Desert, 17, 24–26
Namibia, 17–18, 24–25; balloon trips, 28;
    safaris, 25–26; scientific project,
    27–28
Namib Naukluft National Park, 25
Napo River, 123
Natal Sardine Run, 68–69
National Elk Refuge, 202, 206
National Geographic Expeditions:
    Antarctic, 102; dinosaurs, 234;
    Galapagos, 143–44; safaris, 24
National Humane Society, 282
National Oceanic and Atmospheric
    Administration (NOAA), 81, 83, 84
National Wildlife Federation
    Expeditions, 157
National Zoo (Washington, D.C.),
    242–43, 244, 252, 290
Natural Habitat Adventures: Galapagos,
    145; Monarch butterflies, 157;
    Newfoundland, 150; panda bears,
    246; safaris, 13, 24; sea turtles, 86;
    spirit bears, 192; wolves and elk,
    201–2
Natural horsemanship, 214–16
Nature Protection Trust of Seychelles,
    147
Naturequest: dolphins, 109; Okavango
    Delta, 60–61; safaris, 24
Ndakinna Wilderness Project, 221–22
Nepal: tigers, 254–59
New Brunswick: tide pools, 89–91
Newfoundland, 135, 148–50
Newfoundland Eco Adventures Tours,
    149
New Jersey: tracking, 219–20
New Mexico: pet sanctuaries, 281
New Orleans, 176; insectarium, 152
New York: farm sanctuaries, 282;
    tracking, 221–22
Nez Perce Tribal Lands, 204
Ngamba Island Chimpanzee Sanctuary,
    31, 32–33, 38
Ngorongoro Conservation Area, 11
Ngorongoro Crater, 11, 12–13
Niger: camel festivals, 264–65
Nile crocodiles, 59, 62
Ninja, Emmanuel, 13
Nizke Tatry Mountains, 205
Noatak River, 185
Nomadic Expeditions, 216–17, 236, 264